AMERICAN INDIANS
in Early New Orleans

AMERICAN INDIANS
in Early New Orleans

FROM CALUMET TO RAQUETTE

DANIEL H. USNER

LOUISIANA STATE UNIVERSITY PRESS
BATON ROUGE

Published with the assistance of a grant from the College of
Arts and Science, Vanderbilt University

Published by Louisiana State University Press

DESIGNER: Barbara Neely Bourgoyne
TYPEFACES: Footlight MT Light and Adobe Caslon Pro
PRINTER AND BINDER: Sheridan Books

LIBRARY OF CONGRESS CATALOGING-IN-PUBLICATION DATA
Names: Usner, Daniel H., author.
Title: American Indians in early New Orleans : from Calumet to Raquette /
Daniel H. Usner.
Description: Baton Rouge : Louisiana State University Press, [2018] | Includes
bibliographical references and index.
Identifiers: LCCN 2018015753| ISBN 978-0-8071-7009-0 (cloth : alk. paper) |
ISBN 978-0-8071-7039-7 (pdf) | ISBN 978-0-8071-7040-3 (epub)
Subjects: LCSH: Indians of North America—Louisiana—New Orleans—
History—18th century. | Indians of North America—Louisiana—New
Orleans—History—19th century. | Indians of North America—Louisiana—
New Orleans—History—20th century. | New Orleans (La.)—History—18th
century. | New Orleans (La.)—History—19th century. | New Orleans (La.)—
History—20th century.
Classification: LCC E78.L8 U86 2018 | DDC 976.3/3500497—dc23
LC record available at https://lccn.loc.gov/2018015753

The paper in this book meets the guidelines for permanence and durability of the Committee
on Production Guidelines for Book Longevity of the Council on Library Resources. ∞

For
Jacob Seals Usner
and
Jordan Durel Usner

CONTENTS

ILLUSTRATIONS

MAPS

PREFACE

L ook at the official seal of New Orleans, an image dating back to the mid-1800s. It resembles many city and state seals across the United States. Standing prominently on both sides of a shield are figures of an Indian woman and an Indian man. Inside the shield is a reclining nude figure who faces the rising sun. Above the shield are twenty-five stars, and below rests an alligator. The origin and meaning of the Crescent City's official emblem remain obscure, but along with the iconic Louisiana reptile, those Native Americans clearly represent what was, and still is, a commonly held notion. As the original inhabitants of the land, American Indians are supposed to witness, and thereby certify, the dawn of a new age. The birth of a city, as celebrated in the seal of New Orleans, marked the early and inevitable passing of Indigenous people. Only their tribal legends and names endure. And indeed, the Crescent City is crisscrossed with streets named after long-forgotten peoples: Natchez, Chickasaw, Choctaw, Cherokee, Houma, Opelousas, Seminole, Tunica, and—the most challenging of all for tourists to pronounce—Tchoupitoulas. Chef Menteur Highway even honors a Choctaw chief who was supposedly banished by his tribe for lying too much. And, of course, there is the ubiquitous "Bayou" attached to area waterways and roads. It originated in the Choctaw word *bayuk,* meaning small stream.[1]

The paradox of American Indians being symbolically represented in street names and official emblems, while going almost completely unnoticed as real participants in the city's history, is deeply rooted throughout American history and culture. It reflects a persistent idea—more like a stubborn insistence—that Native people relinquished their possession of land and sovereignty long ago. This belief, thankfully, has been directly confronted by the determination of American Indian people themselves to assert their presence as well as by the commitment of scholars to rescue fact from fiction. When it comes to what we know about American Indians and their relationship with American cities, plenty of progress has been made. The surge in migration of Native Americans into metropolitan areas during and after World War II and the consequential rise of activism there ensured that study of urban Indians would occur. At first this new urbanization of American Indians drew attention mostly from sociologists, anthropologists, and political scientists, with little notice of earlier periods of Native presence in cities.[2] But eventually, historians and archaeologists began to consider how Native Americans participated in urbanization from pre-Columbian times through the twentieth century. Places that were densely populated centuries before European colonization, especially in the Mississippi and Ohio Valleys and in the American Southwest, indicate clearly that Indigenous North Americans had already experienced life in cityscapes. And the documentary records of places like Boston, Philadelphia, Charleston, and St. Augustine are finally being scrutinized by Early American historians for evidence of a dynamic and ongoing Indian presence in colonial towns.[3] Some of the most fascinating new work has even explored the frequent Atlantic crossings made by Indian people to European cities, in roles ranging from stolen captives and scientific specimens to political diplomats and entertainment celebrities.[4]

In this expanding study of American Indians in cities, the long span of time between colonial centuries and the mid-twentieth century still seems sorely neglected. Lately, some historians have produced valuable work on Great Lakes and West Coast cities over the nineteenth and early twentieth centuries, but there is plenty left to do in the history of American Indians for most cities.[5] Definitely falling into the latter category, the city of New Orleans happens to be an ideal place for studying how American Indians utilized urban space in dynamic ways over the centuries. Most obviously, the birth and early growth of New Orleans depended intricately on French relations with American Indians throughout the vast Mississippi Valley. Countless Indian delegations visited North American towns from Montreal to Savannah, from St. Augustine to Los Angeles, to negotiate with colonial officials and perform diplomatic ceremonies. New Orleans was no exception. But long after those towns stopped being centers of Indian diplomacy, an Indian presence in many American cities would persist in various ways. This was certainly the case for New Orleans, which throughout the nineteenth century was visited periodically by formal delegations of Indian leaders and regularly by informal groups of Indian traders and workers. Because all of this occurred on a large scale and over a long time in the Crescent City, plenty can be learned from the city's past about the complicated history of American Indians in urban America.

This book intends to trace that complicated history across the first two centuries of New Orleans, in the hope that other students of the city will dig deeper into that same time but moreover that they will extend much-needed coverage to the twentieth and early twenty-first centuries. American Indians are seldom considered as travelers or tourists to urban places, so my effort concentrates on how Native visitors to one city communicated their identities and their interests in changing forms. There is a long and deep scholarship on how performance of Indianness by non-Indians shaped the evolution of American identity and culture, from theatrical stages and middle-class men's clubs to sports mascots and motion pictures. And performance of Indianness by American Indians in Europe has also received plenty of attention lately. When it comes to the study of Indians themselves performing Indianness on this side of the Atlantic, however, far less has been written—with the exception of work on Wild West shows and world's fairs.[6] Countless Indian delegations to North American cities since the seventeenth century involved public rituals and demonstrations constituting their own expressions of identity and interest. Calumet dances, exchanges of wampum, lacrosse games, and other forms of diplomatic ceremony were regular events in colonial spaces as varied as Boston and Santa Fe. Even when Indian political relations seemed to become less essential to colonies and states, occasional visits to cities by western Indian emissaries provided opportunities for performance, even for spectacle.

Whether engaging government officials in diplomatic ceremonies, peddling cultural objects in marketplaces, playing traditional stickball matches on the outskirts of town, or performing songs and dances before city spectators, American Indians in New Orleans displayed their Indianness in complicated ways that warrant scrutiny. As Peter Nabokov wrote in *How the World Moves*, "Simply by being themselves, whenever Indians traveled outside their home communities they often felt onstage. It was never enough that they *were* Indians, they always had to *be* them as well. That meant satisfying old preconceptions and stereotypes."[7] For this reason, I have constructed a narrative of American Indians in Old New Orleans that self-consciously circulates, as time unfolds, between both the observations made by non-Indian people and the actions taken by Indian people. A recovery of Indian perspectives and interests, especially for the eighteenth and nineteenth centuries, can only be achieved through critical analysis of how white people represented Indian behavior in their drawings, paintings, and photographs as well as in their writings. Closer attention to the motives of observers ought to sharpen our awareness of precisely how evidence available to historians was constructed. This seems essential for breaking through biased language in order to reach as much of Indian motivation and experience as possible. Along the way, a focus on changing perceptions of American Indians in an urban space can add a relatively neglected dimension to the overall study of what historian Robert Berkhofer has called "the white man's Indian." To know how Indigenous people have been viewed and judged specifically in towns and cities is as important as knowing how they are represented in homeland forests, prairies, or deserts.[8]

This book's first two chapters relate how American Indians interacted with colonial officials and residents in French and Spanish New Orleans— in roles as diverse as slaves, traders, diplomats, and soldiers. The eighteenth century was certainly a time of incursion, dispossession, and even enslavement by colonial Europeans, but it was also when American Indians assimilated intrusive spaces into their own sense of place. New Orleans instantly became, and continued to be, a place of Indigenous sovereignty as much as a place of imperial aspiration. Although historians have devoted increasing attention to French relations with Choctaws, Natchez, Quapaws, and Caddos—the most populous and powerful nations in the Lower Mississippi Valley—we still have difficulty imagining what this meant for Louisiana's colonial capital. For days, even weeks, at a time, hundreds of Indians visited officials in the town. The contest between Great Britain and France for trade and alliance with American Indian nations in the interior Southeast, through much of the eighteenth century, especially advantaged the

Choctaws in their negotiations with both empires. But for Chitimachas, Houmas, Tunicas, and other nations in closer proximity to French colonists, Louisiana's lasting reliance on their economic and military services also ensured a strong degree of political autonomy. Diplomatic missions to New Orleans taken by emissaries from all of these nations were a regular feature of the colonial town's public life. When France ceded its claims west of the Mississippi River to Spain and lost everything else in North America to Britain after the Seven Years' War, the Lower Mississippi Valley became partitioned between Spanish and British rulers during the 1760s. With this new borderland of empires enhancing Indian nations' bargaining power, their elaborate rituals of political action, diplomatic exchange, and cultural representation made a significant impact on New Orleans society for a while longer.

The last three chapters of this book then explore how American Indians, in equally wide-ranging ways, maintained a significant presence in the city throughout the nineteenth century. The very survival of Indian communities in areas like the Crescent City, in the face of tremendous adversity and prejudice, actually challenged a dominant narrative that insisted on the inevitability of their disappearance. The "vanishing Indian," in other words, refused to vanish from Louisiana. Although references to this continuing Indian presence in New Orleans depicted them as silent and passive figures—much like those on the city's official seal—American Indians did nothing less than creatively adapt to rapidly changing circumstances. It took resilience and resourcefulness for them to put the growing port city and its surrounding plantation society to their own cultural and economic use. And their persistence, by the way, also had some influence on New Orleans society. Given how recorded accounts so systematically marginalized or obscured the Indian presence, it is difficult to get closer to the individual lives of Indian people. My primary objective, nonetheless, is to capture how real persons experienced New Orleans and *not* how they were imagined. I wish to at least intimate the stories that American Indian people tried to tell for themselves, rather than simply reiterate those that were told about them.

When the importance of Indian diplomacy to government officials in New Orleans waned at the end of the eighteenth century, Indian people relied on different forms of self-representation to maintain a dynamic presence on the cityscape and perhaps also to create a kind of "memory-scape." Back-of-town, as explored in chapter 3, became a fruitful space for perpetuating means of frontier exchange with Africans and Europeans that Native ancestors had developed during colonial times. With the loss of land and leverage that followed acquisition of Louisiana by the United States, American Indians improvised new ways of expressing their autonomy and negotiating their interest inside New Orleans. Playing stick-ball matches, carousing on city streets, or performing dances for urban spectators, however, also brought some risk as white spectators began to view Indian games, parades, dances, and peddling as the performance of a diminishing otherness. And to make the Crescent City's relationship with American Indians even more complex and fraught, for a couple of decades during the nineteenth century it became part of that painful passage for many Seminoles and Creeks who were being forcibly removed from their homelands. The appearance and treatment of these refugees in New Orleans are the main subject of chapter 4.

Meanwhile, nearby Choctaw Indians on the north shore of Lake Pontchartrain continued to maintain their creative relationship with the Crescent City by regularly vending crafts and plants in the French Market. Residents and visitors, not surprisingly, interpreted even this public activity as the residual behavior of a nearly extinct people, virtually erasing Indians from the city's history and landscape while nostalgically describing the survivors' ancestors. But for American Indians, as chapter 5 shows, this presence in urban marketplaces and fields comprised a strategy of persistence—engaging local resources for their livelihood while remembering, for themselves at least, the crucial role they played all along in early New Orleans.

As New Orleans now enters its fourth century, time is long overdue for considering the importance of American Indians to its history. I first and foremost hope that this book will contribute something to their inclusion in the Crescent City's recognized cultural diversity and social complexity, joining what over the past couple of decades has been a remarkable surge in the study of its history.[9] Much work, of course, remains to be done, especially about the city's changing and growing Indian population over the last century or so. My secondary wish, though, is to encourage an altogether new way to understand New Orleans and comparable cities. As the forms of American Indian interaction and presence explored below will demonstrate, how groups of people living nearby or visiting periodically relate to a city is an important dimension of urban development. Whether looking at farmers, gardeners, and seafood harvesters who supply the city from its surrounding area, or at shipping and trucking crewmen, and business and tourist visitors who pass through, there is plenty to learn about their itinerant presence in, and their substantial contribution to, urban life. The sprawl of cities like New Orleans onto fragile environments around them, and how this affects the culture and livelihood of longtime inhabitants in those places, are also subjects that demand greater attention. Clues for this wider inquiry are waiting to be found in the history of American Indians in and around New Orleans.

The seeds of this book were planted almost two decades ago, when for four months in 1999 The Historic New Orleans Collection presented at its Royal Street gallery in the heart of the French Quarter a special exhibition entitled "Romance and Reality: American Indians in 19th-Century New Orleans." I had proposed to Jon Kukla, then executive director of this research museum center, the formative idea for an exhibit and, to my astonishment, was entrusted to serve as guest curator. My hope was to offer visitors a rare look at American Indians in the city of New Orleans during the nineteenth century, as depicted by a variety of artists and writers. But I was not willing simply to display for passing viewers different pictures and words that had never before been assembled. Instead, I wanted somehow to invite them to explore critically the multiple ways that producers of this imagery viewed American Indians still living in close proximity to white society after many years of contact and conflict. Over several years of research in The Historic New Orleans Collection, I had found scattered among its holdings numerous lithographs, drawings, paintings, and photographs from the nineteenth century that captured a long-forgotten presence of American Indians in the Crescent City. Some of this visual material had already been reproduced in local histories, pictorial collections, scholarly books, and museum exhibitions, vaguely suggesting to the viewer that this culturally heterogeneous city included Native Americans among its occupants. In lithographs dating back to the 1820s by Félix Achille Beaupoil, Marquis de Saint Aulaire, an Indian family crosses a street in New Orleans's Faubourg Marigny and another stands beside the

Mississippi River. Illustrations drawn by Alfred Waud and Charles Upham for popular magazines after the Civil War, depicting Choctaw women at the French Market, convey the impression of a fleeting and exotic presence of American Indians on the margins of urban society.[10]

While compiling an extensive list of such pictures held in the collection, I searched in other places for additional glimpses of American Indian people in nineteenth-century Louisiana. To my surprise, I found a wide array of scenes and portraits featuring Lower Mississippi Valley Indians and so began to consider how these images compared to the realities of Indian life in and around an Old South city. Planning and designing an exhibition was certainly an extraordinary experience for a historian like myself, particularly for a social historian who had spent previous years downplaying the need to study ideas about American Indians any further while trying to shift attention more to the agency of American Indian people. The collection of material objects from Indian societies and their display in museum exhibits have played a powerful role in shaping how we think about Native American people. The prominent use of cultural artifacts and human remains in museums of natural history—in the company of animals, plants, and minerals—reduced Indians to a subhuman position. Meanwhile, museums featuring national and local histories relegated them to the distant past. The selective marginalization of Native American history and culture in museum spaces has perpetuated narratives of backwardness and extinction that are inseparable from the physical acts of conquest and domination long endured by American Indian people. Even the display of words and pictures about Louisiana Indians in the past, therefore, should be understood as a pressing concern to Native Americans today.[11]

At The Historic New Orleans Collection, my idea for this exhibition was radically different from what was ordinarily organized inside its Royal Street gallery. This combination research center, archival collection, and tourist attraction had never presented a program or exhibit focusing on American Indians. And the fact that I wanted to design an explicitly interpretive presentation was especially challenging. My desire to elicit critical thinking about the image makers' perspectives and to capture both change and continuity over one hundred years imposed an unusual demand upon an exceptionally talented staff—one already well equipped to highlight the artistic and technical features of the exhibited materials. With approval granted by the board of directors, I proceeded to assemble and arrange a total of seventy-four pictorial images. They were displayed roughly in chronological order alongside brief descriptive texts, and running along the wall above the items were panels presenting quotations from contemporaneous written accounts of the Indian presence in nineteenth-century New Orleans.

I decided from the very beginning of my guest curator role that "Romance and Reality" somehow had to involve American Indians from communities in and around New Orleans today. The nearest Indian nations are Houmas and Choctaws, although the more distant Chitimachas and Tunicas also have a long history of interaction with the Crescent City. My most helpful contact was then-director of the Cannes Brûlée Native American Center in Kenner, Louisiana, Landris Gray Hawk Perkins, whose Houma and Choctaw families are deeply rooted in the New Orleans area and who has many years of experience in public education. I explained my idea to Perkins and requested his input and participation. He helped The Historic New Orleans Collection publicize the exhibition among Louisiana's Indian communities and agreed to present two public programs during its running. An evening slide lecture featured photographs from Indian family albums, allowing the audience to contrast the exhibit's outside glimpses with Perkins's inside memories. In a Saturday presentation, Perkins shared traditional stories and historical accounts with a large number of visitors in the center's French Quarter courtyard. In gathering cultural objects to display along with pictures and words for "Romance and Reality," John Lawrence—director of museum programs and, by the way, a De La Salle High School classmate of mine—introduced me to Mercedes Whitecloud. With her late husband Dr. Thomas Whitecloud, Mercedes collected a remarkable array of American Indian arts and crafts. Her knowledge of Louisiana Indian basketry and devotion to the craft, which she has shared with me since 1999, is largely responsible for the research path that I would eventually follow into Chitimacha history.

Since I curated that exhibit, other research projects—including my current inquiry into Chitimacha basket diplomacy—have demanded most of my attention, but I never stopped accumulating information about American Indians in the New Orleans area or reading new scholarship on Indigenous people in different cities. Whenever working in an archive

or library for another article or book, I would set time aside to probe
for possible sources on New Orleans and add to my collection of notes.
As those notes steadily grew in volume, the idea for eventually writing
a book devoted exclusively to American Indians in New Orleans began
to blossom. It became "the next book," as I would repeatedly tell myself,
but never reached the front burner until the Crescent City's tricentennial
came around. Tempting requests to produce short essays on its American
Indian experience for publications and symposia beckoned me back to
Louisiana's colonial period, which I had left behind as an area of research
years ago. Drawn temporarily away from my current work on Chitimacha
history in the late nineteenth and early twentieth centuries, I suddenly
decided to finally write the New Orleans book that kept getting delayed.
Margaret Lovecraft at Louisiana State University Press agreed to solicit
readers of my manuscript as quickly as possible, two readers generously
and expeditiously responded with helpful and supportive feedback, and
the Press's administrators approved a plan to publish this book in time for
the 2018 tricentennial.

So it is obvious that my debts to many people have indeed accrued over
the two decades of background to *American Indians in Early New Orleans.*
The wonderful staff at The Historic New Orleans Collection has of course
earned my gratitude. John Lawrence, my "old" friend, and Priscilla Lawrence, who succeeded Kukla as executive director, have remained generous
supporters of all my work. I also owe thanks to Gray Hawk Perkins and
Mercedes Whitecloud for many lessons learned from them since the exhi-
bition. Among several research centers whose staffs have been helpful, the
New Orleans Public Library's Louisiana Division/City Archives & Special
Collections, The Historic New Orleans Collection, Tulane University's
Louisiana Research Collection, the University of New Orleans's Archives
and Manuscripts Department, the Louisiana State Museum's Louisiana
Historical Center, and Louisiana State University's Louisiana and Lower
Mississippi Valley Collections deserve hearty thanks. Here at Vanderbilt
University, the Jean and Alexander Heard Library's Interlibrary Loan Ser-
vice always made sure that rare books and articles reached me in timely
fashion. And most of the research that went into this book was made possible by funds provided by the Holland N. McTyeire Endowment.

An opportunity to test some of my ideas for this book came in the spring of 2017, when the program committee organized a special session for the annual meeting of the Organization of American Historians in New Orleans. Thanks go to Alison Games for putting "New Perspectives on Early New Orleans" together and for inviting me to participate. Fellow panelists, all of them highly accomplished scholars of New Orleans history, offered encouragement and inspiration through their own presentations as well as their feedback on my paper. Ginger Gould, Sophie White, and Shannon Dawdy were already good friends, and I enjoyed meeting Ryan Gray. Serving as commentator, Shannon insightfully and forcefully voiced a call for braver treatment of the city's rich but fraught past. I owe deep appreciation to four friends who read the book manuscript in part or in its entirety—Larry Powell, Peter Wood, Emily Clark, and Bruce Duthu. Emily read it as a referee for Louisiana State University Press. Her feedback, along with that provided by an anonymous referee, made a big difference toward improving various aspects of this book. I take full responsibility, of course, for all of its errors and shortcomings.

Ambitious projects undertaken by institutions and organizations in New Orleans to mark the city's tricentennial also contributed to my decision to write this book. Under the careful and knowledgeable guidance of Erin Greenwald, The Historic New Orleans Collection planned a special exhibit, "New Orleans, the Founding Era," to commemorate the anniversary. For the exhibit catalog, I was asked to write a short piece on American Indians in French colonial New Orleans. The Louisiana Endowment for the Humanities—in partnership with the New Orleans Convention and Visitors Bureau, the New Orleans Tourism Marketing Corporation, and the 2018 NOLA Commission—invited me to accompany other historians of the city in producing essays for a wide readership in *New Orleans and the World*. For this opportunity to summarize both the eighteenth and nineteenth centuries of American Indians' presence in the city, I am most grateful to editor Nancy Dixon and other members of the editorial board. As acquisitions editor at Louisiana State University Press, Margaret Lovecraft showed an enthusiastic and careful attention to my manuscript that made publication of this book an exceptionally rewarding experience. Thanks also go to managing editor Lee Sioles for the guidance it took to have *American Indians in Early New Orleans* appear during the city's tricentennial. In designing maps for me, Mary Lee Eggart's fine skill as an artist along with her true knowledge of south Louisiana made a much-appreciated difference. As copyeditor, Gary Von Euer deserves recognition for the thoughtful and thorough attention that he devoted to the manuscript.

I am truly blessed and thankful to have Rhonda Usner as my partner in every possible way. My love for her and my need for her friendship grow each day. Our sons, Jacob and Jordan, have earned the dedication of this book to them. I cannot say how much of their character might be attributed to the fact that both of their parents were born and raised in New Orleans, but there is no doubt that the city made some difference in their own lives—even though their real home was thirteen hundred miles away in Ithaca, New York. Spending summer-long weeks and holiday seasons with countless loving relatives, enduring frequent fieldtrips to south Louisiana historic parks and museums, rushing across town to catch a parade of Mardi Gras Indians on Super Sunday, attending Jesse Jackson's presidential campaign rally in Municipal Auditorium—this is just a sample of New Orleans experiences that Rhonda and I eagerly shared with our sons during their childhood. What I know for certain is that Jacob Seals Usner and Jordan Durel Usner, although marvelously different from each other, have both become remarkably compassionate, inquisitive, and hardworking men who are my deepest source of joy and pride.

AMERICAN INDIANS
in Early New Orleans

CHAPTER ONE

PLACE OF FOREIGN LANGUAGES

In the year 1699, on the Saturday after Mardi Gras, Pierre Le Moyne d'Iberville was slowly ascending the Mississippi River when he encountered a traveling group of Biloxi Indians just below the future site of New Orleans. On the lush but spongy shoreline of the river, covered with thick canebrakes and shaded by cypress and oak trees, one of these Biloxi men treated the French naval officer to a customary show of friendship. He first passed both hands over his own face and breast and then passed them over Iberville's face and breast before raising them toward the sky. In return for knives, glass beads, and axes offered by Iberville, the Biloxi gave him some buffalo and bear meat. This was Iberville's first time voyaging on the Mississippi, and its banks surely seemed exotic to someone born and raised in Canada. But for someone who, along with other members of his family, had accumulated plenty of experience in Indian diplomacy, the Biloxi's greeting would not have appeared so strange. Two days following that initial encounter, Iberville's party, including his brother Bienville, reached a point along the river where Indians portaged to and from Lake Pontchartrain. "They drag their canoes over a rather good road," Iberville reported, "at which we found several pieces of baggage owned by men that were going there or were returning." After his guide, another Biloxi man, pointed out that the distance from river to lake was short, "the Indian picked up a bundle from there." Within only a few days, the importance of both ceremony and commerce was documented right where the Crescent City arose two decades later.[1]

American Indians had mainly used this crescent-shaped bend in the serpentine Mississippi, situated between the river's east bank and a chain of shallow lakes, to transport goods between waterways and to seasonally gather food sources. The natural conditions making this site ideal for portage and fishing, however, also reduced any likelihood of it becoming a place for permanent occupation, an environmental challenge that to this day—as much of the world knows now—demands expensive engineering and constant vigilance.[2] Indigenous people in this alluvial lowland had developed over the millennia a wise rhythmic pattern for exploiting its rich array of animal and plant resources. As the Mississippi River's delta jumped directions every few centuries, American Indian communities easily shifted their uses of new and old channels. During summer and autumn, people occupied natural levees formed by the waterways' spring deposits of sediment, hunting deer, possums, raccoons, swamp rabbits, and muskrats; fishing in backwater lakes; and gathering persimmons, honey locusts, crab apples, sassafras, pecans, black walnuts, wild plums, and hickory nuts. In winter these communities dispersed into camps along bayous and lakes, harvesting plenty of fish, fowl, clams, and oysters. When spring flooding by the Mississippi began, the nearest bluffs bordering the floodplain became centers of occupation. This was the season ripest for group-oriented hunting, for engaging in longer-distance trade and warfare, and for intensifying production of domestic crops over time.

Several centuries before French colonization began, the Pontchartrain Basin—those waters and wetlands lying between natural levees along the Mississippi River and terraced land north of Lake Pontchartrain—had become prime habitat for this seasonal round of activity. East-to-west ridges left by abandoned channels of the Mississippi provided ground for occupation and travel above the floodplain, and a sizable bayou entering the lake offered convenient access to the banks of the Mississippi. Shell middens and mounds formed by Indigenous inhabitants, like Big Oak and Little Oak Islands, are remnants of seasonal camping and collecting across the area that would become New Orleans. A recent archaeological excavation at Bayou St. John has uncovered one mound with pottery fragments and animal bones dating to AD 300–400 (Late Marksville Period), also revealing that it was partly flattened to become the foundation of a French colonial fort built at the bayou's entrance to Lake Pontchartrain.[3]

The early years of the eighteenth century were an especially trying time along the lower banks of the Mississippi River. Deadly warfare between Indian nations since the 1680s was being driven by a Chickasaw alliance with South Carolina, as the purchase of captives by British traders now motivated Chickasaws to commit aggressive raids against other Indians. This commercialization of intertribal captivity meant that thousands of Lower Mississippi Valley and Gulf Coastal Indians—decades before French colonization of the region began—were already transported by Chickasaw captors either to work on Carolina plantations or to be shipped off to other British colonies. Dreadful attacks by Indian nations allied with British traders and armed with guns had a devastating impact on many groups across the Mississippi Valley. When René Robert Cavelier de La Salle traveled down the Mississippi in 1682, he saw at a Tangipahoa village situated near present-day New Orleans "only carcasses of men and women, ruined huts, and others full of dead bodies, a coating of blood on the ground, and all their canoes broken and cut up with axes." Four women who had somehow escaped captivity and death told La Salle's exploration party that it had been destroyed by "Auma, Auma, Chiquilousa," names suggesting that Houmas and Chickasaws were likely responsible.[4]

Raids and counter-raids created a wave of damaging conflicts and destabilizing migrations that shaped the early formation of French and Indian relations. Soon after Iberville reached this region to begin colonization, an English trader led a party of Chickasaw and Alibamon warriors on an attack against Tunica Indians. Sometime earlier this man had been captured by Tunica warriors but managed to escape, so now he was motivated by revenge as well as profit. The Tunicas fled from their village and took refuge among the Houmas. But for reasons that are not clear, they suddenly turned on their hosts, forcing the Houmas to move temporarily downriver to Bayou St. John in 1706. Uncertainty over the intentions of any outsider generated apprehension and hostility toward other Indians as well as newly arriving Europeans. When some Chitimachas assassinated missionary Jean François Buisson de St. Cosme near present-day Donaldsonville, Louisiana, Jean-Baptiste Le Moyne, sieur de Bienville, Iberville's younger brother, feared that more Indian attacks would occur "because of the small fear that they have of the French." Expressing "in great seriousness" their low opinion of the new colony, Chickasaw and

Choctaw chiefs had recently asked Bienville "if there were really as many people in France as here and whether there were many more." Bienville subsequently mobilized French soldiers and Indian allies in a war against the Chitimachas that would last over a decade, with a countless number of Chitimacha people captured and enslaved before it was all over. Peace was finally established in 1718, following mediation by Houma Indians who were closest to the Chitimachas and by French concessionaires whose formative plantations were in constant danger of attack.[5]

The ceremony marking this peace began when a delegation of about forty Chitimacha Indians—including a chief and his wife—landed in several dugout canoes at the Mississippi River's bank fronting New Orleans, a colonial town still being cleared and surveyed. Singing to the cadence of gourd rattles and waving a calumet pipe toward the sky, the Chitimachas marched solemnly to the makeshift cabin of Bienville. Once all of these visitors were seated on the ground, the pipe was lit and presented to Louisiana's governor. After war with the French had ravaged his people for a decade, the Chitimachas' "word-bearer" expressed joy over Bienville's willingness to accept peace. "Our hearts and our ears are filled with it," he declared, "and our descendants will preserve it as long as the ancient word shall endure." After presenting gifts of deerskins to the governor, this orator further elaborated on the causes and consequences of the costly war. With a brief speech, Bienville received this promise of peace, along with the pipe itself as a gift. He commanded the Chitimachas to return all colonists taken captive during the war, but refused to return any Chitimacha people captured and enslaved by the French. Bienville then closed this ceremony by insisting that the chief relocate his village closer to New Orleans, a city that ever since then has taken its rituals quite seriously.[6]

Antoine Simon Le Page du Pratz, while starting a farm along Bayou St. John, benefited from, among other services, his enslaved Chitimacha woman's interpretation of the very ceremony that ended her people's war against the French. His account, eventually published in *Histoire de la Louisiane,* includes a valuable report of the calumet ceremony. In order to establish any new alliance or restore peace after a war, American Indians performed ceremonies centered on the use of a pipe made of river cane or some other reedlike material and attached to a carved bowl made of red or black stone. Waving the pipe decorated with bird feathers during an

Fig. 1. Antoine Le Page du Pratz, *Marche du Calumet de Paix,* engraving in *Histoire de la Louisiane* (1758). Yale Collection of Western Americana, Beinecke Rare Book and Manuscript Library, Yale University.

opening dance and smoking tobacco with the opposite party, as depicted in Le Page du Pratz's engraving *Marche du Calumet de Paix* (figure 1), were standard protocol. This elaborate ritual of diplomacy was actually spreading beyond its geographical origin in the northern Great Plains and western Great Lakes while the French began to colonize the Gulf Coast and Mississippi Valley. Diffusion into the eastern woodlands of a ceremonial complex that linked different levels of the natural world and formed kinship ties between strangers was then under way partly because French explorers and officials like Bienville adopted it for establishing trade alliances with American Indians.[7]

Whether relations between native and colonial groups were violent or peaceful at any given time, representation of American Indian people in early eighteenth-century images and words reveals more about imperial fantasies than about actual interactions. François Jollain's *Le Commerce que les Indiens du Mexique font avec les François au Port de Missisipi* was a copperplate engraving circulated to promote colonization of the Lower Mississippi Valley soon after the founding of New Orleans. The hospitable posture of Native Americans in this picture—looking more South American or Caribbean in aspect than North American—typified attempts to publicize and romanticize the opportunity awaiting investors in trade and settlement along the Mississippi River (plate 1). In one fictional letter published in the magazine *Nouveau Mercure* to promote John Law's Company of the West, a colonial author expects Louisiana to "one day become France's Peru."[8] The supplicatory gestures of some Indians in Jollain's engraving also aimed to solicit from its viewers financial support for efforts at Christianization. European colonizers since Columbus had rhetorically blended commerce and conversion into a Christian imperialism. The French in particular were deriving an imagery of Native joy—expressed through physical gestures in response to European arrival—from medieval and early modern art commemorating ceremonies performed in French cities whenever the king visited.[9]

What was really happening on the ground bordering the Mississippi River, most of it below sea level, did not come close to Jollain's representation—and not only because his picture featured high mountains in the background. While slaves, convict workers, indentured servants, and soldiers strenuously burned dense patches of river cane and chopped down hardwood trees, carving out of perceived wilderness a perfectly rectangular grid of streets designed by royal engineers, American Indians used their deep knowledge of river currents, lakes, bayous, and wetlands to draw the site of Louisiana's new capital into their trade and diplomatic sphere. Europeans might be worrying about its perilous location—fearing floods, insects, hurricanes, and diseases—but Indians were used to blending their harvests, travels, and rituals with the region's natural rhythms. As in other North American colonial towns over the seventeenth and eighteenth centuries, American Indians would now creatively establish their own trade and ceremonial grounds in a place named Nouvelle Orléans in order to negotiate and even resist colonialism.[10] For thousands of years southeastern Indians had been constructing mounds as spaces for ritual

performance and aesthetic expression, even distinguishing in their design between messages intended for outsiders and insiders. In a project
studying many different mound sites that date from the twelfth to the
sixteenth centuries (called the Mississippian Period by archaeologists),
Choctaw writer LeAnne Howe associates ball games, dances, and other
ceremonies with the layering of soils. Descendant Indian societies across
the Southeast perpetuated this tradition on village square grounds, and
eventually on colonial plazas, where gift exchanges and calumet dances
secured political alliances.[11]

Describing one of many ceremonies performed by American Indian
delegates at the governor's house in New Orleans, Marc Antoine Caillot,
a clerk working for the Company of the Indies, vividly captured how they
regularly turned the formative colonial town into their own ritual space.
Numbering anywhere between one hundred fifty and five hundred men
and women, they sang and danced before lining up outside the gate. Chiefs
and other dignitaries then entered, carrying plenty of gifts, and placed a
calumet in the governor's hands. After everyone present took a puff from
the pipe, then through a French interpreter familiar with their language,
the Indian spokesmen delivered a series of speeches that might last for
hours. "Since the great sun of the French sent you here to govern the country, and he has found in you much valor and the necessary qualities to
make you obey," as the lead orator would typically begin, "we come here,
with my nation, to present to you our fealty and assure you that, when
you need our small services, we will always be ready to follow your orders,
whether it is to second you in a war you may have against your enemies, as
well as for any other thing that regards the usefulness of the French nation,
which we have always loved, and which we continue to cherish." Once all
of the speeches had ended, "four worthies get up, along with four Indians,
and dance the calumet dance, all painted and ornamented with different
types of feathers, to the sound of an earthen pot covered with a deerskin,
ornamented with many bells and accompanied by their voices." Writing
about a place already becoming a creative confluence of diverse rhythms
and tones, Caillot added, "This makes music as bizarre as their movements
and dances. When they have danced for a while, by making extraordinary
contortions that make you want to die laughing, they sit down again on
their bottoms, whereupon one of them gets up and takes the calumet."

The pipe was passed around for a final round of smoking, and the gifts were placed at the governor's feet. On the next day at Company of the Indies headquarters, the governor first spoke to the chief and his closest entourage and then in exchange for the gifts he received—usually a large quantity of deerskins—gave them an array of goods that commonly included cloth, combs, mirrors, muskets, and vermillion. "When they return to their village, the chief has it all divided."[12]

During the autumn of 1722, New Orleans residents saw Indian delegations visiting Governor Bienville on a series of urgent diplomatic missions. Tunicas arrived in early October, Acolapissas in early November. Jean-Baptiste-Martin Diron d'Artaguette, located at Cannes Bruslées at the time, was informed that the Acolapissa war chief "was going down to New Orleans to make a present to M. Bienville of some fowl and Indian corn, to the end that he [M. Bienville] should permit his nation to seize the medicine man of the village of the Ouachas, living among the Tensas, ten leagues distant from New Orleans, who had undertaken to cure the great chief of the Acolapissas, but who, on the contrary, had put into his body the teeth of serpents and other evil things." Subsequently, the Acolapissas took "as slaves a great part of the village of the Ouachas." The survivors escaped to the French, and Bienville dispatched an officer on November 19 to demand that the Acolapissas return their captives and reconcile with the Ouachas. Peace was restored, according to d'Artaguette. In the midst of these events, Tattooed Serpent of the Natchez led a large delegation to New Orleans after conflict erupted between the Apple Village and the St. Catherine Concession. A calumet ceremony was held, although illness prevented Bienville from serving as host. Nearly a hundred residents of the city, as journaled by d'Artaguette, were around that time sick "with fevers and with other illnesses." The brother of the Great Sun promised to compensate the concession with regular payments of chickens, and Bienville provided him with eight hundred livres' worth of gifts and munitions to bolster pro-French support among the Natchez.[13]

From a much longer distance, a special delegation of Illinois, Missouri, Osage, and Oto Indians traveled to New Orleans in 1725 to board a ship for France. A chief of each nation, along with a daughter of the Missouris' head chief, were being led by commandant Etienne Véniard de Bourgmont on what had become a standard itinerary for Native American visitors to

European capitals. The spectacle of these Missouri Valley Indians attending theaters and fairs in Paris, between visits to the court of Louis XV and the office of the Company of the Indies, received widespread attention. Witnessing a demonstration of the calumet dance performed by these Indian celebrities, Jean-Philippe Rameau was inspired to compose "Les Sauvages," which eventually became an entrée in his opera-ballet *Les Indes Galantes*. On March 10, 1736, Rameau's *Les Sauvages* was performed for the first time with its newly added fourth entrée. Set in a North American forest, it involves a competing courtship of an Indian girl named Zima by a Frenchman named Damon and a Spaniard named Don Alvar. The plot unfolds in the first half of an act, as Zima rejects both European courters and marries a native warrior named Adario. In the second half, the ballet becomes "Danse du Grand Calumet de la Paix." In this dance *en rondeau*, the opera-ballet expresses its most exotic sound. As Cuthbert Girdlestone describes it, "The piece is given first as a dance by the full orchestra except for trumpets and drums; it is repeated as a duet by Zima and Adario, each return of the refrain being taken up by the whole chorus. The vocal line is simpler and more peaceful than that of the instruments; it seems to hover above it. In the second episode the instrumental part is also varied; this is the most moving section in this very beautiful number." More than half a century earlier, Father Jacques Marquette had compared an Illinois calumet ceremony to "a Ballet in France." "This is done so well," he wrote, "with slow and measured steps, and to the rhythmic sounds of the voices and drums."[14]

Although Indian diplomatic delegations instantly became an important feature of public life in New Orleans, the city's survival and early growth depended more immediately upon goods and services provided by nearby Indian communities. From Indian villages to the new port town, a frontier exchange economy already under way in the countryside began to channel an increasing volume of deerskins for exportation and an essential supply of grain and meat for urban consumption. Within no time Indian people were regularly delivering a variety of goods to New Orleans and occasionally working as guides for travelers and as fugitive-catchers for slave owners. Over the winter of 1722–1723, Bernard Diron d'Artaguette traveled from New Orleans upriver to Illinois, recording in his journal detailed observations of Indian communities and colonial settlements along the way. Louisiana's inspector general of troops remarked how Chaouacha, Colapissa, Taensa, Houma, Chitimacha, and Tunica villagers provided essential services and goods to nearby colonial inhabitants struggling to survive and start their own farms. Although we might still visualize colonial Louisiana as an unbroken stretch of settlements along the Mississippi River, reinforced by the way maps are drawn, it was more like a patchwork of Native and colonial communities. The Acolapissas lived across the river from but near "three little villages of Germans"—"the remnant of that multitude of Germans whom the company had sent here"—and numbering 150 warriors, "their chief occupation is that of planting great quantities of Indian corn which they sell to the French in exchange for merchandise." Also, because of disputes with the Acolapissas, a nearby village of Chaouachas was abandoning its land. Between two Houma villages on the east bank, totaling three hundred warriors, "there are eight French settlements which are engaged in raising food crops." Passing the Chitimachas, who numbered one hundred warriors, D'Artaguette called them "great eaters of the crocodile, or alligator, which they catch with considerable skill." He described how they dove into the water and clenched the alligator's jaws together with their hands. Upon reaching the Tunicas, D'Artaguette estimated that "there may be in this village two hundred warriors who live on hunting and Indian corn, which they raise." He reported that some of them had "a smattering of Christianity, but just as they were commencing to appreciate the Word of god, Father Davion left them, to such a degree did his own interests outweigh those of charity." D'Artaguette spent the evening at the Tunica village, noticing that "there are also in this village fifteen French places which raise rice, beans, maize and other vegetables necessary to life. Their greatest trade is in poultry, which they go to New Orleans to sell." The next morning D'Artaguette's party "purchased some Indian provisions" and "hired an Indian hunter to go with us as far as the Arkansas."[15]

As mentioned in one of Bienville's reports on the colony, Acolapissa Indians on the north shore of Lake Pontchartrain opposite the mouth of Bayou St. John "furnish us almost all the fresh meat that is consumed in New Orleans without however their neglecting the cultivation of their lands which produce a great deal of corn." Chaouachas, downriver on the east bank of the Mississippi, traded mostly in corn, although on at least one occasion they supplied roofing bark for buildings at Balise. Houmas upriver on the east bank "rendered us good services in the famines that we have experienced in recent years by the abundance of provisions that they have furnished us." Chitimachas, "very skillful" at fishing, brought portions of their seasonal catches from surrounding lakes. Marc Antoine Caillot described how every winter as many as three hundred Biloxi Indians hunted along the bayous flowing into Lake Pontchartrain from the north. Colonists living in New Orleans then bartered with them for the fresh game. A "pinch of vermillion," for example, might be exchanged for four or five ducks. Caillot himself "got fifteen ducks and deer for three musket balls." Recent archaeological fieldwork at St. Anthony's Garden, today a picturesque space behind the St. Louis Cathedral, strongly suggests that this site was an early market frequented by American Indians and town residents.[16]

Complexity and diversity of the Indian presence in New Orleans was vividly captured in a drawing made by Alexandre de Batz in 1735 (plate 2). A mason and engineer in the French military, de Batz produced watercolor images on location that are crude but graphic in their depiction of everyday life. In *Dessein de Sauvages de Plusiers Nations Nlle Orléans*, individuals from different nations stand along the Mississippi River. An Atakapa man is holding a calumet, while trade goods commonly exchanged between colonists and Indians—bison ribs, tallow, and bear oil—line the shore. And the young African standing next to the Atakapa is not the only enslaved person depicted. The Fox woman apparently working on a deerskin is also enslaved. The figures behind her are Illinois Indians from the Upper Mississippi Valley, signaling that diplomatic and trade missions from nations across the region were a regular feature of public life in New Orleans throughout the French colonial period.[17]

Early trade with American Indians, especially commerce in furs, also employed occupational traders who lived in New Orleans. A significant number of "voyageurs" kept houses there in 1727, according to an early town census. Pierre Ferand on Rue Bourbon was identified as a trader with the Houmas, while Barbier was "of the Tonicas Indian village." Pierre La Houx "of the Akansas" lived on Rue Orléans with his wife and child. Other traders were identified with posts in upper Louisiana, so their residence in the colonial capital was most likely seasonal. On a journey upriver from New Orleans to Natchez in 1726, Jean-François-Benjamin Dumont de Montigny stopped at the Tunica village, "where the chief, a Christian, although an Indian, received me graciously and served me supper in the French fashion." Staying overnight in this Indian village, the French lieutenant slept "at the home of a Frenchman who had settled there and who was doing very well in trade, since he was the only Frenchman in the place." As reported by Dumont, this French trader "obtained from the Indians all that he wanted in exchange for the supplies he sold and for which he made a nice profit for himself by going down to New Orleans to resell what he had, such as poultry, corn, oil, pelts, etc."[18]

<<<<

Indian labor as well as Indian trade contributed heavily to the city's formative economy, and most American Indians working inside the colonial town were enslaved captives taken during early warfare. Long before New Orleans was founded, tens of thousands of Native North Americans had been captured and sold into slavery, at first by European explorers and eventually by colonial officials and merchants. Many of these captives, mostly taken during war, were shipped to British or French Caribbean colonies; others worked as plantation slaves or household servants up and down the Eastern Seaboard. Many enslaved Indians lived in cities like Montreal, Boston, New York, Charleston, and—by the 1720s—New Orleans.[19] From Louisiana's beginnings, Indian people, especially Chitimacha women and children, formed a substantial part of the French colony's slave population. A 1721 census listed more than fifty Indian slaves living in the vicinity of New Orleans. Twenty-one lived in town, while the rest are listed in the villages of Bayou St. John, Gentilly, Chapitoulas, Cannes Bruslées, and Chaouachas. (The total population of enslaved people in the colony is recorded as 161 Indians and 680 Africans.) Five years later, thirty Indian slaves were residing inside New Orleans. On the Rue Royal two Indian and four black slaves (age and gender not identified) lived with carpenter Thomas Dezery. On the Rue St. Louis, François St. Amand's household included his wife and two children, along with seven Indian slaves. Among residences on the Rue du Quay was that of a hunter named Reboul and his Indian slave.[20] These enslaved people, like the Chitimacha woman owned by Le Page du Pratz, provided a multitude of different services and products for their colonial owners. They even instructed their colonial owners about medicinal and culinary uses of local plants. Useful knowledge about Louisiana flora and fauna in general would have been shared. Le Page du Pratz's Chitimacha servant was most likely involved when he sent to natural scientists in France plenty of herbs packed inside river cane baskets.[21]

By no means did enslaved Indians escape the abuse, torture, and murder that all slaves faced at the hands of owners. After flogging a young Native "sauvagess" so savagely that her death was likely, a colonist named Coupart sold her to another slave owner. The offended buyer, Lasonde, sued Coupart for return of the goods he had exchanged for the Indian woman, telling the court that he had been fraudulently told that she was suffering only from a fever. It is not evident in the proceedings whether or not this young woman survived the brutal whipping.[22] The lives of Indian women working at domestic tasks in New Orleans, of course, varied quite widely, some even marrying non-Indian men who were not always their owners. The earliest marriage on record occurred on July 3, 1731, when Mathurin L'Horo married Marie, a "sauvagess libre" who was the widow of a drummer killed during the Natchez War. Later that same year, Hippolite, "daughter of a sauvagesse named Catherine, formerly the servant of Nicolas Chauvin de La Fresniere," married Canadian Joseph Turpin. La Fresniere, Louisiana's second largest slaveholder at the time (owning one hundred fifteen Blacks and three Indians), served as witness to this marriage.[23] Additional glimpses into Indian women's presence in early New Orleans include the trial of a young African American slave named Jeanne Marie, who when charged with infanticide accused an unnamed "sauvagess" of bearing ill will toward her and of killing her baby. In 1743 an enslaved woman "of the Panis nation" with "an infant at her breast" was sold by Martin Urtubin to Dubois for nine hundred livres; several months later another "sauvagess" was sold by Françoise Jallot to the Ursuline nuns for three thousand livres. In August 1746, an American Indian woman owned by Captain Henri d'Orgon was sold at a public auction. Like most enslaved Indians in colonial New Orleans, this woman's name and origin are not identified in the record. But because D'Orgon had engaged in warfare against the Chickasaws in 1738 and had become commandant of the Natchez fort the following year, she was most likely a Chickasaw woman taken captive during the French campaign against her people.[24]

As in other port towns of colonial North America, there was mounting fear among Louisiana officials and elites that Indian and African slaves might collaborate, or that open interaction between free and enslaved inhabitants could lead to rebellion. From its very beginning, New Orleans was the site of frequent Indian flights to freedom. In May 1723 Antoine Rivard complained to the Louisiana Superior Council about two runaway Indian slaves owned by Coustillas who were killing and eating his cattle along Bayou Chapitoulas. A few years later, an Indian slave belonging to Rivard himself was caught after running away. Sansoucy, as he was named, left his owner because he feared punishment for failing to find a stray ox. This arrested fugitive reported that he had found refuge in a village of about fifteen runaway Indian slaves, armed and ready to defend themselves against capture. In that same spring of 1727, a runaway slave belonging to the Company of the Indies' cashier was arrested and accused of enticing an enslaved Indian woman to rob her owner and flee with him.[25] The flight of African slaves to Indian communities was an additional cause for concern among New Orleans slave owners. When an anonymous visitor from France observed how "the inhabitants, sailors, Indians, and slaves run around freely inside as well as beyond the town," he passed a common judgment about what elites called the rabble. "They meet in a multitude of negro cabarets frequented by slaves who have fled their plantations either due to laziness or want, and who survive by trading stolen goods."[26] As a consequence of such fraternization, numerous African Americans in the Lower Mississippi Valley, as in other colonial regions, became proficient enough in an Indian language to serve occasionally as interpreters for officials and traders. Slaves also worked as rowers and packhorsemen, thereby coming regularly into close contact with American Indians. The overall danger from fluid Indian-black relations as perceived by slave owners, however, far outweighed these particular services in communication and commerce.[27]

Authorities in colonial towns everywhere, whether it be Montreal, Boston, New York, Philadelphia, or Charleston, attempted to implement prohibitions and punishments that would discourage loose interaction among free and enslaved people. In September 1724 Louisiana's attorney general, François Fleuriau, reported to the colonial council that "a number of robbers and scoundrels . . . were convicted [and sent] to this colony . . .

by orders of the king, the intent of which was to punish them by exile from France and to make them change their life. They, on the contrary, continue their wantonness and evil ways, of which we have examples every day in thefts, sedition, and conspiracies and the carrying off of ferries, boats, and sloops, not only done and fomented by these people, but by their corrupting others. Most of these malcontents stay in New Orleans. . . . These sorts of idle people who have no trade debauch and entice the French domestics, Indians, and negroes and get them to steal from their masters. . . . Let them be exiled far from the ports." Exemplifying one way to generate division between potential collaborators, a free black named Louis Congo was appointed as public executioner. When he was attacked by three runaway Indian slaves in the summer of 1726, Fleuriau urged the Superior Council to take prompt and sweeping action against all fugitives, urging assignment of neighboring Indian villagers to seek and capture them. "For a long time now," the attorney general later wrote, "a large troop of Indian slaves have banded together and deserted. Well-armed, they run and thieve around the city and it is feared they plan to do worse." "Let us punish the deserters with a swift blow, acting with impunity," he added. The three men who had attacked Louis Congo—identified as Guillory, Bontemps, and Jean Baptiste—were eventually arrested and severely punished.[28] Incentivizing Africans to distrust and resent American Indians was paired in colonial policy with benefits offered to American Indians for capturing fugitive slaves. When a black woman owned by Madame Lionnais ran away in 1730, for example, Bayogoula Indians apprehended her for a reward.[29] Throughout the next century-and-a-half of plantation slavery in the Lower Mississippi Valley, neighboring Indian communities would be materially rewarded for this service. As late as the early 1860s a "Goula Indian" named Blow-Gun John was assisting in the pursuit of a fugitive slave named Juda, owned by John Hampden Randolph of Nottoway Plantation in White Castle, Louisiana. From his home on a cane ridge up Bayou Tigre, Blow-Gun John rented two dugout canoes to the Iberville Parish sheriff and his posse and provided them with a hindquarter of venison along with precise directions on how to reach a nearby runaway camp.[30]

Tension between needing Indian diplomacy and trade, on the one hand, and fearing too much of an Indian presence in New Orleans, on the other, was greatly sharpened by news of war with the Natchez Indians.

On November 29, 1729, Natchez warriors launched their initial attack 240 miles upriver, under the guise of a calumet ceremony in which the chief was presenting a large quantity of gifts to an arrogant and naïve commandant Chepart. Officials in a highly vulnerable New Orleans not only worried about Indian-black collaboration, but thought—perhaps with more reasonable concern—that Indian emissaries would gather intelligence about the city's weak fortification and fragile populace. American Indian nations geographically situated with some leverage between European empires and competing merchants commonly used this kind of information to decide where to direct their alliance and commerce. Anxiety over Indian visits to New Orleans intensified further when a plot under way by enslaved people in New Orleans was discovered early during the Natchez War. Governor Périer quickly had two black men and one black woman burned at the stake, but rumor of a possible conspiracy by the Chaouachas and other local Indians caused him to take seemingly inconsistent action. For an attack against the Chaouacha village downriver from the city, Périer recruited and armed black slaves from the plantation of Maréchal de Belle-Isle. According to Lieutenant Dumont, "they went to the village and killed eight or nine Indian men, as well as some women, with the result that the negroes became the enemies of the Indians, who no longer trusted them."[31]

Only several days after the Natchez War began, a large delegation of Choctaw Indians approached New Orleans to offer their military assistance to a nervous Governor Périer. Wanting their allegiance but questioning their intention, the governor dispatched an officer to meet them outside the city with a supply of trade gifts. France's alliance with the Choctaws dated back to 1702, when Iberville began arming them against Chickasaw warriors who had subjected many of their towns to raiding for slaves to sell to British traders from South Carolina. Choctaw diplomatic parties since then, however, traveled mainly to Mobile for meetings with French officials; their expanding commerce in deerskins also focused at that Gulf Coast town. Now with the outbreak of war against the Natchez, need and opportunity to negotiate directly with the governor in New Orleans initiated a Choctaw connection to the city that at first was tenuous but that would evolve and endure for two centuries to come. When Périer welcomed several Choctaw chiefs in New Orleans nearly a year after the outbreak of Natchez warfare, condemnation by many colonists provoked a chastising letter from Philibert Ory. Contrary to the governor's claim that this meeting motivated the Choctaws to march against Natchez enemies, they asserted "that you have risked a great deal in that you have taught these people the passages by the lakes and by the rear to come to New Orleans and that you have thereby inspired in them a desire to come and establish themselves on Lake Pontchartrain, which if it were executed would have dangerous results" for the city and surrounding plantations. Instead of acquainting these Indians with the town's lack of fortification, Périer should have met them in Mobile or even at Natchez.[32]

Indian delegations to New Orleans were nonetheless essential for perpetuating and reinforcing alliances with Indians across the Mississippi Valley, and whatever promises and presents Native emissaries might bring back home really mattered. With the Natchez War well under way in 1730, an Illinois chief named Chikagou led a diplomatic party to the city, offering military support to the French. One of those travelers accompanying Bourgmont to Paris several years earlier, Chikagou spread on the ground before governor Périer a deerskin bordered with porcupine quills and placed upon it two calumets along with other ceremonial objects. The pipes, he told the governor, represented two messages—his people's religious devotion to Roman Catholicism and their political allegiance to the French Crown. "We have come from a great distance to weep with you for the death of the French, and to offer our Warriors to strike those hostile Nations whom you may wish to designate." Many Illinois families had been converted by Jesuit missionaries, and Chickagou was seeking assurance that Périer would protect the Illinois as well as "our Black Robes." "When I went over to France," he reminded the governor, "the King promised me his protection for the Prayer, and recommended me never to abandon it." The need for protection, of course, was mutual, as the Illinois would become especially important participants in France's ensuing campaigns against the Chickasaws—powerful allies of the British situated in the heart of the Lower Mississippi Valley.[33] And during the three weeks spent in New Orleans, Chikagou and his delegation dramatically demonstrated their Roman Catholic faith to town residents. Lodging at the Ursuline nuns' residential school, these Illinois Indians impressed Father Mathurin le Petit "by their piety, and by their edifying life." As the Jesuit priest reported:

Every evening they recited the rosary in alternate choirs, and every morning they heard me say Mass; during which, particularly on Sundays and
Feast-days, they chanted the different prayers of the Church suitable to
the Offices of the day. At the end of the Mass, they never fail to chant
with their whole heart the prayer for the King—The Nuns changed the
first Latin couplet in the ordinary tone of the Gregorian chant, and the
Illinois continued the other couplets in their language in the same tone.
This spectacle, which was novel, drew great crowds to the Church, and
inspired a deep devotion. In the course of the day, and after supper, they
often chant, either alone or together, different prayers of the Church,
such as the *Dies irce,* etc., *Viexilla Regis,* etc., *Stabat Mater,* etc. To listen to
them, you would easily perceive that they took more delight and pleasure
in chanting these holy Canticles, than the generality of the Savages, and
even more than the French receive from chanting their frivolous and
often dissolute songs.[34]

Only months before Chikagou's visit, New Orleans was the scene of a
sharply contrasting public ritual. Tunica allies of France brought five Natchez prisoners to the capital, including the Female Sun of the Flour Village. While a colonist smashed the skulls of the others (a woman and three
children) and threw their bodies into the fire, the Female Sun—believed
to be an instigator of the Natchez War—was tortured and burned by her
Tunica captors. As one observer explained, Governor Périer wanted the
Indians instead of the French to commit this gruesome act of retribution.
After preparing themselves with dance and song known as "the calumet
of death," the Tunicas carried the woman from the town watch-house and
tied her to a frame made of river cane poles. The Female Sun "taunted her
torturers with threats and insults," directing much of this at a Natchez man
who had betrayed his own people and joined the Tunicas. Before this terrible spectacle of slow cutting, piercing, and burning ended, both a French
woman who had been earlier captured by the Natchez and an outraged
French soldier added their own assaults against her body. For their role as
captors and executioners on behalf of the French, the Tunicas would soon
suffer a devastating raid by vengeful Natchez warriors that cost the lives of
two of their chiefs.[35]

At that time, hundreds of Natchez men, women, and children were being transported through New Orleans as prisoners and shipped as slaves to the French Caribbean colony of Saint-Domingue. The city is rightfully seen as one of North America's most infamous slave markets because tens of thousands of African and African American slaves were transported there, initially from across the Atlantic world and later from other parts of the United States. But less recognized was its position also as an entrepôt for the exportation of many enslaved American Indians, sharing this role with other colonial cities from Boston to Charleston. On January 24, 1731, French soldiers and their Choctaw allies rounded up a total of 438 Natchez people, but 51 died before the colonial ships were loaded. The first of two vessels to carry the enslaved Natchez to Cap Français, *Le Gironde*, departed New Orleans in January 1731. The number was small, but nearly all were killed while attempting to take over the ship during passage. The second ship, *La Vénus*, left New Orleans in May 1731 with 291 enslaved Natchez, but only 160 were alive when the ship reached Saint-Domingue. On his way back to Louisiana from France in 1733, Bienville happened to stop at Cap Français and speak to some of those same Natchez near the dock. As the returning governor wrote in a letter on January 28, 1733, "I have seen here, my lord, the chiefs of the Natchez who are slaves, among others the man named St. Cosme, who had been made to hope that they would be able to return with me. They assured me that it was only their nation that had entered into the revolt and that the harsh treatment that had been given them had forced them to it and that they had decided upon it without taking council of other nations, and if I am willing to believe them about it, my arrival in the colony will restore to it the tranquility that I had left there."[36]

The Natchez War was a time of heightened apprehension in New Orleans over possible Indian attack and slave rebellion. Fearing that intelligence about the city's vulnerability would be gathered by even allied Indians, colonial officials wanted to discourage diplomatic visits. Despite royal plans for fortification, New Orleans was protected only by a shallow moat hastily dug after war had erupted. And it would soon dry up from neglect. When Périer greeted Choctaw delegates to the city with presents in 1731, his critics claimed that Bienville would never have allowed it. "This has such a bad effect that today," as Jadart de Beauchamp wrote to minister Maurepas, "there are three times as many Indian chiefs as when M. de Bienville shared them [the presents] out and consequently three times as much expense for the presents, in addition to the fact that these barbarians, who are woodsmen [and] had never dared to venture on the water, in this way are going to become boatmen and in a position to make war on the French in whatever places the settlement of the colony may be made." That same year also saw a visit by Atakapa and Opelousa Indians from the west, requesting Louisiana's governor to send traders to their country for peltries, tallow, and horses.[37] Despite lingering anxiety, however, Indian warfare only came near New Orleans when Choctaw civil war spilled onto upriver settlements in 1748. Even then, settlers driven from the German Coast by hostile Choctaws found sanctuary among neighboring Indian villagers. During the threat of a Choctaw attack, however, a small group of slaves in the New Orleans area—including a few enslaved Indians—did flee from their owners and cross Lake Pontchartrain in a pirogue, hoping apparently to join a Choctaw war party and find freedom in Indian country.[38]

⋘

For most of the eighteenth century, peaceful exchange between American Indians and town residents remained the norm in and around New Orleans. Providing the colonial town with foodstuffs and services was the mainstay of nearby Indian communities' relationship with the colonial town, contributing significantly to its foodways, material life, and public culture. Pottery sherds excavated at the St. Augustine Church site in present-day Tremé and at Madame John's Legacy in the Vieux Carré even indicate that American Indian ceramics were being used for decoration and display as well as for cooking and storage inside colonial households. The everyday presence of household wares naturally makes precise documentation rare, but in one reported burglary of a New Orleans home in 1744 there is mention of money being taken from "a small Indian basket."[39] For larger Indian nations located farther inland, like the Choctaws, commerce in deerskins constituted their most important and long-lasting connection with New Orleans. The Choctaws started using the name Balbancha for New Orleans, a "place of foreign languages," a name derived from *balbaha,* their word for talking in an unknown language or for prattling like an infant. American Indian people obviously recognized that the French colonial town had become a pivotal place in intercultural communication and exchange. Strange new sounds and sights had to be carefully interpreted for selective use. From diplomatic and military relations dating to the mid-eighteenth century, the Choctaws drew into their cultural tradition an adaptation of the European snare drum. To this day, a military-style snare drum is played on special occasions among Choctaw people in Mississippi.[40]

An extensive network of trade linked Choctaws, Creeks, Quapaws, Caddos, and other interior nations tightly to the export economy of Louisiana. As merchants or officials, packhorsemen or rowers, traders or interpreters, many city residents participated in what was predominantly a trade for deerskins with Indian people. The volume and value of deerskins annually shipped from New Orleans comprised a notable portion of colonial Louisiana's exports during both the French and Spanish periods, occupying a substantial amount of time of mercantile clerks, dockworkers, and other town residents. Tens of thousands of deerskins left both New Orleans and Mobile every year, sometimes amounting to more than one hundred thousand pounds as Bienville reported in 1743. Midcentury merchants like Gerard Pery and Pierre Rasteau regularly shipped this cargo from New Orleans to La Rochelle, France, from where mostly raw skins headed to tanneries nearby or in Switzerland. And of course, there was the return flow of European manufactures for the region's Indian trade that contributed to the colonial town's commercial activity. Military officers commanding garrisons in the interior, such as Lieutenant François Hazeur at Fort Tombecbé in Choctaw country, managed once in a while to form partnerships with New Orleans suppliers and shippers in order to monopolize trade with particular Indian nations. By 1750 commerce with the Choctaws alone required five thousand ells (or six thousand meters) of Limbourg cloth, nearly two thousand blankets, four thousand pounds of gunpowder, and a hundred fifty muskets—among many other goods—that had to be carried on horses or in boats to dozens of different villages. Even after crops like cotton and sugar far surpassed peltry in overall economic importance, the city continued to be a major outlet for furs and skins produced in the Upper Mississippi and Lower Missouri river valleys.[41]

Indian-colonial relations in the city, though, were watched by colonial officials committed to maintaining social order and preventing defiant behavior. Prohibition against settlers, soldiers, and tavern keepers selling alcohol to Indians as well as slaves proved difficult to enforce, even after stronger regulations were enacted early in 1751. A proliferation of makeshift taverns in New Orleans was drawing settlers as well as Indians and slaves into town. In addition to limiting licenses to only six taverns and to prohibiting them from selling to Indians and blacks in article 3, the new law addressed an apparent neglect of cultivation by colonial farmers who were apparently contributing to "the disorders in New Orleans" caused by the "multiplicity of taverns." Article 9 decreed that within eight days of the new regulations' publication, all inhabitants of the German Coast and of other nearby settlements "who have abandoned their lands to come and settle here" must return to their homes or else be treated as vagrant disturbers of the peace. Complaining about lax vigilance by military officers, commissioner Michel de la Rouvilliere reported later that same year that "the soldiers are allowed to do what they please, provided they drink at the liquor shop designated for them; and they carry out of it wine and spirits, which they re-sell to the negroes and to the Indians. This has been proved ten times for one; everybody knows it, and yet the abuse is not stopped."[42]

It was not uncommon throughout the eighteenth century for colonial officials to focus on the deleterious effects of alcohol on American Indians. Estimating the population of Native communities along the Mississippi River in 1758, for example, Governor Louis Billouart de Kerlérec attributed their drastic decline in numbers to "the quantity of drink that has been traded to them." "Formerly very numerous," the Tunicas had been reduced to sixty warriors, the Houmas to sixty, the Chitimachas to eighty, and the Chaouachas to only ten or twelve.[43] Subsequent governors during both the Spanish and American periods continued to wrestle with the health and social effects of alcohol. In 1798, for example, Manuel Gayoso de Lemos issued a proclamation regulating city life that included prohibition against the sale of liquor, wine, or brandy to American Indians under any circumstances and to slaves unless permitted by their owners. Fines for offenders ranged from four to twelve pesos, and tavern keepers found guilty of violating this ordinance would lose their licenses. As late as 1812, the state legislature of Louisiana saw reason to pass a law declaring, "If any person or persons shall sell or give any spirituous or intoxicating liquors to any Indian or Indians, the person so offending, shall upon conviction thereof before a competent tribunal forfeit and pay the sum of two hundred dollars, one half for the use of the party suing for the same, and moreover shall be liable for all mischiefs, injuries or damages as may be caused by said Indian or Indians, while in a state of intoxication produced as aforesaid to the person or persons sustaining the same."[44] Assumptions about alcohol's influence on the appearance of American Indians in towns like New Orleans and measures taken to police interaction among marginalized groups of townspeople would resonate throughout many representations of the Indigenous presence in urban space.

Shortly into the second half of the eighteenth century, a force beyond the will of colonial and Native peoples in the Lower Mississippi Valley brought political and economic changes to them on a scale significantly greater than those experienced since the founding of New Orleans. After losing the Seven Years' War, France was forced to cede all territory that it had claimed east of the Mississippi to Great Britain. Meanwhile, royal cousins Louis XV and Carlos III secretly agreed to transfer from French to Spanish possession what remained of Louisiana west of the Mississippi. Although resting sinuously along the east bank of the river, the "Îsle d'Orléans"—that important slice of Louisiana between lakes Borgne, Pontchartrain, and Maurepas, and the Mississippi—remained part of Louisiana. How American Indians would adapt to this sudden loss of France as their familiar ally and to newly made claims on their allegiance by Spain and Great Britain after 1763 mattered not only inside and between their own nations, but also in their continuing relationship with the port town that Choctaw people called a "place of foreign languages." Sudden growth in the size of the Lower Mississippi Valley's colonial population—slave and free—and rapid development of its urban and plantation economy began testing their diplomatic mettle as never before.

CHAPTER TWO

BORDERLAND

O n July 14, 1764, thirty-three Tunicas from Pointe Coupée met with Jean-Jacques-Blaise d'Abbadie, the newly appointed director general of Louisiana, who had summoned them to New Orleans to complain about their harassment of English ships on the Mississippi River. In response to the acting governor's stern remarks regarding Great Britain's rightful possession of lands "given them" by King Louis XV, Chief Perruquier said, "My father, the British have always corrupted the ways among all the tribes. They have given them [the Indians] liquor to drink which has killed them. When I learned that they would come to our lands, I said: 'They will put us to death; kill them!' I well know that you had forbidden it. But, as I know in my heart that they would enslave us, I could not refrain from attacking them. If they had put their garrison ashore, we would have killed them all. But they fled, and they did the right thing. Finally, my father, I come to you as an embarrassed child. Chastise me if you wish, but have pity on us." D'Abbadie then introduced the Tunica emissaries to Philip Pitman, a British army lieutenant responsible for exploring and surveying the Florida coast and Mississippi Valley. "Do you see this English chief?" he asked. "He is my friend. I shake his hand. The English will do the same every time that they will meet you." After offering their hands to Pitman, "who promised them, on the part of the English, the same good will and the same friendship as the French," the Tunicas performed the calumet ceremony. Four days later, d'Abbadie gave them the nation's annual presents from France, and Pitman delivered a speech along with wine, brandy, and other gifts on behalf of Great Britain. The Tunica delegation then departed New Orleans.[1]

Although spared from the violence that raged farther north during the Seven Years' War between Great Britain and France, the Lower Mississippi Valley was profoundly affected by the consequences of that imperial conflict. Fear of English warships possibly approaching the Gulf Coast did motivate construction of a palisaded wall around New Orleans at long last, but the city was never attacked by a European or Indian enemy. Louisiana's Indian allies, most pivotally the Choctaw nation, maintained their loyalty to France. The really anxious time for Indigenous as well as colonial people in the region only began when, as a result of the war, France transferred Louisiana to Spain and Spain transferred Florida to England in 1762–1763. Now uncertain about the effects of European remapping, yet determined to protect their own interests, American Indian nations started sending unusually large delegations to New Orleans. It became a time of busy and intense diplomacy inside the colonial city. Before then, more typical diplomatic ceremonies were those reported by Governor Louis Billouart de Kerlérec over the preceding decade. In late winter of 1753 a delegation of "seven honored men of the nation of the Choctaws" brought him seven Chickasaw scalps, "for which I paid at the accustomed rate and in the accustomed manner." Two days of what the governor called "long" and "bad" speechmaking by the Choctaws ensued before he "forbade them to make a habit of coming to New Orleans, assuring them that I would not fail to go to Mobile every year at the time indicated and designated in advance." Anxiety over people who might one day become hostile being familiar with the colonial capital and its surroundings was persistent among Louisiana officials. But their Indian counterparts also insisted that obligations be met, traveling to New Orleans when necessary in order to make their case. France's failure three years in a row to deliver annual presents caused Choctaw emissaries in 1757 to once again visit New Orleans, demanding "very loudly" that gunpowder and other trade merchandise be provided and threatening to receive English traders into their villages.[2]

Visits to colonial cities by Indian delegations were a common feature of public life across early America, as sentimentally remembered by a pair of the nation's founding fathers. Thomas Jefferson described visits by the Cherokee chief Outacity at Tuckahoe and later in Williamsburg when Jefferson was a student at William and Mary. The Cherokee orator's "sounding voice, distinct articulation, animated action, and the solemn silence of his people at their several fires, filled me with awe and veneration," wrote Jefferson in a letter to John Adams. Adams, in turn, nostalgically recalled times that he spent in Braintree with neighboring Punkapaugs and Neponsets, noting however that as the men went to work as sailors and the women as domestic servants these Indians seemed to have disappeared. "We scarcely see an Indian in a year," he informed Jefferson in 1812. The artist Benjamin West, a contemporary of Adams and Jefferson well-known for history paintings that included Indian subjects, fondly told about a group of Native travelers who regularly passed by his home in Springfield, Pennsylvania, just west of Philadelphia, on one occasion showing him how to make pigments of red and yellow ochre for his youthful pictures of birds and flowers. They also taught West, as reported by his early biographer, "to be an expert archer," which came in handy for shooting birds to use as models.[3]

In July 1763, only weeks after reaching New Orleans from France, Director General d'Abbadie was visited by chiefs of the Biloxi, Chitimacha, Houma, Choctaw, and Quapaw nations—all of whom were "friendly and devoted to the French" but came to New Orleans "to sound out rumors circulating among them concerning the cession of fragments of Louisiana to England and, they say, to Spain." A pan-tribal Indian war was raging against British garrisons and settlements north of the Ohio River, and Spain's newly acquired possession of Louisiana would not be officially announced for months to come. Over the autumn months of 1763, d'Abbadie and Governor Kerlérec, soon to be recalled to France for alleged violation of royal orders, received delegations of Apalachee, Biloxi, Pascagoula, Taensa, and other Indian people from the Gulf Coast—all wanting to migrate from what was now British West Florida to what they hoped would remain French Louisiana. Louisiana officials, themselves still unsure about France's sovereignty over the colony, welcomed this opportunity to secure Indian allies and carefully identified destinations of strategic self-interest. In September, for example, the Apalachees were directed to the rapids just above entrance to the Red River. "There," d'Abbadie wrote, "they will be useful for aiding vessels ascending the river towards Natchitoches" and "moreover, through their hunting, they will be able to supply New Orleans." En route to their new home, the Apalachees held a ceremony in the capital city—d'Abbadie called it an "election" by their elders—to replace a chief of advanced age with a younger leader named Martin. In March 1764 a chief named Mastabé and several other Choctaw diplomats reached New Orleans to tell d'Abbadie that they "could not become accustomed to the absence of the French in his village and that everything was melancholy for them." The French official reminded Mastabé of a speech that he had given in Mobile urging the Choctaws to live peacefully with the English—"now our brothers"—and to expect patiently that their needs would be met by British traders.[4]

The establishment of British forts and settlements along the east bank of the Mississippi, starting just above the Iberville River (present-day Bayou Manchac), made both deeply rooted and newly arriving Indian nations nervous about their future. How best to negotiate with European powers in a space that suddenly became a tense borderland between empires remained to be seen. Despite warnings from the Louisiana government not to react militarily, early in 1764 a combined force of Tunicas, Ofogoulas, Chitimachas, and Houmas attacked a flotilla of English ships carrying soldiers upriver. When the Tunica chief sent a delegate to New Orleans a few months later, d'Abbadie expressed anger over how the Indians had disregarded his words. The tribal deputy agreed to the truth of this, but announced that "the English had sinister hearts and that, at Pointe Coupée, they had heard the British speak of the Indians with contempt."[5]

During the summer of 1764, New Orleans hosted a series of diplomatic envoys eager to represent their nations' long-standing allegiance to France. On June 6 a delegation of Biloxis and other Indians from the Gulf Coast "assembled near New Orleans to play ball and for diversions, attracting there numerous spectators." This passing mention by d'Abbadie is the first known reference to Native American stickball being played in New Orleans. This game, now commonly called lacrosse, as many later references will show, became the Crescent City's most popular spectator sport over the next century. A few days following the Biloxi ball game, a Choctaw delegation arrived to express their people's "considerable attachment to the French." A deputation from two Chitimacha villages following suit, "they chanted the calumet for me," as d'Abbadie recorded in his journal, "and we renewed our mutual pledges of attachment."[6] Upon the director general's request, a Quapaw delegation of thirty-seven arrived about a month later, accompanied by the commandant of the Arkansas Post. After "they chanted the calumet for me" the next day, d'Abbadie encouraged the Quapaws to relocate from their homeland, because of its remoteness from New Orleans and because of recent flood damage to the French post. Somewhere along the Red River, near Natchitoches, was the governor's choice, although he admittedly did not yet have official approval to authorize such a move. A Quapaw spokesman replied one day later at d'Abbadie's house: "My father, the roads have always been white for you to come and see us. When I have found them red, I have whitened them. You are surrounded by tribes who do not observe the words of the French. It is not the same with us. We have always listened, and have never reddened our hands with the blood of the French. Here, you see several warriors who please you. They will deliver your message to the village. I shall espouse it in the village, and we shall desire only to follow your advice. If it depended only upon me, I tell you that I am ready to go and establish myself where you will want, but there are other chiefs and warriors at the village, and I do not know their thoughts on this matter. When I shall be in the village, I shall relate your speech to them, and I am convinced that they will comply with your wishes. I will instruct Mr. Cabaret to notify you of their intentions. My father, I recommend to you the warriors and young men who have come to see you." The Quapaws departed from New Orleans on July 9 with gifts provided by d'Abbadie. The Tunica delegation led by Perruquier arrived a few days later.[7]

As of September 1764 d'Abbadie had still not received official communication from the French court, although he already knew about the cession of Louisiana to Spain, and rumors about it were circulating in the colony for months. How the region's largest and most powerful Indian nation might react to the news was a serious concern, so he requested a special visit by Choctaw representatives. After sending a boat to Pass Christian to transport them to New Orleans, d'Abbadie met with a delegation of thirty-three Choctaws in mid-December. Here again the French governor (of a colony that was actually Spanish) mediated between Indian and English authorities. In the presence of Sir John Lindsay, commander of the British squadron, and "Messrs. Stuart and Maclellan," d'Abbadie urged "peace and union which must prevail between the redmen and the whites." The Choctaws immediately "assured me [d'Abbadie] of their attachment to the French" and "extended compliments to the English officers." They proceeded to report, nevertheless, "the terrible treatment which they experienced at the hands of the British traders" who "beat them with clubs, steal their horses, and debauch their women." Stuart promised to relay this complaint to his king and to have the nation's annual gifts ready for an assembly in Mobile. One of the oldest members of the delegation still expressed strong skepticism, "stating that he had been told by persons who speak the truth that they [the English] were bound to poison and destroy the Choctaw nation."[8]

Before the year ended, another diplomatic exchange occurred in New Orleans that demonstrated American Indian uncertainty about changing imperial partners and shifting geographical borders. A Shawnee elder named Charlot Casqué arrived from the Illinois country, conveying to d'Abbadie his people's devotion to the French in the aftermath of deadly war against the English. "I have come from afar," Casqué announced, because "the Master of Life has decreed that I come here, and my heart is pleased to see you." Lacking a retinue, he assured the governor that he was sent to represent his "great chief" and present a wampum "necklace of five branches" containing names of "the forty-seven villages who want to die attached to the French." He hoped the French would help defend their land and never abandon them. "In former times when I have come here, everyone seemed cheerful and content," but now Casqué noticed how "today, all is sorrowful." He saw "many persons whom I do not know" in the city, confessing that "I myself am dejected." The elderly Shawnee ambassador, however, departed on a positive note. "Since I see you," he told d'Abbadie, "my heart is content, and my eyes become clear." He would report this warm reception to his nation.[9]

❦

American Indians worked hard to keep New Orleans within their own economic and political network as much as possible under the region's destabilizing transformation. And even during a period of rapid regime change and colonial growth, Indian trade in and around the city remained important to many townspeople. A failed revolt against Spain's first Louisiana governor in 1768, led by a conspiracy of merchants and planters in the New Orleans area, did not implicate American Indian nations. Arrival of a large Spanish army, under the command of General Alejandro O'Reilly,

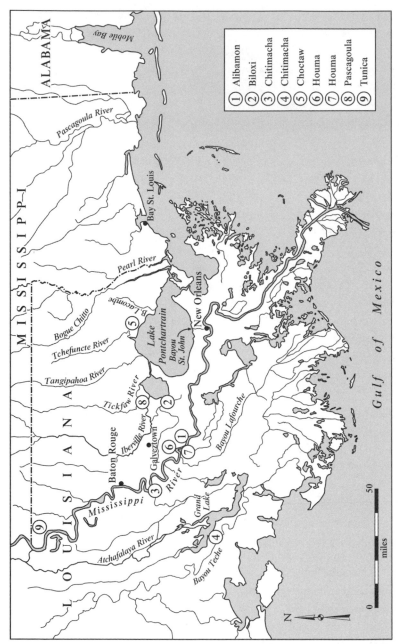

①	Alibamon
②	Biloxi
③	Chitimacha
④	Chitimacha
⑤	Choctaw
⑥	Houma
⑦	Houma
⑧	Pascagoula
⑨	Tunica

American Indian Communities in the Spanish-British Borderland, ca. 1770. Map by Mary Lee Eggart.

speedily ended this colonial rebellion by mid-1769 and initiated fruitful diplomatic relations with most Louisiana Indians. To the dismay of British officials in West Florida, claiming exclusive jurisdiction over the Choctaws, commerce between New Orleans and that populous interior nation also persisted throughout the 1760s and 1770s. Some Choctaw Indians even began to establish new communities on the north shore of Lake Pontchartrain, bringing them closer to the place of foreign languages. One merchant in Mobile urged West Florida's colonial assembly "to have a stop put to the trade that's carried on by the inhabitants of New Orleans with the Indians on the English side . . . to the great prejudice of this Province and particularly those concerned in the Indian trade."[10] But Bayou St. John and Lake Pontchartrain provided much too convenient passage for goods and skins, and Choctaw hunters began spending more and more time on the north shore of Lakes Pontchartrain and Maurepas. The return of West Florida to Spain after the American Revolution would further reinforce Choctaw settlement around New Orleans, and over the next century these so-called St. Tammany Choctaws would exhibit a versatile public presence in the Crescent City.[11]

Over the autumn months of 1769, some of New Orleans's most elaborate Indian ceremonies took place—as delegates were summoned by General O'Reilly once he firmly established Spain's possession of Louisiana. At a single council held in late September, several different communities were represented. Nine chiefs and their interpreters arrived at half past eleven in the morning, "together with quite a number of Indians, singing and playing on their military instruments." Seated beneath a canopy in the main hall of his house, O'Reilly greeted these guests in the company of Spanish officers and town officials. After placing their "military implements" at the general's feet, each chief "saluted him with his flag, which is a small pole decorated with feathers in the shape of a fan, waving it in a circle over his head, and touching him on the chest four times with it, then giving it to him." O'Reilly then took puffs from pipe after pipe held by each chief and concluded the opening ceremony by shaking hands with all of them, "the Indian's greatest sign of friendship." Speaking on behalf of the entire delegation, the Bayogoula chief pledged alliance to Spain and beseeched Spanish authorities to "grant us the same favors and benefits as did the French." "I am afraid of displeasing thee, great chief of chiefs," he further said, "so I close, assuring thee that all these red men, warriors and chiefs of the tribes will be inviolably faithful to thee, both here and in all the posts where there are people at thy orders." In response to this speech, O'Reilly explained the close family ties between Spain and France and discouraged Indian hostility toward the English "because, although they were not related by the same bonds as was the French nation, they were friends of His Majesty." He then rose from his chair "to place about the neck of each one of the chiefs the medal which hung from a silk ribbon of deep scarlet color." And before departing the city, each tribal delegation also received gifts from the royal government.[12]

Although translated and recorded language found in colonial documents for this and other New Orleans meetings that autumn might sound overly deferential to us, Indian diplomats were clearly asserting themselves as sovereign allies in accordance with their own rituals. To optimize their own advantages in the newly configured imperial borderland, they strategically dodged colonial demands from Spanish and British officials for exclusive allegiance and sought convenient arrangements with both sides. After the American Revolution began and Spain entered the war against Great Britain several years later, however, Governor Bernardo de Gálvez was able to recruit fighters from some of these Indian nations for successful campaigns against British forts on the Mississippi River and Gulf Coast. Open conflict between empires now became a potential opportunity for restoring stable relations with a single, and the more familiar Louisiana-based, ally. One hundred sixty Indians, mostly Houmas, Alibamons, and Pacanas, alongside some six hundred militiamen, joined Gálvez's army on his march from New Orleans to Manchac. "Sickness and fatigue," he later reported, "had diminished more than one-third part" of his regular troops. The Tunicas avoided recruitment because of the more vulnerable location of their village, and the Chitimachas reported fear of a Quapaw attack as reason not to join Gálvez's army.[13]

Doubt over which side some Indian nations might take and distrust of neutrality claimed by others persisted nonetheless, so meeting their expectations in both commerce and diplomacy would be urgently required. Representing rather starkly the volume and variety of goods needed on hand, in the autumn of 1779 Governor Bernardo de Gálvez sent to his uncle José de Gálvez, Spain's minister of the Indies, a "Memorandum of merchandise, which is needed at the warehouses of New Orleans, to entertain the friendship of the Indians and furnish the traders, who are sent to trade with them":

4000 Ordinary blankets 2 ½ thread.
1000   "   "   3   "
600   "   "   2   "
400   "   "   for cradle
100 gross awls
100   "   steel to strike fire with a flint.
100 Worm for drawing wad.
4000 Rifles 3 ½ foot barrel, caliber 28 to 32 shot per pound.
100 Gross large knives with 3 nails in Handle.
100 Gross pocket knives with horn handle.
100 lbs. copper wire.
50 Gross scissors.
100   "   wooden combs.
500 lbs. glass beads, all colors.
800 Copper kettles, English style, all sizes.
500 lbs. vermillion.
300 Hatchets with handles.
1000   "   [without handles]
500 Axes.
2000 Hoes 7 inches wide at bottom, because those which came last year
     were useless, on account of being too narrow.
300 Pieces of blue limbourg.
100   "   " red   "
200 Dozen looking glasses.
30000 lbs. of shot, 28 to 30 pound.
10000 lbs. of small shot.
2000 Pieces of linen for shirts.
50 Pieces of handkerchiefs, regular.
48 Large medals.
48 Small   "
500 Gorgets, half gold and half silver plated.
100 Pieces of red ribbon.

30 Doz. Adorned men's shirts.

150   " untrimmed   "   "

50   " women's shirts.

450 Doz. Hats.

100 lbs. silver plated gallons.

500 Pairs bracelets.[14]

Fully maintaining this inventory of goods and gifts in the city's warehouses proved impossible for government officials, but trade with Indian allies remained as essential for colonial security and prosperity as ever. The war now under way between Great Britain and its Atlantic Seaboard colonies caused exceptional apprehension and disruption in the New Orleans area, even though Spain's campaigns against British forts occurred farther upriver and eastward along the Gulf Coast. While Governor Gálvez was bombarding Baton Rouge in 1779, American privateer William Pickles landed his sloop, *The Morris,* on the north shore of Lake Pontchartrain. He subdued the British frigate *West Florida* on the lake, raised the American flag on shore, and gathered oaths of allegiance from residents between Bayou Lacombe and the Tangipahoa River. On September 26, Pickles ferried 122 Choctaw Indians across the lake to Bayou St. John.[15] Over the ensuing winter Gálvez hosted Indian delegations to follow up on his military conquest of English forts along the Mississippi River. When Payamataha led a Chickasaw delegation to New Orleans in December, Gálvez received them with "all possible display and pomp" and gave the chief a Spanish medal and written commission along with gifts. This commission assigned Payamataha the role of persuading other Indian groups that "all of the Nations should live together in good accord under the orders and law of the Great King of Spain." In a June 1780 letter to his uncle, Bernardo de Gálvez wrote that "the multitude of Indians who come to this city since His Majesty gained the devotion of the numerous Choctaw nations, has been an object of many embarrassments which absolutely take up my time which is needed in the various affairs of the government." The governor then requested authorization to create a separate official position for managing Indian affairs.[16]

<<<

Contributing plenty to irritability and instability in Indian relations with colonial officials in New Orleans was an oftentimes vexing competition between merchants and nations for trade. Official efforts to secure order by monopolizing Indian commerce, usually with the added incentive of benefiting family or friends, seldom made headway in Louisiana—or in any other North American colony for that matter. This goal came closest to being reached in the hands of Gilbert Antoine de St. Maxent, a soldier who left France for New Orleans in 1747 and soon thereafter opened a store on Conti Street to supply fur traders. Marrying Elizabeth de la Roche, a well-to-do New Orleans widow, also enhanced his financial position. By the 1760s he brought into his business Pierre Lacléde, who started the town of St. Louis and expanded the company's reach up the Missouri River. Slave-owning planter as well as merchant-soldier, St. Maxent not only helped Spanish officials suppress local rebellions against their takeover of Louisiana, but became father-in-law to Governors Luis de Unzaga and Bernardo de Gálvez. After serving Spain as commander of colonial militia during the Revolutionary War campaigns, St. Maxent was appointed by son-in-law Gálvez as commissioner of Indian affairs and lieutenant governor of West Florida. In 1782 he partnered with New Orleans merchant Michel Fortier to contract with King Carlos III an agreement to ship 380,000 pesos' worth of French and Spanish goods to Louisiana's capital for trade and diplomacy with Indians, especially urgent because of treaties negotiated after conquest of the British forts in West Florida. Nearly two decades earlier, when St. Maxent had received from Director General d'Abbadie monopoly privileges over trade in the Illinois country, other Louisiana merchants raised strong objection and accused that colonial officer of profiting from the deal. Now for maintenance of peaceful relations with Indian nations throughout the Mississippi Valley, this latest and more extensive agreement declared, "it is necessary to have a sufficient supply of merchandise on hand in the city of New Orleans, in order to attract the Indians by means of gifts, and to provide the merchants who trade with them." This plan obviously reflected the persistent value that Indian trade held both politically and economically, but began to unravel when St. Maxent's ships carrying the merchandise back to Louisiana were captured by the British—still at war with Spain—and he and his crewmen were imprisoned in Kingston, Jamaica. Little was recovered from the confiscated goods, and St. Maxent's fortunes steadily declined before his death in 1794.[17]

In the immediate aftermath of revolutionary conflict, the north shore of Lake Pontchartrain and its adjacent Gulf Coast continued to be a theater for expressions of American Indian uncertainty and discontent generated by the war. In September 1782 a few Choctaws demanded food and stole chickens from a German inhabitant near Galveztown, the Spanish post on the Iberville River. "A Negro who serves as interpreter" told Gilbert Antoine de St. Maxent that "these same Indians said we are trembling with fear, and that Spain was not good, because it killed them with hunger and did not give them anything to eat." St. Maxent was inclined to send to New Orleans "all the Indians of this nation who came here," but hesitated without "the opinion of my superiors."[18] A few months later St. Maxent reported to Governor Esteban Miró that there were more than four hundred Choctaws at Galveztown, "not taking into account those who have gone down to that capital." With farmers in the countryside obviously suffering damages and thefts committed by Choctaws traveling to and from New Orleans, St. Maxent worried that "by the coming year the inhabitants will be absolutely prevented from getting any crops."[19] Five years later Marios de Villiers wrote to Miró, informing him "that the great chief named Aviberna with ten Indians presented himself to me and said through the interpreter Francisco Boni that fifteen days from now the Great Chief Franchimastabe would come with one hundred Indians. They say these Indians are not coming to do any harm, but that they are on the road to new Orleans to extend the hand to the Spaniards and deliver to Your Lordship the medals of the English. Throughout the month of September all the rest of the chiefs are coming for the same purpose. To each party of these Indians it is always necessary for me to give something for their journey, such as maize, brandy, and paints for their dances, although I have given them very little. I have not ventured to do more until I inform Your Lordship to ascertain whether it is your desire that these Indians be given anything."[20] In 1792 Governor Carondelet received a petition from colonists living along the Gulf Coast, from the Pascagoula River to Bay St. Louis, complaining "that the continued presence of the Indian nations along this coast in their journeys to and from that capital results in considerable damage to them, not only in the crops which they raise for the maintenance of themselves and their poor families, but also in the cattle belonging to them which the Indians kill and wound."[21]

In the long run, particularly in the New Orleans area, trade with American Indians continued to operate rather haphazardly. As first commandant of the new district of Tchefuncte, landowner and livestock raiser Charles Parent, along with other residents across Lake Pontchartrain from the city, was suspected in 1788 of purchasing horses and sheep allegedly stolen from other settlers by Indians. Two years later he was instructed to find two African American fugitive slaves supposedly being held by Choctaw Indians. Parent's other activities in regard to Choctaw Indians included entertaining and providing transportation for delegations on their way to meet the Spanish governor in New Orleans.[22] In 1792 William Panton, owner of a large Indian-trade company, complained to Governor Carondelet that Parent was interfering with his firm's Choctaw commerce by selling rum and other goods from his location on the lake. It was John Turnbull, however, who posed the greatest threat to this company. Well established as an Indian-trade merchant, especially in the Chickasaw nation where he had already fathered two sons, Turnbull was starting a plantation at Baton Rouge, from which he intended to continue "his underhand trade." According to John Forbes, Panton's partner, this illicit competition would encourage Indians and some traders "to fly from one [merchant] to another when in debt."[23]

Carondelet was feeling pressure, however, to permit trade by Turnbull and other merchants. The increasing chance of Indian allies turning to Americans for trade intensified the Spanish governor's concern about meeting their demand for affordable merchandise. Carondelet even considered opening trade with New Orleans for all Indian nations "in order that the residents here can be able to give the Indians a more advantageous trade than the Americans and so hold them entirely dependent on Spain and form of them a powerful Barrier against the Americans." Some New Orleans merchants were aggressively seeking this opportunity. But instead of permitting such wide-open commerce, Carondelet authorized the Panton company to establish trade posts closer to the Chickasaws (present-day Vicksburg and Memphis) and allowed Turnbull to trade freely from his store at Mobile. Choctaw people were indeed returning to their villages dissatisfied about inadequate trade in New Orleans. "They don't say anything in the City," agent Jean de la Villebeuvre reported to Governor Carondelet, "but in the Nation they murmur very much."[24]

⤚⤚⤚

Besides transforming diplomatic and economic relations around New Orleans, the transfer of Louisiana from France to Spain had an even more direct effect on some American Indians living inside the city. Although enslavement of American Indians through warfare had virtually ceased in the Lower Mississippi Valley, a number of Native people still worked as slaves on plantations and in city households. One of these slaves was "Jean Baptiste, Indian," owned by Robert Antoine Robin de Lorgny, an indigo planter owning properties close to New Orleans. In November 1765 Jean Baptiste hanged himself from a peach tree in the courtyard of the city's government house. He was apparently being held for an unspecified offense, and his tribal origin was not identified. Jean Baptiste taking his own life was not viewed as a sign of one slave's despair or apprehension, but rather as an "infamous crime" that deserved further punishment. After a trial of Jean Baptiste's deceased body quickly took place—it was even assigned a defending curator—he was found guilty of committing suicide. "In reparation," the Superior Council of Louisiana condemned the memory of Jean Baptiste in perpetuity and ordered "the public executioner to tie the corpse on a hurdle to the back of a cart head downward and face to the ground and to be thus dragged through the streets of this city to the place where he will be hung by the feet to a scaffold for that purpose erected at said place and after having remained there twenty-four hours to be thrown into the public sewer."[25]

French law in Louisiana had always permitted Indian slavery, but Spain had prohibited the enslavement of Native Americans since the mid-sixteenth century. This did not mean that Indigenous people across Spain's empire had been spared bondage-like exploitation of their labor, but it did require Alejandro O'Reilly to issue an official proclamation extending Spanish law against Indian slavery to Louisiana in 1769. For the first time in this colony's history, its inhabitants were forbidden "to make any Indian a slave or to possess any such, under any pretext whatever, even though there be an open war against that Indian's nation." Current owners of enslaved Indians also were required to provide their names, tribal origins, and values to the record office and were prohibited from parting with them "except to give them back their liberty." There were sixty-one Indian slaves in New Orleans at the time, with a total population of Indian slaves across the colony numbering as many as three hundred. Although O'Reilly's decree motivated numerous slaves claiming Indian identity or descent to sue for their freedom, enforcement of this Spanish law was weak and Native Americans continued to be held, bought, and sold in Louisiana. Opposition from slave owners, led aggressively by Julien Poydras, virtually halted consideration of Indian claimants' freedom suits by the mid-1790s, but not before some succeeded in the pursuit.[26]

The tragic experience of a Chickasaw woman named Mary Ann illustrates both the determination brought by some claimants and the difficulty they faced in appealing to Spanish law. Mary Ann fled to New Orleans from her owner's plantation in St. James Parish to plead with Governor Francisco Luis Hector, baron de Carondelet, for her freedom, claiming that she had been "entrapped and conveyed to M Songy, a planter . . . under the dominion of Spain." Among many complaints raised by slave owners against the 1769 proclamation was that slaves were leaving their plantations for the colonial capital in order to file freedom suits. In this Chickasaw woman's case, Carondelet "gave her a letter to the commandant of the parish of St. James, which produced her liberation from all restraint, and she died a free pauper, in the hospital of New-Orleans." We know this only because Mary Ann's four children—who remained enslaved on Songy's plantation—later filed a lawsuit for their freedom. After Songy died, Ulzere, Françoise, Marie Therese, and Casimer brought the heir of his estate, J. B. Poeyfarre, to trial for unlawfully keeping them in slavery. A parish jury actually decided in favor of these children of a Chickasaw woman, but the decision was overruled by Louisiana's Supreme Court in 1820. The opportunity for slaves of Indian descent to sue for freedom was long past, and the number of enslaved Indians fast diminishing.[27]

During a period that is commonly called the Spanish Dominion in Louisiana history, American Indians at first had to negotiate between rival empires that faced each other across the Mississippi River. Pursuing their separate interests on this volatile borderland, tribal leaders faced new difficulties as well as potential opportunities. Diplomatic missions to New Orleans became more important than ever, and the outcome for most

Indian nations was maintenance of their independence and commerce. As Tunica chief Perruquier well understood when he traveled to New Orleans in the summer of 1764, freedom to maneuver between rival empires was an indispensable aspect of sovereignty. With the end of the American Revolution and Spain's recovery of Florida from Britain, however, Indian nations along both banks of the Lower Mississippi River were once again encircled by a single colonial power. Making matters even more difficult for Native people, both Britain and Spain had been accelerating expansion of plantation agriculture and immigration of settlers and slaves. With a colonial population, mostly concentrated along the Mississippi, numbering above thirteen thousand whites, sixteen thousand slaves, and one thousand free people of color in 1785, American Indian power and influence began to erode. A diminishing diplomatic presence of Indian people in New Orleans, then a city of some six thousand residents, was among the consequences.[28]

By the end of the eighteenth century, most Indian delegations visiting colonial New Orleans on a routine basis came from communities that the French called petites nations—Native nations drastically depopulated by smallpox and other epidemic diseases but still inhabiting banks of the lower Mississippi and its distributaries. Houmas, Chitimachas, and Tunicas had occupied this land for ages, while Biloxis, Pascagoulas, Chahtos, Apalachees, and Alibamons represented groups of people recently migrating from British Florida to Spanish Louisiana. Altogether during the 1770s this population numbered about a thousand people, living in at least eight villages interspersed among spreading colonial plantations. Although their numbers continued to decline, these communities would try to maintain a beneficial relationship with New Orleans as long as possible. Meanwhile, American Indian people mainly from the Six Town district of the Choctaw nation began to form new communities along the north shore of Lake Pontchartrain as well as the Mississippi Gulf Coast. This migration by Choctaws closer to New Orleans guaranteed persistence of an Indian presence in the city. Paddling their dugout canoes down the Mississippi River or along the shore of Lake Pontchartrain and into Bayou St. John, persons from the petites nations and nearby Choctaw villages would continue bringing foods as well as furs seasonally to New Orleans after its acquisition by the United States in 1803. In this regard they resembled more recent

Acadian and Canary Island immigrants who also provisioned the city from their nearby settlements. Well into the nineteenth century, American Indians would also still work occasionally as hunters, rowers, and patrollers for their white neighbors—holding on to a frontier exchange economy they had helped build in and around the Crescent City.[29]

The geopolitical transformation of the Lower Mississippi Valley at the dawn of the nineteenth century is a well-known story, even in regard to its effects on American Indians. The late 1790s seemed to duplicate the borderland situation of the 1760s and 1770s. This time the Choctaws and other interior nations east of the Mississippi found themselves positioned between Spain and the United States. When a Choctaw delegation led by Todohamo visited New Orleans in the winter of 1799–1800, they were told by a representative of the Spanish government that "the Spaniards and Americans are now at peace, but are like two Traders in the same Town in their Nation, who are struggling who can get the most Skins—when they meet they Speak to each other, and behave with seeming friendship, though there is still a sourness in their hearts and in his most, who has the Smallest share of the Trade." This opportunity for Indians to regain diplomatic and commercial advantage between rival empires, however, quickly unraveled. Spain's secret cession of Louisiana to France in 1800 momentarily raised the possibility of that once familiar power returning. A few months after Pierre-Clément de Laussat reached New Orleans as French colonial prefect, he was visited by a Creek chief, "Tastiki of the Topalca." "After a few vague speeches"—delivered through the chain of a Choctaw and a French interpreter—Laussat "proposed refreshments." Glass in hand, Tastiki revealed that he "often thought that a huge cloud covered our horizon, but that wind blowing from the other side of the great lake would arise and disperse it." Although the prefect and chief then "clinked glasses" to that warm sentiment, any hopes that France might protect Indian nations from American aggression were quickly dashed, when Napoleon decided to sell Louisiana to the United States in 1803.[30]

Less known than these transfers of jurisdiction between empires are the ways that American Indian people confronted, and adapted to, the encompassing possession of the Lower Mississippi Valley by the United States. The Louisiana Purchase treaty committed US territorial officials to respect Indian sovereignty and land rights, but rapid encroachment by an expanding plantation society and the government's promotion of that expansion relentlessly weakened Indian control over their lands and resources. Following a century of sustained participation in global commerce through heavy trade in deerskins, Indian people in this region now found themselves being marginalized by a new economy—not unlike what farm communities or industrial-worker families have faced in many other times and places. With their political leverage virtually gone and their economic value diminished, Native Americans began to pursue different strategies for maintaining their cultural autonomy and securing a viable livelihood. No longer an official center of Indian diplomacy, New Orleans nevertheless continued to be a laboratory of Indian adaptation and resistance. Communities closest to the city, even as they faced the deleterious effects of the severest political and economic transformation yet experienced, would not retreat from urban streets and markets.

CHAPTER THREE

BACK-OF-TOWN ACTION

O n February 21, 1809, a New Orleans audience watched the performance of a new French comedy written by Louis Emmanuel Dupaty, *Les Deux Pères; ou, La Leçon de Botanique*. Following this main attraction at the Théâtre de la Rue St. Pierre, attendees were treated to the first production of a five-act tragedy written in verse by a well-known New Orleanian named Louis LeBlanc de Villeneufvre. In *The Festival of the Young Corn; or, The Heroism of Poucha-Houmma*, the main character is chief of the Houmas—an American Indian nation then still living upriver from the Crescent City. As the story unfolded on stage, viewers learned that Poucha-Houmma's son Cala-be had killed a Choctaw man while intoxicated, taken refuge farther west among the Atakapas, and married a daughter of that nation's chief. Back in the Houma town on the east bank of the Mississippi River, chief Poucha-Houmma is tormented by a ghostly vision foreshadowing imminent revenge by the Choctaws. On the day set for celebration of the tribe's Festival of Young Corn, Cala-be and his Atakapas bride surprise his father with a visit. Joy over this reunion, however, is darkened by news of a Choctaw war party fast approaching to demand the life of Cala-be—in accordance with a blood-law practiced by Houma as well as Choctaw people. Fearing not only the loss of his beloved son but also destruction of his entire nation, Poucha-Houmma commands Cala-be to flee with his wife and sacrifices his own life in order to secure a future for his son and people. This turned out to be the one and only performance of Louis LeBlanc's play, probably receiving a tepid reaction from the audience and definitely reflecting weakness in the playwright's first effort at producing a formulaic version of French neoclassical tragedy.[1]

Although this performance and reception of *The Festival of the Young Corn* reveals nothing about real Houma people during the first decade of the nineteenth century, it does suggest how non-Indian people were choosing to remember a century of cultural interaction in and around New Orleans. Louis LeBlanc de Villeneufvre was born in the French province of Dauphiné in 1734 and orphaned at the age of thirteen. As a sixteen-year-old ensign, he traveled to Louisiana to serve in the colonial infantry. From 1752 to 1758, LeBlanc was stationed among the Choctaws and grew to admire these people for their courage and dignity in the face of many threats. He also engaged in a lucrative deerskin trade with his hosts, and—like Gilbert Antoine de St. Maxent—did well enough to marry into a prominent colonial family (Marie Jeanne Avart) and get promoted to a higher rank in the military. As a career officer, Lieutenant LeBlanc readily transferred his allegiance to Spain and was stationed by Louisiana's new sovereign to Natchitoches, where he traded profitably and negotiated effectively with Indians on the northwestern edge of the colony. His wife and children, meanwhile, stayed on the family's plantation near New Orleans. When Spain declared war against Britain during the American Revolution, LeBlanc saw action in the campaigns against Galveztown, Baton Rouge, Mobile, and Pensacola. Continuing to demonstrate adaptability to changing regimes, he befriended prefect Pierre-Clément de Laussat and his wife Marie Anne Péborde Laussat during Louisiana's brief transfer back to France and then William Claiborne after its purchase by the United States. Within the next few years, LeBlanc decided to write a tragic play out of anger over what he measured as a rise in the slandering of American Indians by fellow citizens.[2]

Dedicating his play to Madame de Laussat, LeBlanc credited the former prefect's wife with inspiring him to write *The Festival of the Young Corn*. He remembered how, upon seeing "a family of these unhappy people who are called barbaric, whom prejudice rejects, whom pride despises, but whom a soul like yours appreciates and pities," she "helped them forget their sufferings" and "found in the suffering family none of the hideous and sinister traits that Europeans attribute to them, but only the pitiful marks of the harm that Europeans had done to them." Since Laussat had only seen Indian people in passing, LeBlanc wished to offer "more about them" by drawing from what he knew since being generously welcomed by the Choctaws more than a half-century earlier. "Whatever they are today, Madame, I have not forgotten what they were once, nor what they deserved from me." Pleading ignorance of any profession other than military service, he nonetheless wanted to "decrease the prejudice which weighs upon them." To achieve this, LeBlanc selected one episode out of many from Indian history that would demonstrate "the vigorous mettle that their souls received from nature." Only a few days after the young French ensign had reached Louisiana, a Houma chief named Poucha-Houmma supposedly sacrificed his own life to save that of his son. "This chief had often been to New Orleans where he was much admired," according to LeBlanc's preface to the play. "His death was talked about, and many versions circulated," so Governor Vaudreuil, "who esteemed him great for his good qualities and his loyalty to our flag, decided to find out the truth." LeBlanc happened to be present when an interpreter sent to learn the truth reported back to the governor. Over the ensuing years, he also conversed several times with Cala-be, Poucha-Houmma's son, "about the details of his father's death." With "these details engraved in my memory," the aged and amateur playwright wrote "only that which the facts aver."[3]

Three months after the first and last performance of LeBlanc's play and at the author's request, William Claiborne, governor of the Orleans Territory, sent a manuscript copy of it to Thomas Jefferson, who by then was out of the White House and back in his Virginia home. "I do not know," Claiborne wrote, "that this production as relates to the stile and manner, possesses a particular merit; But when we bear in mind, that the tragical Scene which it is designed to perpetuate, was really exhibited (and to which several aged Citizens can testify) I trust, the perusal will be found interesting." We do not know what the Sage of Monticello thought about the play, although some Louisianians considered it worthy enough to purchase when copies were published by subscription in 1814, a year before LeBlanc's death.[4] When it came to the actual presence of American Indians then and there, Claiborne was having less contact than did any previous governor of Louisiana. In April 1806, however, he did present "two uniform Coats" to two visiting chiefs of the Houmas, "a friendly Tribe of Indians." "They reside on the waters of the Mississippi in the County of Acadia within this Territory," as Claiborne reported to Secretary of War Henry Dearborn, "and have been in the habit of receiving small presents from Governors." In another letter to Thomas Jefferson, written several months before sending LeBlanc's play, the governor had this to say: "We have in this Territory, many little tribes to whose happiness and prosperity, (under the orders of the President) it would be my pride and pleasure to contribute: With these Tribes, hunting continues a favorite pursuit; Agriculture and the raising of stock are but partially attended to; But the men are often useful, in assisting Boats in navigating the Mississippi and its waters; And the women have of late turned their attention to manufactures. They make a variety of Baskets and mats which are exchanged with the white Citizens for provisions and clothing. I have obtained a Basket and a mat manufactured by the Attakapas Indians, which are transmitted."[5]

⋘

Since the last decade or so of the eighteenth century and what American officials like Claiborne seemed to ignore, the Houmas and other *petites nations* in the orbit of New Orleans were confronting severe pressure to sell their land to encroaching white planters and to relocate away from the Mississippi River's banks. Displacement from their villages and loss of territory reflected an accelerating rise in the region's non-Indian population, but also signified a quickening evaporation of these small nations' value to New Orleans—following nearly a century of playing an influential role in the city's security and economy. Biloxis and Tunicas migrated northwestward to the lower Red River, and Alibamons left for the Opelousas district farther west. With the sale of land to Alexandre Latil and Maurice Conway at the site of present-day Houmas House, Houma people began abandoning their village sites and migrating southward along Bayous Lafourche and Terrebonne. The Chitimachas concentrated their population westward along Bayou Teche and Grand Lake. Although many non-Indian claimants received confirmation from the US Land Office by documenting purchase from Indian owners, the government showed no signs of supporting claims made by Indian people themselves. The Houmas' claim to land along Bayou Boeuf, for example, was denied by district commissioners who reported to Congress in 1817 that "we know of no law of the United States by which a tribe of Indians have a right to claim lands as a donation."[6]

Although the *petites nations* lost their diplomatic weight and presence in New Orleans entering the nineteenth century, the Choctaw nation held on to its formal relationship with the city a bit longer. Choctaw negotiation with US officials over territory, trade, and sovereignty now mostly occurred inside tribal boundaries, with Native delegations occasionally traveling to Natchez or Nashville. The persistence of a Spanish presence in Florida also drew some Choctaw diplomacy and commerce into the port towns of Pensacola and Mobile. Despite New Orleans's decline as an embassy for Indian diplomats, its role as a nexus of Indian trade continued. Expansion of the fur trade with American Indians across the Mississippi and Missouri Valleys during the early nineteenth century meant that deerskins, beaver and other small-mammal pelts and buffalo robes were being shipped through the Crescent City to European and other American cities. In addition to involvement of New Orleans merchants in the private sector of this commerce, the United States relied upon the city for warehousing and selling furs and other products being purchased through a network of government-owned trade houses. Although peltry, tallow, and beeswax sold by Choctaws at their government house on the Tombigbee River went through the port of Mobile, federal posts at Natchitoches (Louisiana), Chickasaw Bluffs (Tennessee), Arkansas, Fort Osage (Missouri), and Fort Madison (Iowa) shipped what they acquired from different Indian nations to a warehouse in New Orleans. These and other trade houses were established to meet Native expectations for fair pricing and to facilitate US treaty relations with Indian nations. During 1807 the factor at Chickasaw Bluffs shipped a total of thirty-five pounds of deerskins downriver to the Crescent City; 87,000 pounds came from the same place eight years later. In the month of February 1810 there were 109 tons of skins in the government's New Orleans warehouse, being managed by an agent named Joseph Saul. From 1809 to 1813 the two posts at Fort Osage and Fort Madison sent to the city 178,000 pounds of deerskins, 21,000 raccoon furs, 17,000 pounds of tallow, and 133,000 pounds of lead. The merchandise sold to Indians in exchange for these and other products also passed through the ledger books of merchants and the hands of dockworkers in the Crescent City.[7]

The outbreak of war between the United States and Great Britain in 1812 led to the last formal, but dramatic, act of Choctaw diplomacy to occur in the history of New Orleans. Choctaw men fought in the Battle of New Orleans mainly as an extension of the role they played in the Creek War. When the Creek Confederacy slipped into civil war and slid into open

conflict with the United States, Choctaw leaders diverged over what policies to pursue. Some attempted to stay out of the war altogether, although
individual Choctaw warriors did join the Creeks' Red Stick resistance
movement. Others chose to provide military assistance to the American
government's invasion of Creek country. Alliance with the Choctaw nation was a crucial part of US strategy in the Gulf South, as it had been
for France and Spain over the previous century. "All the friendly Indians
should be organized, and prepared to cooperate with your other forces,"
Secretary of War James Monroe wrote to General Andrew Jackson in September 1814. Underscoring evidence of "some dissatisfaction among the
Choctaws," he warned Jackson that "their friendship and services should
be secured without delay." "The friendly Indians must be fed and paid,"
as Monroe further instructed, "and made to fight when and where their
services may be required."[8]

At a council hosted by Pushmataha in the town of Apuckshunubbee a
year earlier, Choctaw men had already formed special companies to fight
alongside American soldiers during the Creek War. Working closely with
Pushmataha was Pierre Juzan, a trader married to the chief's niece who
had an interest in bolstering alliance with US officials and merchants. After
contributing to campaigns against Creek Indians and to the occupation
of Spanish Pensacola, Juzan led a portion of the Choctaw force—as many
as sixty men—to New Orleans for Andrew Jackson's defense of the city
against Great Britain's invading army. Most of these Choctaws patrolled
Chef Menteur Road to prevent a British approach from Lake Borgne, but
Juzan brought about eighteen of them to join Jackson's main line below
New Orleans just in time to rescue a group of Tennessee riflemen from
being outgunned by British snipers. Juzan's Choctaws secured an advantageous position to the left of Jackson's defensive line, firing elusively from
a cypress swamp at British soldiers marching toward the Americans. According to one estimate, about fifty redcoats were killed and many more
wounded by these Indians at the Battle of New Orleans. Although this
heroic military operation in defense of New Orleans marked the end of
the Choctaw nation's long-lasting political presence there, by no means
did Choctaw people abandon their intricately dynamic relationship with
the city.[9]

≺≺≺

The widening distance of Indian communities from New Orleans reduced the frequency and scale of Indian visits by the early nineteenth century, but a significant Indian presence continued to be made on the urban landscape. Losing political and economic influence on the city, after nearly a century of practicing prominent diplomacy in its public life, American Indian nations put other forms of performance to public use. Stickball games played by Indians, for example, arose as a source of entertainment for non-Indian residents as well as a means of cultural self-representation by Indian participants. As mentioned in chapter 2, the earliest documentation of this Indigenous precursor to lacrosse being played for colonial onlookers here dates back to June 1764. Before his death in 1794, longtime city resident Guy Soniat du Fossat wrote: "The Indians are exceedingly fond of sports. It is common to see them lose all their possessions on the hazards of a game. Their favorite game is called 'Raquette,' and it is a ball game in which they display skill and bodily strength and speed in foot-racing. The contestants form sides. The winners tear off the clothes of their adversaries." A month before officiating Louisiana's transfer to the United States, Pierre Clément de Laussat witnessed one Sunday "Negroes and mulattoes, in groups of four, six, eight—some from the city, others from the country"—playing "raquette des sauvages" against each other: "I was invited to one of these contests, where bets rose from five to six hundred piastres fortes. Each team distinguished itself by ribbons of motley colors. The game was dangerous. Rarely did it happen that there were no accidents, no arms or legs broken. Metairie, more commonly called the Plaine labarre, usually served as a tilting ground. The road was full with an unbroken line of traveling coaches, *cabriolets,* horses, carts, spectators, and players. The escorted winners retired triumphant. By a strange inconsistency, only too common, the spectators cheered and encouraged the skill and triumph of those very athletes whom they dreaded having to fight someday."[10]

The Choctaw game of stickball, or *ishtaboli,* encompassed a ceremonial complex known for settling conflicts and avoiding wars, so it was a somewhat consistent replacement for the calumet dance. Matches between clans, towns, and nations were usually preceded by ritual preparations, accompanied by conjuring and gambling, and followed by special songs and dances.[11] As explained to anthropologist John Swanton by Mississippi

Choctaw Simpson Tubby in the early twentieth century, the Choctaws valued stickball as the "peace game," and the first Choctaw to make ball sticks was named Musholeika, meaning in rough translation "'to go out' or 'to put out' like a light." Tubby credited non-Indians with the introduction of gambling into the sport, which by the late nineteenth century became more volatile, although Swanton noted earlier and more widespread evidence of betting in American Indian games.[12] Interaction with colonial people would have certainly introduced some new elements for adaptation and innovation, well exemplified by Choctaw incorporation of the European snare drum into stickball ceremony. It also offered new public spaces for performance and self-representation.[13]

Like playing stickball, marketing select wares persisted as a form of displaying Indian identity and culture to a rapidly growing and diversifying city of 8,500 residents by 1805. Although losing political and economic importance to New Orleans, American Indian people put the Crescent City to whatever use they could find for their own livelihood and survival. Instead of formal diplomacy, they now practiced informal diplomacy. And as New Orleans became more susceptible to outbreaks of yellow fever because of its rapid growth, these Native visitors tended to concentrate their presence in the city during healthier winter and spring months. Certain places in back of town, especially along Bayou St. John and the road leading from it, became campgrounds for Indians seasonally visiting the city. Particular features of New Orleans's physical environs played a notable role in encouraging open exchange with Indians. "The inhabitants, sailors, Indians, and slaves run around freely inside as well as beyond the town," as one mid-eighteenth-century visitor from France put it. "They meet in the thick and intruding woods that border the town almost all around." Well into the next century, the wetlands around New Orleans provided optimal space for what city elites and officials considered illicit and dangerous activity. Drinking, gambling, bartering, and dancing brought diverse people together in ways that especially troubled slave owners, who came to expect stronger prohibitions and police action in a city rapidly approaching a population of thirty thousand by 1820.[14] As a child growing up along Bayou St. John at the time, Father Adrien Rouquette even thought "there were more Indians in the city than there were whites or negroes," perhaps because this stream "was lined with their encampments." When "a place was built on the Bayou Road to serve as a market," he later recalled, "the Indians took possession of it as lodging place, and their claim to do so was not disputed."[15]

Early nineteenth-century visitors to New Orleans commonly described this changing presence of American Indians with different degrees of disparagement. Strolling outside the town gate behind the present-day Vieux Carré on a Sunday afternoon in 1799, Fortescue Cuming observed "upwards of fifty Indians" encamped near a brickworks in temporary housing covered with palmetto leaves. Although he emphasized "disgustful" signs of intoxication and indolence in his travel account, the Pennsylvanian did not overlook evidence of cultural activity. Singing and dancing occurred under the brickyard's large circular shade, while a group of women were weaving baskets, mats, and sifters for sale in the city. Another visitor to the city at that time, Berquin-Duvallon, described a scene this way:

> Every winter, are seen a great number of the savages from different nations assembling at New-Orleans. These various hordes repair hither, the chief place of the colony, in order to receive their annual gifts from government, in token of their friendship; consisting of woolen garments, blankets, fowling pieces, powder and shot, vermillion, &c. Each band has its own encampment in the vicinity of the town, composed of huts covered with the skins of bears and other beasts. The squaws are to be seen busy in making baskets and moccasins, which they sell to the colonists. The men kill wild fowl, drink rum, or sit on the ground in a pensive posture doing nothing, retired in the shade if it is warm, and courting the sun if it is cold. Their dress is a piece of coarse cloth, or a blanket thrown over their shoulders; but they decorate themselves with broaches, earrings, and even nose jewels. They paint their faces with streaks of red and blue, which with their dress and accoutrements gives them an air of masquerade, and suits the carnival, at which season they assemble.

Paul Alliot, perhaps overestimating that "some hundreds of savages with their wives and children live on the outskirts of New Orleans," noted that the men sold game in the city "for excellent prices" while the women sold firewood and reed baskets "at good prices." He nonetheless judged that they "have no care or troubles," "greatly love taffia," and "especially enjoy

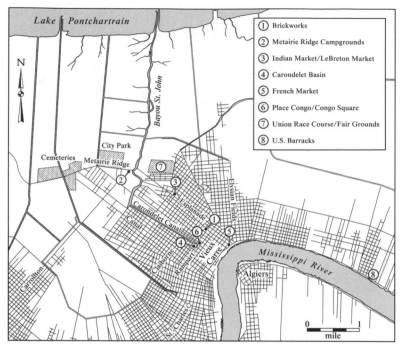

Sites of American Indian Presence in Mid-Nineteenth-Century New Orleans.
Map by Mary Lee Eggart.

the protection of the government which makes them annual presents."
Christian Schultz in 1808 saw residing in the vicinity of New Orleans "a
gang of poor miserable naked wretches," people he thought were "outcasts" from the Tunica, Alibamon, Chitimacha, and Atakapas tribes, exhibiting "daily scenes of riot, obscene dances, and intoxication."[16]

A specific site selected by some Indians for encampment near New
Orleans by then was the former Lepers' Hospital on Metairie Ridge, close
to present-day cemeteries and City Park. Established in 1785 and closed
in 1807, this building—according to Mayor James Mather—was now "the
headquarters of a band of Indians who have already all the lumber which
could be detached therefrom without destroying the roofing." The mayor
asked city councilmen to consider leasing out the property or making it
a "public pound" because "the whole neighborhood is complaining of
the annoyance they experience from the sojourn of the Indians about

them, and you may well conceive the disorder which such vagabonds are apt to commit."[17] Indian camps along the road between Bayou St. John and the Vieux Carré continued to be a regular feature of the New Orleans landscape. At its intersection with Gentilly Road near the former home of Daniel Clark—as recalled by Henry Castellanos—a market originally called "the Indian market" and renamed Le Breton Market in 1867 was "the bivouac of the vagrant Indians that abounded in that vicinity."[18] Construction of a canal and basin linking Bayou St. John with the main part of town, a project that began in the 1790s and was completed in 1817, increased the volume of travel and commerce from the direction of Lake Pontchartrain. Docking in the Carondelet Basin at the end of Toulouse Street, boats brought lumber, naval stores, bricks, crops, shellfish, and game directly into the present-day French Quarter. And as reported in the city directory and register for 1822, "a great number of Indians come by this route to New Orleans, with their furs and peltries, which they trade for such necessaries as they stand in need of."[19]

A handful of drawings and paintings depict this everyday presence of American Indians in New Orleans during the early nineteenth century. *Vue d'une Rue du Faubourg Marigny*, one of a few watercolors by marine painter and lithographer Félix Achille de Beaupoil de Saint Aulaire, depicts a street scene that includes an Indian family (plate 3). Although better known for his spectacular paintings of western Indians, Swiss artist Karl Bodmer also produced vivid images of Choctaws along the Mississippi River. Based at the utopian colony of New Harmony, Indiana, with Prince Maximilian, Bodmer traveled alone to New Orleans in 1833. He stayed for a week in January with druggist Joseph Barralino, who arranged for him to paint with watercolors several individual Choctaw men and women (plate 4). Maximilian later recorded in his own diary Bodmer's impressions of Indians who frequented the Crescent City. "Some of them make their fires on the streets," he wrote, "and, like the Negro women, also cook their coffee as well as their somsé, an overboiled meat dish." On his return trip to New Harmony, Bodmer spent three days in Baton Rouge and a week in Natchez, painting additional images of Indians in those places.[20]

Although seldom identified as such today by historians, Choctaws and other American Indians were regular participants in back-of-town interaction with New Orleans slaves and working-class whites. In 1831 a French traveler, Georges J. Joyaux, described how "every Sunday, the negroes of the city and of the surroundings meet in a place called *The Camp*," a large space on the shore of Lake Pontchartrain reached by either canal boats or steam-driven railcars. Distinct groups of dancers performed a variety of "attitudes and expressions," which Joyaux called "lascivious," to the beat of drums echoing back from a thick cypress forest. He also noticed that "several Indian families—settled not far from the Lake—also come to The Camp to share these ludicrous pleasures."[21] From the very beginnings of frontier exchange in and around New Orleans, a notable number of African Americans interacted regularly and intimately enough with local Indians to learn their languages. Some knew enough to serve as interpreters for colonial and municipal officials, but black slaves' ability to communicate directly with Indian people was also self-serving. As late as 1850, a fugitive slave named Henry who fled his owner's plantation in St. Charles Parish was described as "a bright mulatto, five feet six or seven inches high, strongly built, speaking English, French and the Choctaw dialect." Previously owned by Mr. Beauregard and employed for a while in the *New Orleans Bee* office, Henry was likely in New Orleans when a twenty-five-dollar reward for his capture was advertised in the *Daily Picayune*. "He will try to go to the other side of Lake Pontchartrain, or Westward," his owner suspected.[22]

White observers of back-of-town action predictably insisted upon compartmentalizing fluid social gatherings into racialized categories. Traveling through New Orleans on his way from Westphalia to Texas in the mid-1830s, Friedrich Wilhelm von Wrede entered a tavern where African Americans were singing and dancing. In "a glaring contradiction to this boisterous gaiety," as the Prussian put it, were several Indians sternly and quietly leaning against the wall and observing the scene "with gloomy eyes." Although reluctant to answer questions raised to them, their conversation "became exceedingly lively" under the influence of more drinks. Some even "stepped forward and in deep-ringing voices boasted of the exploits of their tribe, their chieftains, and also their own glorious accomplishments." Von Wrede was impressed enough by this display to judge "these haughty red people who even in their intoxicated state still had a respectable demeanor . . . while many others of my own white race through brutal wantonness and impudence disgraced their own color and fatherland."[23]

One cannot be certain about the actual influence that intoxication had upon American Indian behavior on the streets of New Orleans, although we know about the particular vulnerability to alcohol suffered by many Native people. Drinking, no doubt, adversely affected the health and demeanor of everyone who imbibed, and white observers tended to overassociate public demonstrations by Indian people with drunkenness. But there was more going on in most cases. New Orleanian Adrien Rouquette, who became a missionary priest among Choctaws across Lake Pontchartrain, remembered from childhood hearing "their songs as they reeled along through the streets, carrying bottles of whiskey in their hands, and their faces painted blue and bright red." Residents would close their doors and pedestrians would run out of their way as these Indians approached, although he "always mingled among them without being harmed." Some of this boisterous parading, however, occurred for specific social purposes. Whenever a Choctaw wedding was under way and the bride appeared in splendid dress, as also recounted by Father Rouquette, "a little drum was beaten and a basket was carried around, in which all who were met were requested to drop in a contribution for the benefit of the newly wedded twain." "Men and women who performed this ceremony," he added, "drank freely and made their rounds singing. The shrill voices of the squaws mingling with the warlike base [sic] voices of the men would make you shudder."[24]

Contrasting with numerous perceptions of disorderly conduct by American Indians, there is only a scant record of them seriously disturbing the peace or being arrested for vagabondage. In May 1805 Governor Claiborne was hoping "to relieve the Inhabitants of the Sixth District of this City, from those vexatious Indian visits of which they complain." A few years later four "Ouachinans" were detained in prison for violating the city's ordinance against vagabonds. But in defiance of Mayor James Mather's will, Daniel Clark considered this arrest "illegal and arbitrary" and successfully appealed for their release by writ of habeas corpus. Although the exact location and occurrence of the alleged crime cannot be determined, an "Indian Called Annetto . . . aided and assisted the escape of Negro's—from their masters." Annetto, however, was pardoned by Claiborne on October 9, 1807.[25] Recalling Choctaws in camps along Bayou St. John and in various New Orleans markets, Henry Castellanos believed that "the police never arrested them for misdemeanors or crimes, but turned the offenders over to the chief of their tribe for punishment, the exemption, it was claimed, being based upon treaty stipulations or immemorial usage."[26] In 1817 Edouard de Montulé wrote: "One sees many Indians in New-Orleans, but these have in general lost their spirit of national unity and distinctive character through their proximity to the city. They are even scorned by their compatriots. A few of them find work at the port, and as soon as they have earned a little money they immediately get drunk, and there usually follows a bloody scuffle. They are exceedingly jealous of their women. Whenever it happens that a white man or a Negro takes one of them by surprise, the husband pursues him with such perseverance that it is difficult to escape his vengeance—which consists, if I can believe what I hear, in cutting off the ravisher's ears." Ironically, Indians were then included in a state law mandating a sentence of death for any person of color accused of raping a white woman or girl.[27]

The prevalence of orderly and peaceful conduct among Indians visiting New Orleans did not spare them from condemnatory remarks made by many observers. An extreme version of such commentary came from Benjamin Latrobe, an English-born architect best known for designing the US Capitol in Washington, who was also responsible for various buildings and projects in New Orleans. He moved to New Orleans in 1819 to complete construction of its municipal waterworks, but died the following year from yellow fever. Vehemently dismissive of newly emerging concern about "our Red brethren," Latrobe recorded in his journal nothing but scorn for Indians seen on Crescent City streets, calling them Choctaw "outcasts, the fag end of the tribe, the selvage, the intermediate existence between annihilation & savage vigor." At a New Orleans dinner party with Bolling Robertson, Captain Walsh, Judge Dominick Hall, and other gentlemen, the architect learned about some "positive virtues" possessed by local Indians: "They are most scrupulously honest," and "their women are most scrupulously chaste." Transgressions committed by these people were so few and far between that "the laws seem to take no notice whatsoever of them." This meant, furthermore, that "the few laws, or customs rather, which they have, they are permitted the full execution of practice, without interruption." Latrobe's dinner companions even recounted several episodes in which an Indian who had murdered a fellow tribesman presented himself for execution. Only a few years preceding Latrobe's visit, a confessed killer "came to the Market place, laid his head upon a block, & his companions took up brickbats, stones, or whatever they could find, & pelted him till he was dead." A quarter century earlier, another had surrendered himself near Canal Marigny "with great courage, painted & dressed for the Solemnity," but he suddenly began pleading for his life. Enraged by this cowardice, his executioners "declared he was not worthy to die" and "stripped him stark naked, tore his blanket & every other part of his apparel to shreds, & distributed it among them, and ordered him to run. He did not wait, but took to his heels." When Captain Walsh had asked for the meaning of this disrobing, "the answer was, that he was a *Hen*, & not a *Cock*."[28]

These were Choctaw rituals that became standard lore in nineteenth-century travel journals and correspondence—almost as commonly cited as were quadroon balls and gentlemanly duels. More importantly, they were a means for Indian people to enact their own kinship and justice systems in momentary spaces. They were performing a degree of autonomy—even for money in some cases. Nevertheless, the popularity of describing in detail episodes of Choctaw men (mostly) giving themselves up for execution was consistent with the romantic era's preoccupation with how Indians viewed death and dying. The "dying Indian" had become a versatile subject in novels, plays, poems, and paintings that dramatized "lastness" among Indians in one way or another. Most commonly a noble brave mournfully and courageously confronted either the loss of a loved one or the end of his tribe. Over time, this theme became subsumed by the overall assumption that all Indian people were naturally vanishing. Writings by François-René de Chateaubriand and James Fenimore Cooper are perhaps the best-known versions, yet a short story written by southern author William Gilmore Simms specifically used the trope of a Choctaw willingly appearing for his ritual execution after murdering another Choctaw. The lead character in "Oakatibbe, or the Choctaw Sampson," published in 1841, killed Loblolly Jack in a drunken fight. The victim was considered to be dishonest and violent, especially by the Mississippi planter who was seasonally employing Oakatibbe's group as cotton pickers. But despite

Colonel Harris urging the more virtuous murderer to flee, Oakatibbe sto-
ically faced the death penalty meted out by Loblolly Jack's relative in accordance with Choctaw law. "Never did man carry with himself more simple
nobleness," wrote Simms. The moral and physical nobility demonstrated
by fictional characters like Oakatibbe was a common feature in the "last
Indian" theme that appeared in literature across a long span of time and
a wide array of genres. From local histories and poems to popular plays
and novels, one encountered the stoic Indian—usually a man—readily
accepting the demise of his people and thereby reinforcing assumptions
about the inevitability and innocence of white replacement.[29]

American Indians, however, did not always perfectly mirror white
Americans' romantic imagination when it came to how they faced the
death penalty. Perhaps adapting what had been a customary alternative to
execution, the murderer of a fellow Choctaw sometimes collected money
from sympathetic whites in order to satisfy the victim's kin. In one New
Orleans–based episode of Choctaw justice purportedly occurring in 1832,
as recounted many years later by Henry Castellanos, a group took possession of a schooner docked at the Old Basin and demanded that the skipper
take them across Lake Pontchartrain. A young Choctaw found guilty of
homicide was being returned by his victim's relatives to the St. Tammany
community, where they would execute him. Lt. Bonseigneur Dutillet of
the City Guard managed to rescue this man from his Indian escorts and
interview him inside the guardhouse. Undemonstrably in broken French,
Eh-he-lum-abe told how he had shot and killed one of three young fellow tribesmen who were attacking him. When the city official expressed
sympathy for his plight, the Choctaw "begged to be taken back to the
schooner, where his squaw and children had been left," explaining that
otherwise his father, brother, or son would face death in his stead. But in
apparent accordance with Choctaw law allowing material compensation to
replace execution, Dutillet raised among fellow citizens a hundred dollars
for his ransom and thereby satisfied the victim's kin.[30]

Five years later, the *New Orleans Picayune* reported that "a few weeks
since, one of our Indians accidently, in a drunken frolic, killed one of his
tribe, in the vicinity of this city, by striking him upon the head with a bottle." The Choctaws assembled in council to try the murderer and sentenced
him "to be shot this day, or raise the sum of three hundred dollars." One

day before the scheduled execution, "notwithstanding the pressure in the money market" the newspaper writer was quick to note, "the prisoner with two of his brothers who had him under guard, succeeded in collecting this amount from the liberal citizens of New Orleans." The final dollars were obtained inside Hewlett's Arcade, where one of the condemned man's brothers "mounted a table, and returned thanks to the crowd around him." Although the speech was made in the Choctaw language, so "we could not tell whether it was good or otherwise," in the prisoner's tears and in all three brothers' faces, "joy was plainly depicted."[31]

Disparaging and patronizing characterizations of American Indians living in scattered communities and appearing occasionally on city streets were fast becoming the nation's official position toward Native people who had survived centuries of colonialism. Labeling them "small remnants of tribes," Secretary of War John C. Calhoun believed that removal far away from population centers was their only alternative to extinction. In the opening paragraph to his annual report for 1831, President Andrew Jackson's commissioner of Indian affairs, Elbert Herring, declared that "the humane policy" adopted by the government "with respect to the Indian tribes residing within the limits of the United States . . . is progressively developing its good effects; and, it is confidently trusted, will at no distant day, be crowned with complete success." Native Americans, he opined, were "gradually diminishing in numbers and deteriorating in condition." "Incapable of coping with the superior intelligence of the white man, ready to fall into the vices, but unapt to appropriate the benefits of the social state," they would naturally be engulfed by "the increasing tide of white population." The disappearance of "tribes numerous and powerful," according to Herring, foreshadowed the fate "of those that still remain, unless counteracted by the substitution of some principle sufficiently potent to check the tendencies to decay and dissolution." And that "salutary principle" was, of course, the government's newly inaugurated "system of removal; of change of residence; of settlement in territories exclusively their own, and under the protection of the United States; connected with the benign influences of education and instruction in agriculture and the several mechanic arts, whereby social is distinguished from savage life."[32]

The boundary that ideologues and policy makers imagined between "savagery" and "civilization" was hardly a real line between interactive people, but even intimate contact between Indians and whites could be subjected to creative and performative othering. Thanks to the regular appearance and close proximity of Indians, a simple case in point, New Orleans was the scene of a significant event in American theater history. Edwin Forrest was the most celebrated American actor of his lifetime, performing Shakespeare's plays and other popular drama and comedy across the United States. Beginning with its debut at New York City's Park Theatre in 1829, Forrest's most profitable and popular performances were the lead role in *Metamora; or, The Last of the Wampanoags*—a play written by John Augustus Stone in a contest sponsored by the actor himself for "the best tragedy, in five acts, of which the hero, or principal character, shall be an aboriginal of this country." This winning script was based on the seventeenth-century Indian war led by Metacom against New England colonists, a staple story in history books and popular writings. Forrest's powerful representation of this historic Indian character, as he explained to his friend and biographer William Alger, owed plenty to the relationship the actor had forged with a young Choctaw in New Orleans during the mid-1820s. Edwin Forrest lived in the city while performing at James Caldwell's American Theatre. Only eighteen years old then, he socialized in a circle of local characters that included slave trader, land-grant counterfeiter, and sugar planter James Bowie. Forrest struck his most influential local relationship, however, with a young man named Pushmataha—son of the Choctaw chief with the same name who had mobilized warriors to assist the United States during the Creek War and the War of 1812 and died during a diplomatic mission to Washington in 1824. "In the custom of paying long visits to New Orleans," the young Pushmataha was remembered by the actor as "the first cause of his deep interest in the subject of the American Aborigines, of his subsequent extensive researches into their history, and finally of his offering a prize for a play which should embody a representative idea of their genius and their fate." When Forrest clashed with theater manager Caldwell over their competing affections for actress Jane Placide, he accepted Pushmataha's invitation to spend a month among the Choctaws in 1825. Probably lodging at one of the Six Town villages in south-central Mississippi, Forrest followed Choctaw customs, taking part in "all their doings, their smokes, their dances, their hunts, their songs." On at least one evening in the forest, the actor asked his Indian friend to "strip himself and walk to and fro before him between the moonlight and the firelight that he might feast his eyes and his soul on so complete a physical type of what man should be." Students of Edwin Forrest's famed career would later attribute the remarkable verbal and bodily authenticity in his staging of Metamora to the actor's New Orleans–based friendship with Pushmataha.[33]

An American performing artist of another kind offered a somewhat different perspective on his interaction with Native people near the Crescent City. In the 1830s the family of Louis Moreau Gottschalk, New Orleans–born composer and pianist, spent time at a cottage in Pass Christian on the Mississippi Gulf Coast. Choctaws regularly passed through this resort town to sell game and wares, stopping at the Gottschalk residence on occasion. Recalling one such visit during his early childhood, the virtuoso musician stereotyped American Indians to comment on a lack of refinement among his critics and audiences in the United States:

> One evening when I was playing "Hail Columbia" a large Indian stopped at the door and watched inquisitively my hands running over the keyboard. My father (although a man of great intelligence, he was not without that weakness in which all fathers participate, who think their children phoenixes) said to the Indian, "You see what this little pale-face can do." The vanity of the savage was so much the more wounded as he could not deny that the child did what neither he nor his had ever done. He came in and attentively examined the box from whence the strange sounds proceeded. Tea was ready. We passed into the next room without thinking of the Indian. I alone secretly observed him. His great size and hoarse voice inspired me with childish fear. I saw him, after satisfying himself that he was not observed, slowly approach the piano; he looked attentively at the keyboard, then carelessly, and as if by accident, he let his hand fall upon a key which returned a sound. Scarcely had he heard it, when his countenance, which had remained morose, brightened, he sat down at the piano, and with all the force of his arms he began to beat the keys, calling out triumphantly to my father, "You see, I never tried before, and I make more noise than he."
>
> Do you understand my comparison? "No!" Very well then. Go to B——, and when you shall be told what some one told me—"Mrs. ——

is the best singer here, because you can hear her a mile off"—recall to yourself the Indian of Pass Christian. "This gallery of paintings is the largest which we have in America." The Indian of Pass Christian. "Mr. Such-an-one is an excellent judge of music; he has spent six months in Europe." Again, my Indian. "Our hotel is as good as the 'Fifth Avenue' or the 'Continental'; look at the number of dishes on the bill of fare." The Indian, always the Indian.[34]

⤙⤙⤙

Behind the Indian presence in and around New Orleans, there was a much wider network of exchange and travel. And when taken into account, this circuit of activity reveals something about what American Indians themselves thought and felt beyond what others said about them. Like many other Native Americans who found themselves surrounded by a rapidly growing non-Native population, Lower Mississippi Valley Indians blended traditional livelihood practices with new forms of work and production. Pursuit of this intercultural alternative to either open resistance or full retreat became a means of retaining some degree of sovereignty.[35] Throughout the first half of the nineteenth century, Indian people moved through a seasonal round of hunting, fishing, gathering, and trading activities that brought them into regular contact with white and black Louisianians. Some even picked cotton on plantations during harvest season. In many cases, itinerant groups of Indian people forged strong personal relationships with particular non-Indian families. Houmas, for example, had virtually become a part of the Michel Bernard de Cantrelle household in St. James Parish. According to Laussat, this sugar planter's children went hunting with their Houma neighbors and even spoke a bit of their language. In 1811 Cantrelle facilitated a meeting of Houma chief Chachouma and his attendants with Governor William Claiborne in New Orleans. Although diplomatic visits from nearby Indian communities to the city occurred less frequently by then—and were even being discouraged by US officials—Claiborne on this occasion treated Chachouma's delegation with ceremonial respect and granted gifts worth a hundred dollars along with provisions for their journey back home. "At the present day," he reported to Secretary of War William Eustis, "the number of this Tribe is greatly diminished; it does not exceed 80 souls,—but their conduct is exemplary and the late visit of the Chief being the first he paid me, I thought it a matter of policy to make him a small present."[36] As a guest at James Pirrie's Oakley Plantation near St. Francisville, Louisiana, John James Audubon recorded in his journal, "Yesterday the 25th of July 1821 an Indian of the Choctaw Nation, who habitually hunts for Mr. Perrie— brought me a femelle of the chuck Will's Widow [*Caprimulgus carolinensis*] in full and handsome plumage." Regularly seeing American Indians in such a relationship with planters, the naturalist-painter was of course more interested in the bird's features. "It Measured," he went on to write, "One Foot in length, 25 Inches in breadth, the tail composed of Ten Feathers is rounded."[37]

As late as 1845, according to a perhaps exaggerated recollection of Felix Leche, "thousands of Indians" from up north spent their winters "hunting and making baskets" along the German Coast. "Like the migrating swallows, these Indians for generations visited at the same farms and became well acquainted with the white families, and much attached to them." Leche described how "on their arrival, the red men kissed the white children, and on returning from their hunting trips, they never failed to give them choice pieces of their booty." Their seasonal departure caused "deep regret to the white boys, some of whom used to accompany the Indians on their hunting trips, and learned much about hunting from them." Meloncy C. Soniat recalled from his childhood on the Tchoupitoulas Plantation a large grove of magnolia trees called "Terre Haute," where every winter a group of Indians from a village near Mandeville camped in palmetto huts to hunt and fish "without Interference from the whites." Whenever the women visited Soniat's plantation home "to sell their beautiful baskets, sassafras and gumbo filé," his mother "would always give them flour, sugar, coffee and bacon; and the Indians in turn would give me either a blow gun made of cane reed or some other small object such as bow and arrows." Soniat fondly remembered these guests departing with their goods, and sometimes a small child, inside a large basket strapped around their foreheads.[38] James Morris Morgan, who was five years old when his family moved from New Orleans to Baton Rouge at midcentury, reminisced about one group of Choctaws living on the Amite River, a few miles east of Baton Rouge. These Indians regularly brought into town, "for sale or barter," their beadwork along with baskets and blowguns made from river cane. "The arrows of these blow-guns were made of split cane with a tuft of thistle at one end," Morgan wrote, "and we boys delighted in the ownership of these long and apparently harmless weapons. I say apparently harmless, but in the hands of an Indian they were very deadly to birds and squirrels. The Indians were wonderful shots with them and at twenty or thirty paces could hit a small silver five-cent piece; always provided they were promised the coin if they hit it."[39]

This itinerant movement of American Indians across the landscape was partly captured in undoubtedly the most familiar image of Lower Mississippi Valley Indians from the nineteenth century. With oil on canvas, Alfred Boisseau painted *Louisiana Indians Walking along a Bayou* in 1847, depicting a man with a rifle on his shoulder followed by a boy with a blowcane, a woman carrying a basket on her back, and another woman with a baby (plate 5). As in other paintings that included American Indians as either central or marginal figures on the landscape, this image romantically conveyed their harmony with the natural world. The Paris-born painter also seemed to be expressing a common attitude toward the condition of Indian women. While Native men were described as idle and lazy, although respected for their hunting skills, viewers assumed that their wives and sisters were burdened with all of the work. "I have seen the squaws bending beneath their burdens," one visitor to the New Orleans area wrote, "while the men walked gravely before, painted with vermilion, and carrying on their shoulders only a light fusee." The notion that Indian women were dispirited drudges, however, tells us more about white society's own anxiety over proper gender roles than about the real relationship between Indian men and women.[40]

Even if white landowners and townsfolk understood their relations with itinerant Indian camps largely as expressions of tolerance or kindness, plenty more was going on. Although unwittingly to some extent, these white patrons actually accommodated the American Indians' way of preserving their material and spiritual relationship with the land and its resources. Seasonal movement across the landscape, transgressing newly marked boundaries of property or jurisdiction, not only secured access to plants, animals, and other natural resources and commerce with other people, but it maintained contact with sacred places and features. There is also no doubt that itinerant groups of American Indians occasionally participated in a shadow economy operating behind the plantations and within the wetlands of south Louisiana. Like many riverside peddlers and even some small farmers who traded illicitly with slaves away from their owners' sight, Indians exchanged goods and socialized with enslaved workers when it suited them. Frontier exchange dating back to the colonial period was being partly preserved in spaces of communication now considered unlawful.[41]

Over the early months of 1840, a few Choctaw families were camping at Pierre Sauvé's plantation six miles upriver from New Orleans. A twenty-five-year-old traveler from Clermont-Ferrand, France, staying with the Sauvé family, was invited by these Choctaws, some of whom could speak French with him, to partake in their meal of *sagamité* [stew made from cornmeal mixed with beans, pumpkins, or other plants]. Victor Tixier proved to be a courteous but ungrateful guest. First of all, the appearance of his hosts did not match the Frenchman's romantic image of "real savages." Wearing a "soiled wool blanket" and "a black hat decorated with circles of trim and red feathers," one of the men seemed flushed in the face and unsteady on his feet from too much drinking. More appealing to Tixier's wish for the authentic Indian, "All of the men and women were tattooed with a sinuous blue line which started at the corner of their mouths and which reached the lower back part of the jaw." Weaving river-cane baskets when he first approached the camp, a few girls shyly hurried into their palmetto-covered huts. When Tixier offered the Choctaws some of his tobacco, "they drew from a skin bag a pipe which I thought would be, if not a beautiful calumet, at least a pipe of red stone with a stem of reed; it was, alas! But a poor pipe made of white clay perfectly similar to those which are called in France *brule quele.*" In time the women became more sociable and resumed their basket-weaving outside. "All were small, had good figures," Tixier thought, "but were perfectly ugly and untidy."

Tixier was smitten, however, by the wife of Baptiste, who seemed to be the group's leader. His wife Outamié's face was "expressive rather than beautiful," with a graceful smile and soft eyes that were "very difficult to describe." Baptiste welcomed Tixier inside his hut, where they smoked first from the Choctaw's pipe and later from cigars provided by the Frenchman. When Outamié handed the French guest a dish of sagamité, he tasted it out of courtesy but had no appetite for "her poor cooking." Baptiste then proceeded to tell Tixier something about his people's history and culture, in what the Frenchman thought was a French-Creole dialect resembling that spoken by black Louisianians. From eighteenth-century wars against the Chickasaws to their recent relocation to Indian Territory, Baptiste emphasized that the Choctaws were the oldest and largest of all "red tribes." He described how kinship groups like his now spent "the snow season" in south Louisiana, traveling in a straight line through prairies and cypress groves and knowing—unlike white people—how to maintain their direction without becoming lost or getting bitten by poisonous snakes. Tixier also learned about the many different medicinal plants used by the Choctaws, sometimes to heal the ailments of non-Indians. The men in this winter-camp of Choctaws on the Sauvé plantation hunted deer, rabbit, and other game for sale in "the settlements or in New Orleans," where the women sold plenty of their baskets. Plantation owners, for the most part, tolerated these Choctaw groups because with great discretion "they never harm the settlements and never take the liberty of cutting sugar cane in the fields near which they build their huts." Only those non-Indians determined to optimize their own hunting would "not allow them on their lands."

When Baptiste's group left the Sauvé plantation "for their big village," they burned down the huts but did not carry back the remains of anyone who might have passed away during their winter stay. Learning about "a burying ground for the redskins in the woods of a nearby settlement," Tixier received help from the landowner, "aware of my great desire to visit the tombs of the savages." During their walk to this cemetery, accompanied by a slave who carried "the necessary excavating equipment," the planter told the Frenchman there was no reason to fear Choctaw anger. "On their return," he said, "they will engage in their medicine to find out what became of the bones you will take away, for it is impossible to conceal from them the violation we are going to commit." With obvious derision, he described how the Indians would carry out a ritual that included drinking "the juice of cassine" in order to ascertain who had desecrated their burial ground. Tixier's host hinted, however, that they might alternatively identify the grave robber "by information cleverly gathered." Also in the course of this conversation, as recalled by the Frenchman, "we began to talk about the Indian women whom the Creoles find to their taste and whose virtue seldom resists the temptation of a few piasters." The rest of Tixier's account of his "expedition," as he called this desecration of an Indian grave, is worth quoting in full:

> We were then walking through a wood of magnolias in full bloom. The half-light, the delightful fragrance, the pleasant coolness of the place made us wish to rest in this grove. I admired these beautiful trees with dark shiny leaves covered with beautiful flowers so white and delicate, with the pretty cone with scales they have in their center, the garlands of creepers in bloom among which cardinals and Florida jays were playing. There was something both sweet and grandiose about the scenery. When I got up to leave, I saw a rattlesnake quite close to me; at the foot of magnolias a hideous rattlesnake: contrasts as always.
>
> We soon arrived at a thicket of brushwood in flower, among which the *tom-beck-be* opened its red clusters covering some pieces of bark laid side by side. We raised them, and the Negro, after digging a foot deep, found a second layer of decayed bark, then another under which lay the skeleton of a woman still wrapped with rotting rags. I took the head without digging any deeper and we put the pieces of bark back into their previous position. My guide assured me that in spite of these precautions the savages would easily find out that their tombs had been violated.[42]

❮❮❮

Many, if not most, of the Indians who developed close ties to non-Indian households and communities were people resisting pressure to leave their homeland. "They obstinately refuse to abandon the different parishes of Louisiana," Dominique Rouquette said about Choctaws, "where they are grouped in small family tribes, and live in rough huts in the vicinity of plantations, and hunt for the planters, who trade for the game they kill." While raising chickens and planting food crops around their homes, women made baskets of various shapes, sizes, and colors "from which they derived a good profit." They also sold medicinal and culinary plants gathered from the forest. Choctaw women regularly selling these items in New Orleans marketplaces fast became an attraction for the city's visitors. "Nothing is more interesting to the tourists than to see them wandering along the streets . . . with their cheap small wares, in their picturesque costumes, half savage and half civilized," wrote Rouquette in 1850. "Some-

times, they squat in a circle, at the big market place, on the banks of the
old river, patiently waiting with chaste downcast eyes, for the customers
who buy what they offer, more for the sake of charity than from necessity."
From their homes on the north shore of Lake Pontchartrain, Choctaw
families traveled on small schooners often captained by slaves of the boat
owners who charged for the trip.[43]

On December 30, 1849, Lady Emmeline Stuart-Wortley, third daughter
of the Duke of Rutland, was waiting for the train that would take her and
her daughter Victoria to Lake Pontchartrain, from where they would take
a steamboat to Mobile. As she described it, she saw "an interesting procession of Indians—an Indian encampment on the move." The men leading
this group into New Orleans "seemed a magnificent-looking set, splendidly
rigged out in very brilliant picturesque habiliments." Dressed in clothing
that resembled from a distance the costume of Highlanders, "they stalked
along with extreme dignity, and their haughty walk reminded me of the
theatrical, yet bold strutting march of the Albanians, the finest steppers I
ever saw." In the eyes of European and American travelers, Choctaws in
New Orleans were obviously becoming another tourist attraction. And as
suggested already in reference to Alfred Boisseau's painting, their perception of Indian women's status and condition was predictable. While the
Choctaw men observed by Stuart-Wortley walked "upright as their arrows,
or the tropical palms," the women were "unlucky squaws, who followed
after, bowed under the weight of papooshes, lodge-poles, pots, pans, kettles, all sorts of luggage and lumber." "How wearily they seemed plodding
along after the ungallant gentlemen of the party," exclaimed the daughter
of an English duke.[44] While regular travel to New Orleans to peddle goods
in its market satisfied some of American Indians' own economic and even
cultural interests, the consequential exposure to the curious eyes of racial
supremacists was nonetheless difficult and even painful to endure.

When Indians once in a while landed in city news for their own kinds
of boisterous behavior, writers always seized the opportunity to deliver
dehumanizing commentary about their condition. With the transition
from diplomacy to entertainment as the principal form of American Indian
performance in cities like New Orleans, white spectators would increasingly view Indian games, dances, and peddling as demonstrations of Native
American otherness—satisfying their own need to marginalize and even

wish away American Indian people. From the perspective of American Indians in and around New Orleans, however, adapting song and dance into ritualized solicitation of gifts was a modification of diplomatic performance. After more than a century of imperial intruders pressuring Indigenous people for everything from their allegiance to their land, conditions now warranted at the very least a playful inversion of expectations and demands. Across centuries and continents, other people have similarly ritualized expressions of protest and subversion in seasonal or spontaneous celebrations. And in a city that would soon attain a global reputation for its residents' performative antics of carnival masking and parading, this should not have been too perplexing or surprising.[45]

"A gang of ragged Choctaw," the *Daily Picayune* reported on December 16, 1837, "were pow-wowing and drumming about the streets yesterday, entering stores and coffee-houses, drumming citizens out of their small change. These vagrants have some ceremony to celebrate two or three times a year and tax the whites to raise funds in order to keep it up. The lazy rascals should have a bucket of cold water distributed over them every time they enter a house. All they want of money is to raise liquor with it. Cold water would do them more good." An article under the headline "Loafing Indians," dated April 2, 1839, described a group of Choctaws "pow-wowing, hooting and dancing about our streets, entering every man's house, and by their noise and dancing levying a direct contribution from all whose premises they encroach upon." In what obviously resembled the charivari tradition of Europe, these Indians "make such a confounded fuss and racket that any one will pay them in order to get rid of their outrageous noise. It is a marriage party, and a bigger set of loafers we have seldom seen."[46] A month and a half later, the same newspaper printed this report:

NOON-TIDE SERENADE.—Just as the sun reached its meridian yesterday, and while we were running our fingers over our head to find out the bump of paragraph-ativeness, a subject for one came right under our office windows in the shape of a band of lazy, loafing Choctaws, with their squaws and little ones of high and low degree, all of whom saluted us with a serenade of most unearthly music. The instrumental department consisted of a miniature kettle drum about the size of one half a musk melon dissevered in the centre, an empty whiskey bottle as mute as a convict under the silent system discipline, and a quarter dollar placed in the hand of a red skinned urchin, on which he let the handle of a jack-knife fall to mark time with the single stick drummer. The vocal performers, who were of both sexes and various ages, sounded every note on the gamut from D flat to X sharp, and pitched in every modulation of voice, from the *aporonso* of Brough to the *contralto* of Madame Caradori Allan. They were dressed as gaudily as red paint, feather and figured calicoes could make them. We thought their musical powers were called into requisition to pay us an especial compliment, till we learned that a pair of the tribe had got married, and that they availed themselves of this mode of "raising the wind" to buy fixings for the happy couple. From the good humor which seemed to sit on their brown faces, and to have taken up abode in the corners of their dark eyes, we could not suppress the exclamation of "Lo! The contented Indian!"[47]

A description of Choctaw Indians camping along Bayou St. John and Bayou Road in the mid-1840s, under the headline of "LO! THE POOR IN-DIAN," imagined that the smoke rising from their "miserable huts" and "cooking fires" now replaced "the smoke of the calumet." "They wander about like ghosts of departed greatness," the writer thought. The more that white Americans indulged in nostalgic fantasy about a distant Indian past, the more spectral did Indian people living in the present become to them. In another article titled "THE LAST OF THE CHOCTAWS," a group of Indians singing, drumming, and dancing on city streets—apparently to raise some money—were called "poor, degenerate puppets" who have "fallen from the high estate which their proud independent ancestors enjoyed!"[48] Recalling episodes like these years later, Henry Castellanos more thoughtfully attributed them to the discontinuation of Louisiana governors' giving gifts annually to their diplomatic delegations. "When by the lapse of time and the effect of prescription these resources were not forthcoming, the Indians would resort to *padegaud* shooting. The sport consisted in carrying about a wooden rooster decked with ribbons for target practice, around which they would dance and shout, begging from house to house a few picayunes for the 'powder and shot' necessary to the warriors and squaws. That meant 'whiskey and ration.' They were wont to keep up these carousals for several days in the outskirts or suburbs of the town. The same performances accompanied their Indian weddings and other ceremonies, from which they reaped rich harvest, as their exhibitions naturally attracted throngs of sojourners and sightseers."[49]

Condescending observations about Choctaw people came fast and furiously from a newspaper that had just been started by George Kendall and Francis Lumsden (early in 1837) and was rapidly becoming New Orleans's most popular newspaper. The *Daily Picayune*'s references to Choctaws regularly seen on Crescent City streets became commonplace in reports and observations that actually had little or nothing to do with American Indian people. Relaying to New Orleans readers some news from London about a visiting group of "Bayaderes" (Hindu dancing girls) in that city, the *Picayune* noted that "their style of dancing, so far as we can learn from the papers, is pretty much the same as that of the *Choctaw* girls on the Levee—merely a hop-up-and-down." In a brief story about a wealthy Philadelphian socialite appearing at a ball in Saratoga with a diamond necklace supposedly worth twenty-five thousand dollars, the writer claimed to have seen "a Choctaw lady the other day on the Levee with a necklace that might have cost *twenty-five cents*, not over, and we'll venture to assert that she felt just as proud of her red beads as the Philadelphia belle with her sparkling diamonds."[50]

Two *Daily Picayune* items in particular reflect how Indians could be woven into narratives about everything from urban business to female beauty. In "A Mercantile Contrast" the reporter wanted to dramatize how even in a "truly commercial place," there is great variety in grades of activity. Standing at a New Orleans street corner one day, he found himself "momentarily between two persons, of similar pursuits yet oh! How different, even in their similarity!" Both "were engaged in traffic," but one was a leading export merchant who operated "upon a grand scale" worth millions. He "was rushing on as hard as he could drive, and we imagined that he was on the way to an insurance office, to renew an expired policy." The other trader, in contrast, was "nothing but a shriveled Indian lad (one of the Choctaws from beyond the Lake), apparently about ten years of age." Sitting on the shelled pavement, he dealt in an inventory "of about a dozen and half peaches, green and shriveled like himself, and a bunch of aromatic herbs plucked from the banks of the Bayou." A "little pig fastened with a tether" completed the Indian boy's investment. "It may be considered a forced comparison that we have drawn," the reporter wrote, but "the same ruling passion, that of selling to the best advantage, and realizing the most upon his investment, seemed to actuate both merchants."[51] Local Indians were forcibly drawn into another account four years later, this time for a very different commentary:

> Low in the scale of humanity as have sunk the Indians who occasionally perambulate our streets, they have not yet lost the faculty of admiring beauty; that is a trait of character which cannot be easily annihilated.— Though in the region of civilization they have parted with most of the ennobling attributes of the untamed son of the forest—"pleased with a rattle and tickled with a straw,"—still there are forms of loveliness which extort from them a heavy tribute.
>
> We were much amused yesterday by the movements of three Choctaws, who passed down Camp street. There were two males and one female, bedaubed with paint like the *paieile* of an artist, and rigged out in all the tawdry ornaments in which they so much delight. About half a rod behind them were two young ladies. Here in New Orleans our sight has become accustomed to female beauty, but we have seldom gazed upon two more attractive specimens than those in such close proximity to our savage visiters. One of the Choctaws turned his head accidentally, and with an abrupt exclamation attracted the attention of his companions to the lovely girls who followed them. We watched their motions while they walked the distance of a square. Every few paces they nodded their heads together, talked in low tones, and then gazed again upon the faces which so singularly please them. Their admiration, though annoying, was respectful, and any belle on earth might have been proud of homage to her charms so honest and unaffected.[52]

While self-serving observers caricatured American Indians in print, on the ground Indian people continued adapting to the urban landscape. A New Orleans resident for more than two decades, Jean Boze mentioned casually in a May 1830 letter that "80 hearty Chasta Indians, in costume and armed with their rackets, came to the ballgame to play against the 80 Creoles of color—mulattoes and blacks—strongest at this game in this country." Stickball games were indeed becoming popular occasions for cross-cultural interaction and competition in New Orleans. For centuries Choctaw people had been playing *ishtaboli*, their name for lacrosse, in association with a rich ceremonial tradition. By the end of the eighteenth century, colonial Louisianians were watching and embracing this Native sport with much enthusiasm. Walking along the French Quarter's vegetable market one November Sunday in 1834, John H. B. Latrobe (attorney and son of architect Benjamin Latrobe) noticed "immediately in front of it on the Levee, or raised mount, interposed between the river at high water and the city, a crowd of men and boys were engaged at a game of Ball—which gave rise to every species of vociferation. Among others were three Indians, their legs bare and coarse shirt on their shoulders, which did not cover the seat of honor. A cloth apron of about eight inches deep scarcely answered to make them absolutely decent." The northern visitor considered this crowded public gathering "unique for Sunday afternoon."[53]

Just outside the city's Vieux Carré, there was an open area called "Congo Plains." On Sunday afternoons, as described by George Washington Cable, "the Indian villagers of the town's outskirts and the lower class of white Creoles made it the ground of their wild ball game of *raquette*." Because of rapid urban expansion around it, this "wide room for much field sport" was soon reduced to "Place Congo." Black and white New Orleanians formed their stickball teams, sometimes playing across the nineteenth century's thickening racial divide but mostly competing within separate leagues. A native of the Crescent City, who like his brother Adrien grew up deeply interested in Choctaw culture and history, Dominique Rouquette identified the city's Algiers neighborhood, directly across the Mississippi from the Vieux Carré, as a site where "the negroes and mulattoes of New Orleans, almost every Sunday, have a game of raquettes." "It is a game of which they are passionately fond."[54] Occasionally a traveling team of Choctaw raquette players would come to New Orleans from their Indian Territory or Mississippi homes to hold a match. On the Sunday afternoon of April 24, 1853, a team of Choctaw Indians, "direct from the Choctaw Nation," challenged to "their celebrated Game of Ball" any team of "Creoles" for a purse of one hundred dollars. Omnibuses carried spectators to and from the Union Race Course every fifteen minutes. For an admittance price of fifty cents, they were also treated to the Choctaws' "celebrated WAR DANCE in full costume, seldom if ever witnessed in this country."[55] On a Sunday afternoon fifteen years later, some two thousand spectators gathered at that same race course, by then renamed the Fair Grounds, to watch a "great match game of raquette between twenty-five Indians and twenty-five Creoles." The Indians, most probably Choctaws, wore "full costumes," while the Creoles wore "black pants and white shirts." All players were barefooted. In what one newspaper writer decided was "the most spirited contest ever witnessed in New Orleans," the Indians defeated the Creoles twelve points to two. A rematch was immediately arranged for the following afternoon, with heaving bets laid on this game. Whether or not the Creole team satisfied its grudge against their Indian opponents does not appear in the record.[56]

For New Orleanians who could not get enough raquette in the city, there was the periodic opportunity of crossing Lake Pontchartrain for a contest among the north-shore Indian communities. Dominique Rouquette recounted one delightful day on the banks of the Bonfouca, where "the Choctaws had assembled from the four parts of the country, and the farmers and planters of the surrounding country, with a large number of their slaves." After an "animated, spirited . . . [and] stubbornly contested" game, the victorious and defeated teams and their families "had a grand joyous feast together in the shade of a grove of oak trees, and the firewater having gone to all the heads, kindled all imaginations. The joyful savages formed groups and danced; native songs were sung, orators harangued the assembly! Everything passed in the most perfect order."[57] American Indian stickball was being played in other parts of Louisiana, especially in the area around Alexandria where groups of Choctaw and Biloxi Indians lived. Over a couple of summer weekends in 1848, for example, teams representing these two nations faced off in a series of games. At stake, as reported in the local newspaper, was a prize of "beef, which the neighbors are to give the victors." Readers were encouraged to witness, if they had never seen a match, "the dexterity with which the Indians use the racket, and their agility and fleetness." A traveler learned in 1860 that the Biloxi Indians near Marksville "go forth once a year, with others of their tribe from adjoining parishes, to join in a great ball play with the Choctaws from Rapides and elsewhere, the place of meeting being generally down in St. Landry."[58]

By the mid-nineteenth century, American Indian nations in the New Orleans area, although economically poorer and politically weaker than they had been a century earlier, had managed to improvise resourceful means of survival. Their continuing presence in the Crescent City was a pivotal part of this ongoing adaptation, as was true of other American cities for similar Indigenous communities around the country. Pursuit of exchange and performance activities on the cityscape, however, did expose them to a judgmental gaze by urban residents that in multiple ways perpetuated marginalization of Indian people and trivialization of their appearance. It must have been excruciating at times to face calmly and quietly those many people who so eagerly felt scornful pity and arrogant superiority. Adding to this regular Indian presence on its streets and in its marketplaces, New Orleans was struck quite dramatically during the 1830s by an escalation of the federal government's policy of removing larger Indian nations still in possession of their homelands. With the outbreak of the US war against the Seminole Indians, the Crescent City instantly became a launching point for soldiers and volunteers sent to fight in Florida. But even more notably, it saw at extremely close range the thousands of Indian refugees who were suffering a painful passage to the West.

CHAPTER FOUR

PAINFUL PASSAGE

A Seminole woman named Mary, being held at a US army barracks on the outskirts of New Orleans in the spring of 1838, unwittingly entered the annals of New Orleans medical history when Dr. Charles A. Luzenberg operated on her for cataracts. Mary's stay in the Crescent City was the consequence of a forced migration of her people from Florida that was well under way. She was among hundreds of Indian people already traumatically driven from their homelands and now waiting for further transportation up the Mississippi River. Luzenberg's brief encounter with Mary at the refugee camp, in the meantime, provoked a sensationalized and heated conflict among the city's physicians. Born in Austria and a graduate of the Jefferson Medical College of Philadelphia, Luzenberg was an ambitious surgeon who established the Franklin Infirmary in New Orleans and cofounded the Medical College of Louisiana. In mid-April he went to the barracks to remove supposedly congenital cataracts from the eyes of thirty-year-old Mary. To boost his reputation, Luzenberg allowed a reporter to publish an account of this surgery in the *New Orleans True American*. In what critics considered an "immoral and criminal" misrepresentation, the story told of a successful operation witnessed by several physicians and some Seminole chiefs. Luzenberg's patient was depicted as a blind "savage of the wilderness" whose "mental agitation" made the doctor's task exceptionally difficult and his willingness to perform it all the more wonderful. Mary, who allegedly could not speak English, reluctantly consented to undergo surgery only after her chief expressed complete confidence in Luzenberg's ability to do what the Seminoles' own medicine men could not. Suspicious of Luzenberg's version and outraged by his self-promotion, the Physico-Medical Society of New Orleans appointed a committee to investigate the case by visiting Mary at the barracks. Physicians on that committee "found that the statements in the [*True*] *American* were nearly all false; that the woman had never been afflicted with blindness from congenital cataract; that on the contrary she had seen from her birth up to the time of the operation, and that she had even seen so well as to sew garments for herself and her children; to observe birds in the air, &c.; that the operation had not only [not] proved successful, as had been asserted, but had utterly failed, the woman having been deprived altogether of vision in the left eye which she had previously enjoyed, and having had the sight of the right eye seriously impaired." The committee also reported that, as personally told to them by Mary, "she had lived two years with a family in Tallahassee, and that she had spoken English from her infancy," proving the surgeon's story "false, as to Mary's life having been passed in the wilds of Florida." Although Luzenberg aggressively mobilized allies from New Orleans's medical profession to testify on his behalf, he was found guilty of "immoral and unprofessional conduct" and expelled from the society. The surgeon's brashness over the years had made enemies among many fellow physicians, but this ruling had no adverse effect on his future standing and career. A year or so after his treatment of Mary, Luzenberg cofounded the Louisiana Society of Natural History and Sciences. But for Seminoles encamped outside New Orleans during the exodus from their homeland, his controversial operation on Mary's eyes revealed plenty about the vast distance between what they actually experienced and what whites thought about them.[1]

By the time of Mary's medical encounter with Dr. Luzenberg, the various forms of Indian presence in New Orleans featured in previous chapters were diminishing—at least in visibility and regularity. During the early decades of the nineteenth century, the Crescent City grew rapidly in population and expanded suddenly in size, with frequent outbreaks of yellow fever and other diseases. The arrival of Haitian, German, Irish, and other immigrants further diversified the urban populace, and they eventually outnumbered Creole and Anglo residents. The number of slaves and free people of color living in New Orleans also rose—although not as fast as other groups—while the migration of slaves through urban space accelerated with the proliferation of slave-trade markets across the city. The development of New Orleans into the nation's second largest port as well as point of entry for immigrants, of course, was based largely upon work demanded from tens of thousands of African American men and women producing the cotton and sugar on the region's plantations. It also derived, however, from the millions of acres of land being expropriated from the country's Indigenous people.

No longer a diplomatic hub for Indian emissaries after the Louisiana Purchase, New Orleans would still see formal parties of Indian people passing through. The removal of nations from their homelands in the East, as a matter of fact, brought the largest groups into the city—mostly as prisoners of war. Other major cities in the United States continued to host Indian delegations, although such visits increasingly became events of spectacle. As the seat of the US government beginning in 1799, Washington was of course continually visited by tribal delegations on official business. But other eastern cities also saw these same travelers once in a while. In 1802 a Philadelphia theater manager paid a group of Shawnee and Delaware leaders to perform dances in the Chestnut Street Theatre. A decade later, his successor offered a hundred dollars to a group of Northern Plains Indians in Washington at the time to appear on the same stage. The mayor of Baltimore persuaded some Osages and Pawnees on their way to Washington in 1804 to demonstrate their "grand national War Dance" at Mr. Leaman's Rural Gardens. An estimated two thousand spectators attended. Public squares and parks, theaters, museums, and even hotels in New York City also provided occasional stages for Indian performers to entertain large crowds.[2]

Although diplomatic visits by Indian delegates became a thing of the past, passage of notable Indian groups through New Orleans did occur periodically during the nineteenth century. In 1827, for example, a delegation of twenty-seven Osages traveled on the steamer *Commerce* from St. Louis to New Orleans, where they boarded the US ship *New England* for Le Havre to tour parts of France with David Delauney. These emissaries, like many groups preceding them, became quite a sensation on European soil. Greeted officially by King Charles X, invited to fashionable salons, and attending opera and theater in various cities, they performed "savage dances of the Missouri" at one widely publicized event that included their chief going up in a hot-air balloon. Dolls dressed in Native costumes, bags and bronze figures depicting the Osage visitors, and even bread shaped into Indian figures were sold by Parisian street vendors, shops, and bakeries. Composer Auguste Panseron was inspired to write what became a popular song, "Chant national des Osages."[3] Some thirty years later, a deputation of twelve Kansas Indians visited New Orleans on what the *Daily Picayune* called "a pleasure trip to see the sights of this great place." They ceremoniously met with Mayor Gerald Stith, expecting to receive lodging during their stay from this "chief of the great people of New Orleans," but he instead passed them on to a federal official to see if they might be quartered at the army barracks.[4]

≪≪≪

It was the United States' warfare against the Creeks and Seminoles that drove most Indian travel through the Crescent City during the second quarter of the nineteenth century. Separate wars to remove both of these southeastern peoples tragically overlapped and intertwined in ways that brought trauma to many African Americans as well as American Indians. Over many months at a time, thousands of Indian and black prisoners of war were confined to Fort Pike on a narrow spit of land at the entrance to Lake Pontchartrain or to US army barracks on the downriver outskirts of New Orleans. There they waited until steamboats were ready to pick them up in New Orleans and transport them upriver to strange new lands assigned by the United States. According to Major Isaac Clarke, assistant quartermaster for New Orleans, 1,150 prisoners were stranded at the army barracks on March 30, 1838. Half of them were sick, and a contractor responsible for attending to them could not be found.[5] For one group of people stuck at the time in their passage through the city, known as "Seminole Negroes," the wait lasted especially long because of much deeper and more insidious circumstances.

When the Seminoles in Florida rejected a dubious treaty signed at Fort Gibson in 1833, runaway slaves of African descent were instrumental in their opposition to removal. Fear of enslavement by being returned to former owners, turned over to fraudulent claimants, or captured by enemy fighters was certainly enough motivation for blacks to engage heavily in Seminole resistance. An estimated fourteen hundred African Americans were living within and around Seminole towns. US officials repeatedly voiced the opinion that even those who were owned by the Seminoles, as one Florida governor put it, "have a controlling influence on their masters, and are utterly opposed to any change of residence." What would become known as the Second Seminole War began with the assassination of agent Wiley Thompson in December 1835 and lasted until August 1842, costing the United States more than twenty million dollars and the lives of some fifteen hundred soldiers and uncounted militiamen and settlers.[6] Once open conflict broke out, removing African Americans to the West along with the Seminoles was a matter of military necessity. In negotiating with the Seminoles, General Thomas Jesup promised to let them leave Florida with their black slaves as well as their black comrades. By March 1837 he agreed that "the Seminoles and their allies who come in, and emigrate to the West, shall be secure in their lives and property; that their negroes, their bona fide property, shall accompany them to the West." White planters in Florida and adjacent states, however, interfered with such agreements by insisting that alleged runaways be returned to them. Doubtful about the legitimacy of many of these claims, Jesup also had reason to worry about the insurrectionary influence that slaves who lived and fought with the Seminoles might have if sent to different plantations across the Deep South. Consequently, he favored expulsion westward of Africans and Seminoles altogether.[7]

With matters growing even more complicated, New Orleans became an especially tragic theater in African and Native American struggles for freedom. In what is called the Second Creek War, open conflict erupted in Alabama during the spring of 1836. Intimidation and encroachment by white settlers along with fraudulent sales of land reserved by remaining Creeks provoked Indian retaliation. The Creek Nation and most of its people had already relocated to the West, but some decided to stay in Alabama and occupy personal allotments of land. Outbreak of war with those still living inside the state gave President Andrew Jackson a rationale for mobilizing troops to drive all Creek people away. As the war achieved this objective, several detachments of forced migrants were organized for travel overland and by water.[8] John James Audubon happened to be traveling from Georgia through Alabama during this exodus. At one location he saw a hundred Creek warriors "confined in irons, preparatory to leaving forever the land of their births!" Farther along his own route to the Gulf Coast,

Plate 1. François Gerard Jollain Jr., *Le Commerce que les Indiens du Mexique Font avec les François au Port de Missisipi*, ca. 1720. The Historic New Orleans Collection, 1952-3.

Plate 2. Alexandre de Batz, *Dessein de Sauvages de Plusiers Nations Nlle Orléans*, 1735. Gift of the Estate of Belle J. Bushnell, 1941. Courtesy the Peabody Museum of Archaeology and Ethnology, Harvard University, PM# 41-72-10/20.

Plate 3. Félix Achille Beaupoil de Saint Aulaire, *Vue d'une Rue du Faubourg Marigny, N[ouv]elle Orléans*, ca. 1821. The Historic New Orleans Collection, 1937.2.2.

Plate 4. Karl Bodmer (Swiss, 1809–1893), *Choctaws at New Orleans,*
watercolor and pencil. Collection of Joslyn Art Museum, Omaha,
Gift of the Enron Art Foundation, 1986.49.329.

Plate 5. Alfred Boisseau, *Louisiana Indians Walking along a Bayou*, 1847. The New Orleans Museum of Art: Gift of William E. Groves, 56.34.

Plate 6. François Bernard, *Choctaw Village near the Chefuncte*, late 1850s. Gift of the Estate of Belle J. Bushnell, 1941. Courtesy the Peabody Museum of Archaeology and Ethnology, Harvard University, PM# 41-72-10/27.

Chactaw indian squaws.

Plate 7. Léon J. Frémaux, *Chactaw indian squaws,* from *New Orleans Characters* (1876). The Historic New Orleans Collection, 1951.78.

Plate 8. Alphonse J. Gamotis, *Indian Village on the Shores of Lake Pontchartrain*, ca. 1900, oil on canvas. Courtesy Roger H. Ogden.

Audubon "overtook about two thousands of these once free owners of the forest, marching toward this place [Mobile] under an escort of rangers and militia mounted men, destined for distant lands, unknown to them." The sight "of warriors, of half-clad females and of naked babies, trudging through the mire under the residue of their ever scanty stock of camp furniture and household utensils" produced in Audubon's mind "an afflicting series of reflections more powerfully felt than easy of description." Hoping never again to witness such a scene—"the masked countenances of some and the tears of others, the howlings of their numerous dogs and the cool demeanor of the chiefs"—he nevertheless thought that had his son Victor been there, "ample indeed would have been his means to paint Indians in sorrow."[9]

One group of Creek exiles, mostly Upper Creek townspeople who aided the US military campaign against hostile Lower Creeks, negotiated a special deal with the army. Its warriors agreed to join American troops already at war with the Seminoles in exchange for a promise that their families could stay in Alabama until their service ended. Supposedly because of violent harassment still being suffered at the hands of neighboring whites, however, the government decided to proceed with removing these families in March 1837. They were first transported to Mobile Point, where many died from yellow fever, dysentery, and other illnesses while being harassed by local residents. Throughout these Creek Indians' ordeal, individuals like James C. Watson, a planter and banker based in Columbus, Georgia, profited from their removal. Watson was a leader among white Georgians and Alabamans guilty of fraudulently buying Creek land way below market value. Despite objections raised by other white speculators as well as by many Creek people, President Jackson approved this deal. Watson was also a member of the Alabama Emigration Company, which contracted with the federal government to manage the transportation and sustenance of removed Indians—including steamboat travel up the Mississippi. Unhealthy conditions at Mobile Point had been significantly worsened by inadequate supplies from Watson's company. In July 1837 the Creek families at Mobile were sent westward to a slightly healthier spot at Pass Christian, and by October the warriors completed their tour of duty in Florida and joined them there before heading to New Orleans for transportation up the Mississippi.[10]

During three months of encampment at Pass Christian, on the Mississippi Gulf Coast, Creek migrants wittingly and unwittingly became the object of much fascination for Crescent City residents. Ball games played by these refugees were watched by New Orleanians who took boat rides over Lakes Pontchartrain and Borgne for the spectacle. On October 16, 1837, Tustennuggee Emathla, a leader of the Creeks at Pass Christian also known as Jim Boy, visited New Orleans to attend performances at the St. Charles Theater and to drink with "some good natured fellows" whom the *Daily Picayune* editor reproached for "making this big child of the forest royally tipsy." That same day, it just so happened, one hundred sixty Delaware and Shawnee Indians arrived from west of the Mississippi and lodged at "the New Barracks below the city" before heading to Florida as auxiliary soldiers in the US war against the Seminoles. Nine days later, Creek refugees from Pass Christian began traveling into New Orleans on the Pontchartrain railroad in order to board steamboats waiting to transport them to Indian Territory. "To a sensitive mind," a *Picayune* writer noted, "the appearance of these poor Indians, cold and shivering, is painful." This sensitivity, however, was largely felt because "we do not see the North American Indian now, as he once was. The white man has invaded his wigwam and ruined his peace and pride." And with this nostalgic contrast, of course, came the predictable adherence to its inevitability as the reporter observed, "But a few years more, and the remote shores of the Pacific will receive the miserable remnants of countless tribes, that once in their native majesty ruled the fairest and richest continent under the sun."[11]

While white observers wistfully insisted that extinction of American Indians was inevitable, the steamboat voyage of this same group of Creeks from New Orleans marked a terribly traumatic moment in what was already a long ordeal of forced removal from their homeland. On a cold rainy evening in late October 1837, three crowded boats embarked from the city's docks, carrying more than a thousand Creek men, women, and children toward Arkansas. Shortly after passing Baton Rouge, the *Monmouth* was struck by a sailboat being towed downstream by another steamboat. With 611 Creeks on board, the boat split into two and sank rapidly. Crewmen and passengers on the accompanying steamers, the *John Newton* and the *Yazoo,* picked up many survivors, but more than half of the *Monmouth's* passengers drowned in the Mississippi River. Among those were four of the leader Jim Boy's children and three of his slaves. The *New Orleans True American* blamed "this vast sacrifice of human life" on the contractors, who in order to maximize profits chartered "rotten, old, and unseaworthy boats" and crowded Creek Indians on them without any regard for their safety and comfort. "The crammed condition of the decks and Cabins, was offensive to every sense and feeling." Although later chroniclers would emphasize its tragic scale—"the largest number of human beings sacrificed in a steamboat disaster" as *Lloyd's Steamboat Disasters* reported two decades later—and would even cast blame on irresponsible officers and crewmen, coverage of the *Monmouth* passengers' fate quickly faded from local and national news at the time.[12] But for Creek people exiled from their homeland, there would be no forgetting. A daughter of Tustennuggee Emathla, when an elderly woman, recalled hearing from a woman who survived the steamboat wreck about this and other painful episodes from a time known as "never no more to live in the east." The woman carried a small bundle of her belongings on the journey. Untying and retying her bundle over and over again, she began a mournful song and was joined by others on board the *Monmouth:* "I have no more land, I am driven away from home, driven up the red waters, let us all go, let us all die together and somewhere upon the banks we will be there."[13]

≪≪≪

Meanwhile, other Indian refugees were drawing the same kind of attention from Crescent City residents that Creek people had received. Passing through New Orleans the following March as prisoners of war, Micanopy, Jumper, and a few other Seminole "war chiefs" attended two different theaters and "attracted a large audience." During the "comicalities of Holland Barrett" at the St. Charles, they "broke forth in boisterous whoops and yells, as amusing to the pale faces as were the performances on the stage." At the Camp Theater they watched, perhaps with less mirth, the performance of a play called *Orenaska, the Mohawk Chief.* Micanopy had already attended theaters in Washington and New York City, and the phenomenon of theater audiences watching Indians watch staged performances goes far back in time. Indian delegations to European cities since the colonial period commonly attended theatrical events and drew intensive interest from spectators. An especially volatile example occurred in 1710 when three

Mohawks and one Mahican visiting London attended a performance of the opera *Macbeth* in the Queen's Theatre. An angry audience demanded a better view of the four Indians before permitting the opera to begin, so the manager placed their chairs on the stage.[14] Soon after attending those performances at the St. Charles and Camp Theaters in New Orleans, Jumper passed away from what was likely respiratory illness at Fort Pike, a bleak and damp fortress situated on a narrow spit of land at the mouth of Lake Borgne. The Seminoles had already lost another valuable leader a few months earlier, when Osceola died as a prisoner at Fort Moultrie on Sullivan Island, South Carolina. At Fort Pike the body of Jumper was ceremoniously buried with his rifle, pipe, and tobacco in the presence of Indian and non-Indian witnesses.[15]

Even in the face of sadness and loss, Seminole refugees stranded in New Orleans were themselves not reluctant to perform before city residents in pursuit of their own tastes and interests. Resilience and improvisation had carried them this far through hardship. In early May 1838, as sarcastically reported in the *Daily Picayune*, a procession of Seminoles appeared on the road from the army barracks to the city market in celebration of a wedding. Leading the parade "was a stout athletic sample of a red man, painted with a rainbow or something else containing all sorts of colors, and hung about with as many rings and bells as a Chinese Pagoda." With the married couple walking at the end of this column, the Seminole strollers stopped at shops and stores and "went through a performance which may be considered very good among that nation to which the performers belong, but in our opinion it would suffer aside an Italian opera." This comparative judgment notwithstanding, "they were treated with the utmost kindness and lots of money was presented." Whether this was "to compensate for the music or to get the amateurs to depart," the writer could not say with certainty.[16]

Seminole prisoners of war being held at the barracks were visited by Matilda Charlotte Houstoun, a wealthy Englishwoman who wrote novels and travel literature. Traveling to this large encampment of refugees several times, she noted in detail their appearance and demeanor—adding to evidence of American Indians' resourcefulness on the New Orleans landscape as well as of white elites' condescension toward their behavior. "Fine athletic looking men, muscular, and well proportioned" and women "not remarkable for their personal charms," with "pretty and interesting" children playing about, reminded Houstoun of "the Gypsies we are in the habit of seeing in Europe." Struck by "the extreme gravity and silence preserved by the whole party"—"even in their amusements"—the English lady "often found the young men playing at a game, which greatly resembled the old English sport called 'Hockey.' They displayed much skill and activity at this exercise: the old men in the meantime looking gravely on." One evening she watched the Seminoles perform "their national war dance." With lit torches in their hands, they moved their feet in a "stamping" motion and at intervals shouted "the most discordant whoops." "The whole ballet, though extremely curious," in Houstoun's opinion, "was anything but a graceful exhibition." When Houstoun would hand coins to some of the refugees, "they appeared to set but little value on" money and, she had "no doubt," would have preferred whiskey or rum.[17]

One group of wartime refugees was stranded in the New Orleans area for nearly an entire year, returning to those Creek warriors who had joined US troops in Florida. In addition to regular monthly pay for their military service, the Creek regiment of seven hundred fifty men were apparently promised by General Thomas Jesup extra compensation for capturing slaves in the war—slaves owned by Seminole enemies as well as slaves claimed by white owners. Retrieving runaway slaves for American citizens and ending collaboration between Indians and blacks were intertwined goals of this second major war against the Seminoles and of their removal from Florida. What a century earlier slave owners had feared for the New Orleans area was now a frightening reality for Florida. Jesup agreed to pay Creek captors twenty dollars for each slave claimed by a white owner and a lump sum of money for all slaves owned by Seminoles. Of course, deciding whether an African American might be a runaway slave or a Seminole-owned slave or a free black living and fighting alongside Seminoles was the crucial problem for the institution of slavery's security in this borderland region.

By July of 1837 about a hundred "Negro Prisoners captured by Thomas S. Jesup, owned (or claimed) by Indians" were being held at Fort Pike, becoming increasingly uncertain about their destination and fate. Honorably discharged and with their families at Pass Christian the following September, Creek warriors were offered $8,000 by Lieutenant Searle for eighty of the captured African Americans at Fort Pike. They refused to accept this payment, however, because they had sold their right to them for $14,600 to none other than James C. Watson, the Georgia planter and banker who was already benefiting from Creek removal as a land speculator and crony contractor. In what fast became a protracted conflict between civil and military authorities, General Edmund P. Gaines doubted the legitimacy of Watson's claim to the captives despite the fact that Secretary of War Joel Poinsett and Commissioner of Indian Affairs Carey A. Harris favored it. During a visit to Washington, Jim Boy and four other Creek leaders authorized Nathaniel P. Collins, Watson's brother-in-law, "to demand and receive all the negro slaves belonging to ourselves and warriors." So in mid-May 1838 the Orleans Parish sheriff went to the US Army barracks, where the "Seminole Negroes" were now being held, with a writ of sequestration issued by the city's civil court. The commanding officer there, however, turned him away.

While in Washington to finalize his sale of "Seminole Negro" prisoners to Watson, Jim Boy was interviewed for a project that had lasting effects on how American Indians would be represented and even studied for generations to come. As head of the Office of Indian Affairs, Thomas McKenney compiled portraits and biographical sketches of American Indian leaders who visited Washington with the purpose of preserving a record of people he assumed would inevitably vanish. He commissioned James Hall to write the biographies and Charles Bird King to paint most of the portraits. The three volumes were originally published, with support from private subscribers, between 1836 and 1844. A portrait and biography of Tustennuggee Emathla (Jim Boy) appeared in volume two (figure 2). Although his interview with Hall occurred in 1838, when he was about forty-five years old, his portrait may have been painted during an earlier visit to Washington. In the biographical sketch of Jim Boy, Hall wrote, "When the Creek nation became divided into two parties, one of whom were friendly to the American people and government, and disposed to yield to the settled and inevitable policy which demanded their entire separation from the white race, and the other hostile to our country and unwilling to emigrate, Tustennuggee Emathla attached himself to the former party." The Creek leader's service to the United States in its war against the Seminoles was then detailed by Hall. Tustennuggee Emathla used the

Fig. 2. *Tustennuggee Emathla (Jim Boy), a Creek Chief,* in Thomas Lorraine McKenney and James Hall, *History of the Indian Tribes of North America* (1842–1844). The Historic New Orleans Collection, Gift of Mrs. Rose M. Monroe, 86-534 RL.

opportunity of his conversation with the biographer to voice resentment over the government's failure to keep its promise that, in gratitude for the military assistance provided by him and his warriors, their families would be allowed to remain in their Alabama homeland until the end of their service. Instead, they were forced to leave sooner than promised. The drowning of Tustenuggee Emathla's four children in the tragic sinking of the steamboat *Monmouth* was included in Hall's narrative. "Melancholy as such an occurrence would be under any circumstances," he wrote, "the catastrophe is infinitely the more deplorable when happening to an ignorant people while emigrating unwillingly under the charge of our public agents, and to a people whose whole intercourse with the whites has tended to render them suspicious of the faith of civilized men." Notably absent from James Hall's account, however, was any mention of Tustennuggee Emathla's demand for possession of the eighty or more black captives taken by his Creek regiment in the Seminole War and being held at Fort Pike outside New Orleans.[18]

The ongoing dispute over the perilous status of eighty African Americans at New Orleans reflected a confluence of major issues confronting the United States. Watson's deal with Jim Boy and other Creeks exemplified what was candidly called "Indian business," referring to sordid financial and commercial advantages all too commonly undertaken by rapacious elites. And in the Deep South, speculating in Indian lands and profiting from removal contracts were entangled with slave stealing and trading. Fundamental questions regarding "plunder" and "prisoners of war" were also raised by the tension between civil and military officials. General Jesup's agreement to purchase captured slaves from Creek fighters, his consideration even of shipping such property of the United States to Liberia in order to remove them from the country, of course fueled the intensifying debate between antislavery and proslavery activists. Perhaps above all other concerns, the vague identity and harsh circumstances faced by the black prisoners themselves underscore their complicated role in the Seminole War—a blend of alliance and subordination in a joint Indian-African freedom struggle. Among these inmates at Fort Pike was Abraham, identified as "the principal negro chief" and considered "a good soldier, and an intrepid leader." Abraham had fled from slavery in Pensacola to freedom in the Seminole Nation during the War of 1812 and was now married to the widow of a former Seminole chief. As a slave owned by an Indian trade company, he had already acquired plenty of experience interacting and communicating with Seminole people. Also known as Sc-aahk-tuste-nugee and Chief of the Istelustes, Abraham served for years as a crucial interpreter between US and Seminole spokesmen, and so he and his family were released from the fort and moved freely through New Orleans during his remaining days in the Gulf South. After much delay in the limbo of military confinement, most of the other eighty captives embarked at last for Arkansas on May 19, 1838. The remaining survivors left the New Orleans barracks a month later—close to an entire year after arriving at Fort Pike. In the midst of all this controversy, the Seminoles finally prevailed in their insistence that these "Seminole Negroes," whether slaves or not, be returned to them. General Jesup had indeed promised them this during their negotiations in Florida. Watson's claim to the slaves, however, would linger for months and years to come. Nathaniel Collins even traveled with the "Seminole Negroes" all the way to Little Rock, Arkansas, hoping that officials would deliver them to him. That never happened, but as late as 1852 US congressmen would engage in heated debate over a claims bill to compensate Watson's heirs with $14,600 plus interest from the treasury.

With opposition to the government's support of slavery feverishly rising, this did not happen either.[19]

᯾᯾᯾

While Seminoles, Creeks, and African Americans were being forcibly relocated to the American West, New Orleanians were being treated to a rather sublime representation of that still remote region—a representation that concealed more than what it revealed about what was really happening west of the Mississippi. In the spring of 1835, George Catlin's national tour of American Indian portraits and landscapes reached the Crescent City, conveying an imagery of societies exotically and sentimentally frozen in time. The Northern Plains Indians depicted in these paintings, however, were altogether producing every year more than a hundred thousand buffalo robes for passage down the Missouri and Mississippi Rivers for shipment through the port of New Orleans. And within two years of Catlin's exhibit in the city, the smallpox virus carried by merchandise and crewmen aboard an American Fur Company steamboat would spread throughout the buffalo-robe trade system and devastate those same societies with illness and death. Meanwhile, George Catlin accompanied his paintings at No. 78 Chartres Street in the Vieux Carré with in-person explanations of them and also displayed a collection of clothing and other cultural objects made by Great Plains Indians—"much admired by the ladies present for the taste and beauty of their execution," as reported in the *New Orleans Courier.* The artist passionately promised his audience that "if his life is spared, he will be enabled to give the world, a work on a race of men who will cease to exist in a few years, and who if not totally destroyed, must sink into vice and thus lose every vestige of those ennobling virtues which their ancestors once possessed."[20]

As this belief became more and more popular, Indian people still living near cities like New Orleans were viewed mostly as only pathetic remnants of a once nobler race. Later performances of a romanticized and remote Indianness, especially in traveling Wild West shows, would further reinforce this skewed perception, while residents of New Orleans contributed in their own special way by adding the garb of stereotypical Indians to their array of Mardi Gras costumes. Describing the New Orleans Carnival that he witnessed in 1849, Scottish geologist Charles Lyell noticed some revelers wearing "feathers in their heads." A few decades later, the editors of the *Daily Picayune* cast an all-too-typical aspersion on American Indians' actual presence in the city when it reported seeing on Mardi Gras Day 1885 "a string of feathered Indians, far more agreeable to the eye than the occasional real brave who pushed his way stolidly through the crowd." By the end of the century, as observed in the same newspaper, "one of the favorite disguises . . . for promiscuous maskers was the Indian warrior's attire." "A few feathers stuck in the hair and a long switch or wig, of black hair," claimed the writer, "and any kind of an old costume constituted the disguise, which was intended to represent 'Poor Lo.'"[21]

Visiting the city a few years after Catlin's exhibit, Matilda Charlotte Houstoun "expected to find every sort of Indian fancy work in plenty at New Orleans." She was disappointed, however, by how little could be found in the stores and by the "unconscionable" prices being demanded— fifty-two dollars for "a small hunting pouch worked with beads!" In a rather strange contrast with the scarcity of Indian objects seen inside city shops, the Englishwoman "often met Indians, both men and women, wandering about the streets" who were most frequently seen early in the morning attending the markets. Offering no comment about the things being sold by these Indians, Houstoun did notice that they were "scantily clothed, with an old blanket wrapped about them" and "often seen in a state of intoxication, (with their long shining black hair falling over their faces) and shivering with cold." Walt Whitman remembered Indians at the market quite differently, although no less superficially, from when he briefly wrote for the New Orleans *Crescent*, as "fine specimens of Indians, both men and women, young and old."[22]

Viewing American Indian bodies, as well as American Indian things, as specimens to collect and study was emerging as a respectable science during these middle decades of the nineteenth century. Phrenological measurement of skulls, though, was mainly a pursuit driven by racialization of human beings and societies, powerfully serving white supremacists' justification for enslavement and conquest of supposedly inferior peoples. When a leading English phrenologist, George Combe, visited George Catlin's Indian Gallery at Boston's Faneuil Hall, not long after it appeared in New Orleans, he observed from scrutiny of the portraits that "the great mass of pure Indians present the deficient anterior lobe, the deficient coronal region, and the predominating base of the brain, by which savages in general are characterized."[23] Gathering American Indian skulls and skeletal remains from battlegrounds, or digging them up from burial sites, became a source of income for soldiers and citizens who sold their desecrated harvest to physicians like Samuel Morton of Philadelphia and Josiah Nott of Mobile. From fellow phrenologist-physicians in New Orleans, Morton received skulls that had been unburied from a Natchez mound near Vicksburg, Mississippi and from a Chitimacha cemetery along Bayou Teche in Louisiana, featuring them in his infamous 1839 publication *Crania Americana*. Among the nearly thousand crania collected by Morton from around the world was also the skull of Athlaha Ficksa, "a full-blooded chief of the Creek nation." Athlaha was one of those Creek warriors who fought alongside US troops in Alabama and Florida. When he died at Mobile in 1837, a navy doctor removed his head, cleaned off the flesh, and mailed it to Morton, who judged it a "remarkably fine head."[24]

In the city of Mobile itself, physician Josiah Nott also devoted research to the racialized science of phrenology—going so far as to promote a heretical theory of separate origins. Skeletal remains and skulls of deceased Indian people became part of Nott's international collection of human crania as he aggressively advanced white supremacy in defense of slavery. Even living Indians fell under the racist gaze of Doctor Nott. As in Louisiana and along the Mississippi Gulf Coast, Mobile was visited regularly by Choctaw peddlers—in this case mostly by women selling firewood to city residents. During the spring of 1853, Nott led Louis Agassiz around Mobile's streets and markets so the Harvard zoologist could observe for himself the "cranial uniformity" among "at least 100 living Choctaw Indians." "The most striking anatomical characters of the American crania are," Nott believed, "small size, averaging but seventy-nine cubic inches internal capacity; low, receding forehead; short antero-posterior diameter; great interparietal diameter; flattened occiput; prominent vertex; high cheekbones; ponderous and somewhat prominent jaws." And as he wrote in a book coauthored with George Glidden, *Types of Mankind:* "Throughout the winter season, in Mobile, at least one hundred Indians of the Choctaw tribe wander about the streets, endeavoring to dispose of their little packs of wood; and a glance at their heads will show that they correspond, in every particular with the anatomical description just given. They present

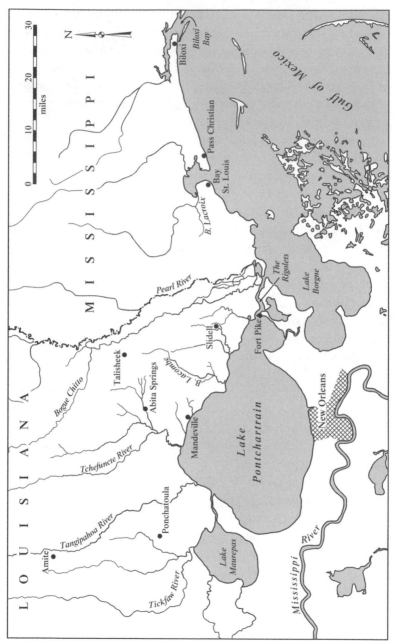

Area Inhabited by Choctaw Communities into the Early Twentieth Century. Map by Mary Lee Eggart.

heads precisely analogous to those ancient crania taken from the mounds over the whole territory of the United States; while they most strikingly contrast with the Anglo-Saxons, French, Spaniards and Negroes, among whom they are moving."[25]

While American Indians were being removed physically to distant places and metaphorically to distant times—even being reduced to scientific specimens—Native people still living around the Crescent City continued to improvise and innovate. By adapting their customs and adjusting their roles in a rapidly changing urban environment, they acted steadily to secure a distinct identity as well as a viable livelihood. Choctaw Indians had customarily hunted along and traveled down the Pearl River, passing then through the Rigolets into Lake Pontchartrain to trade at New Orleans. One British merchant in 1804 observed how the banks of the Pearl remained unoccupied by whites due "in part to the probability of intrusions by the Chactaw Indians, whose hunting parties make much use of its waters."[26] By then, some Choctaw people from the Six Town district of their nation were even forming new communities along the Mississippi Gulf Coast and the north shore of the lake, which they called *Okwá ta* or "large water." A half-century later, about two hundred Choctaws in St. Tammany Parish and another hundred or more living east of the Pearl River in Hancock County, Mississippi, were the principal groups of American Indians still maintaining a close relationship with the Crescent City.[27]

These communities near New Orleans were a small and separate segment of a much larger population of Choctaw Indians who had not left the Southeast during removal. The Treaty of Dancing Rabbit Creek in 1830, which removed the Choctaw Nation and most of its citizens to Indian Territory, had promised to those Choctaws deciding to remain in Mississippi that they would receive individual tracts of land, without losing their tribal membership. This promise of land was not fulfilled, but Choctaws staying behind could still choose to join their people out west and thereby benefit from tribal rights. Although some families did pursue this path over the years, the longer other families stayed in their homeland, the less likely would they be able to claim rights and land in the Choctaw Nation in Indian Territory. Remaining in Mississippi and Louisiana meant suffering discrimination and impoverishment as marginalized residents of

94   AMERICAN INDIANS IN EARLY NEW ORLEANS

those states, while going without educational and economic resources developed in the meantime by Choctaws in Indian Territory. Attachment to their home country had to be strong under these circumstances, and some communities would eventually acquire recognition from the federal government as distinct Choctaw tribes: the Mississippi Band of Choctaw Indians and the Jena Band of Choctaw Indians in Louisiana. Very few members of Choctaw communities along the Gulf Coast and on the north shore of Lake Pontchartrain would partake in this process, mainly because of their separate locations. Their relationship to New Orleans nevertheless remained important and continued to evolve.[28]

Accounts of this ongoing Choctaw presence in New Orleans, however, were filled with a persistent contradiction between form and content. The tragic theme of vanishing Indians almost always framed words and pictures that described—albeit in a limited fashion—actual evidence of Indian resilience and resourcefulness. While American Indians worked hard just to survive in their homeland over the nineteenth century, white observers casually played at representing them as relics from the past or remnants of a people. Contributing further to this impression, no doubt, were periodic passages by Seminole refugees through the Crescent City that continued until 1859.[29] For American Indians still living within the New Orleans area, however, a different kind of mobility provided a means for them to piece together different economic activities and to maintain a cultural relationship with a familiar environment now undergoing new pressures and constraints. But as historian Paige Raibmon has said about Pacific Northwest Indian communities for the same period, even such "tenacious and often ingenious" strategies did not crack "the thick crust of colonial assumptions." American Indians were certainly aware of, and most likely even annoyed by, the view that most white people were taking of them. By the late nineteenth century, however, they had little choice. As the next chapter will show, they had to engage the assumptions and expectations held by onlookers in ways that both utilized and reinforced the colonial gaze.[30]

CHAPTER FIVE

ACROSS THE LAKE

Ernest and Josephine Favre, a young married couple, were two of about fifty Choctaw Indians living in or around Mandeville, Louisiana. One mid-August afternoon in 1901, their cabin in the woods was visited by a stranger named Stewart Culin. An ethnologist employed by the Brooklyn Museum in New York, Culin had traveled to New Orleans to examine the archaeological collection of the late Dr. Joseph Jones. He spent time in the Crescent City, also visiting Tulane University's museum, French Quarter antiquity shops, and the old St. Louis Cemetery. From a gravedigger working at the cemetery one Sunday morning, Culin learned that the old game of raquette was still being played on Sunday afternoons at a field just east of town. It just so happened that the anthropologist was undertaking a comprehensive study of American Indian games, so he rushed to watch that day's match. In a contest that Culin would vividly describe in *Games of the North American Indians* (1907), two teams of "french-speaking negroes" played "with much vigor and no little violence" in a manner nearly identical to what Culin had seen among Choctaws. The players carried a racket made of hickory in each hand and tossed the ball back and forth between single-post goals six hundred feet apart. The winning team sang Creole songs, "reminding one of the same custom at the close of the Indian games."

Stewart Culin decided to take a trip across Lake Pontchartrain to Mandeville, on the steamer *Lawrence*, after he learned that "a small fragment" of Choctaw Indians living there "still come on Sundays to the market to sell baskets and the powdered sassafras leaves that form an essential ingredient in the well known 'gumbo.'" By 1901 Mandeville and other towns along the north shore had become a favorite leisure destination for New Orleanians who could afford recreation time away from work. Reaching the first Choctaw household with help from a guide, Culin "found men and women seated about their little cabin, the women plaiting baskets from strips of split cane." At first they appeared "listless and indifferent," but to this visitor's delight they "soon became interested and animated." Culin already had a reputation for being a relentless, if not ruthless, collector of Indian things, acquiring sacred and profane cultural objects by whatever means he thought necessary for the sake of science. This day at Mandeville was no exception, as he eagerly began inquiring and photographing. Before his visit was over, Culin managed to purchase ornamental, winnowing, and large carrying baskets, blowguns, and even a "rude fiddle" made of cane, and "one of a pair of old rackets, *ka-bu-cha,* precisely like those used in the game I had witnessed in New Orleans." The last item was acquired "with much difficulty," according to the anthropologist's candid report.

Ernest Favre was a generously informative host to Stewart Culin. Like other Choctaw families, he and Josephine combined traditional skills and subsistence farming with intermittent wage labor for their livelihood. While men hunted deer or cut timber to sell, women made baskets or gathered medicinal and culinary plants for income. Favre provided Culin with estimates of the sizes and locations of different Choctaw communities in the area, and indicated that he had recently come close to leaving Louisiana for the Choctaw Nation in Indian Territory. He also told the ethnographer about old dances still being performed. He and his brother occasionally performed for spectators at Mandeville homes and hotels. Josephine Favre was the daughter of a Choctaw named Prince Pisa, who had passed away just over a year earlier. She showed Culin a photograph of Prince Pisa wearing a dance costume, taken a quarter century earlier in a New Orleans studio. Josephine also brought out the blue calico shirt and red flannel baldrics, "ornamented with white bead work in characteristic scroll design," that her father had worn for the picture. Ernest "kindly put on the costume and allowed me to photograph him," and afterwards the ferocious collector "purchased one of the bands and borrowed the photograph for reproduction." Returning to New Orleans, Culin "hunted up the photographer, whose name, Daliets, appeared on the back of the old picture." He no longer possessed the negative, but "distinctly remembered Pere Roquette bring the Indian prince to his studio many years before."[1]

≪≪≪

Between Prince Pisa's trip to Daliets's studio and Stewart Culin's trip to the Favres' home, urban development was undoubtedly making an Indian presence in New Orleans harder to maintain, or at the very least harder to see. Population sprawl encroached on wetlands behind the city, while accelerating construction of canals and railroads facilitated recreational and commercial travel. For at least another half-century following the Civil War, however, Choctaw families like the Favres, living just north of Lake Pontchartrain, continued to integrate the New Orleans French Market into their livelihood, tapping into consumer tastes of city residents and visitors that were currently becoming more sentimental than material. American Indians could now be seen almost exclusively in the Vieux Carré's French Market, across Lake Pontchartrain. During the late 1850s French portraitist François Bernard painted *Choctaw Village near the Chefuncte,* capturing a leisurely mixture of preparations for household needs and market sales during families' relaxed time together (plate 6).[2] From this and other communities "across the lake," as New Orleanians once referred to the area, Choctaws regularly traveled to peddle culturally distinctive wares in open spaces between meat, fish, fruit, vegetable, and bazaar stalls. And occupation of this liminal space, in what was fast becoming the Crescent City's major tourist site after the Civil War, exposed mostly Choctaw women to a fresh set of pejorative or patronizing observations. For Indian people themselves, nonetheless, selling baskets and plants to curious onlookers still constituted a meaningful form of identity as well as a helpful source of income.

Among the "picturesque groups" often seen "under the shadows of the markets," as *Emerson's Magazine and Putnam's Monthly* informed its readers, one would see "a party of Indian girls, ready to sell their small wares and willing to be gazed upon." "In the hottest spot of the whole market," as reported in an August 1866 issue of *Harper's Weekly* with a large and detailed illustration, "the most picturesque subject is found, namely, the Indian dealers in herbs and baskets." Predictably, the sight of these Indians invoked assumptions about the fate of their race. "Years ago," the magazine writer declared, "a larger number of these aborigines ornamented the city, but as they grow tame, they disappear from the city as fast as from their ancestral grounds." Several months later, visiting the market early one Sunday morning, Italian tourist Giulio Adamoli described Choctaw families as "brownish, indolent creatures who sell vegetables, a kind of green powder which I could not identify, and baskets of their own weaving."[3]

The "green powder" that Adamoli did not recognize was, of course, ground sassafras leaves, called filé and used in south Louisiana kitchens to thicken gumbo and other dishes. After gathering *kombo ashish,* the leaves of *Laurus sassafras,* during autumn, Choctaws over Lake Pontchartrain would dry them outdoors under the sun, pound them in a wooden mortar into a fine powder, and pound this powder even finer after sifting it through a basket. More than any other culinary herb or medicinal plant purchased from Indian women, filé would have a lasting influence on regional culture. Also entering many non-Indian households in New Orleans during the nineteenth century were "Indian baskets of every conceivable shape, size, design and coloration," as observed by Léon Grandjean. By the last quarter of the century, while more and more people settled north of Lake Pontchartrain, Choctaws were visiting New Orleans less frequently partly because their goods could now be sold to closer consumers. As Grandjean pointed out, "many New Orleans homes contain examples of Choctaw basket weaving—round baskets, square ones, conical baskets and V-shaped ones—either purchased from the squaws in the French Market years ago, or more recently in their home parish, St. Tammany." Other examples reached homes and even museums farther away. An assistant curator of ornithology spent three months in 1896 collecting bird skins along the Gulf Coast for the Field Museum in Chicago. In addition to the nearly one thousand skins brought back to Chicago, G. K. Cherrie donated to the museum's anthropology department a couple of river-cane baskets—one heart-shaped and the other elbow-shaped—apparently purchased from Indian women during his stay in New Orleans.[4] Born in 1864, future New Orleans mayor Martin Behrman was the son of a single mother who sold dry goods from a stand in the French Market. Prominent in Behrman's memory of a childhood spent at the market were the Choctaw women selling their wares. "I remember standing there and watching the Indians

Fig. 3. Alfred R. Waud, *Sunday in New Orleans—The French Market,* from *Harper's Weekly,* August 18, 1866. The Historic New Orleans Collection, The L. Kemper and Leila Moore Williams Founders Collection, 1951.68.

by the hour," he wrote. The political machine that Martin Behrman would help create and that would back his ascent to City Hall was named the Choctaw Club.[5]

Throughout the second half of the nineteenth century, illustrations of Choctaw women selling filé powder and dried laurel leaves, scrub brushes made of palmetto roots, and baskets woven from river cane and palmetto appeared in many magazine articles about New Orleans—mostly aimed at prospective visitors and tourists. Prominent artists working for publications like *Harper's Weekly, Putnam's Monthly,* and *Frank Leslie's Illustrated Newspaper* drew some of the most detailed pictures of Indians in the French Market. To accompany his *Sunday in New Orleans—The French Market* (figure 3), Alfred R. Waud wrote how, "grouped around in stolid indifference to the heat, with heavy folded wraps resting on their heads," they "patiently await customers for their okra, and other herbs and roots." While attending the 1877 annual meeting of the American Society of Civil Engineers in New Orleans, illustrator Frank Hamilton Taylor drew *Indian*

Fig. 4. Frank Hamilton Taylor, *Indian Gumbo Sellers, French Market,*
New Orleans, ca. 1870. The Historic New Orleans Collection,
Gift of Mr. and Mrs. Albert Louis Lieutaud, 1950.56.

Gumbo Sellers with pencil and wash (figure 4). This image appeared in
Taylor's illustrated record of the engineers' excursion through the South.
When Léon J. Frémaux, a former colonel of engineers in the Confederate
Army, illustrated people commonly seen on the city's streets and levees
for his book *New Orleans Characters,* he made sure to include a sketch
of Choctaw women (plate 7). Among the few photographs of American
Indians in the New Orleans marketplace that have survived are Edward L.
Wilson's *Indian Filé Vendor at French Market* and Paul Hammersmith's
French Market N.O. Feb. [18]91 (figures 5 and 6).[6]

Much of the language used to describe the Choctaw families peddling
their goods in New Orleans was derogatory, condescending, or romantic—
representing a genre of literary and pictorial discourse over the presence
of Indian people peddling or laboring in cities, tourist resorts, and along
transportation routes across nineteenth-century America. Observers
deployed a language asserting ownership of Indianness on top of taking
possession of Indian land. As larger Indian nations were being exiled from
their homelands, smaller groups that remained were being erased from the

Fig. 5. *Indian Filé Vendor at French Market,* by Edward L. Wilson.
The Historic New Orleans Collection, 1982.127.88.

historical record. As Friedrich Ratzel wrote about New Orleans Choctaws, "These Indians are pitiful remnants of Atala's tribe" whose "sad, shy manner contrasts sharply with the lively cheerfulness of the Negroes, mulattoes, and Creoles." With heads and shoulders covered by cloth that hardly exposed their faces and with their hair tied in a knot on top and hanging straight down their backs, Choctaw women in the marketplace seemed to this German geographer to be uncomfortable "even in this very diverse crowd"—"a sight that arouses sympathy." Another German traveler felt

Fig. 6. *French Market N.O. Feb. [18]91,* by Paul Hammersmith. The Historic
New Orleans Collection, Gift of Mary Louise Hammersmith, 1977.79.13.

that "they very much deserve attention from the foreigner because of the
originality of their tribal life. Wrapped in blankets, selling laurel or sassafras
leaves, they show in their faces all the marks of their race's character—as
well as all the apathy." In the eyes of Lafcadio Hearn, "the sadness that
seems peculiar to dying races could not be more evident than in them." A
guidebook produced for the 1885 world's fair reinforced this image of Indians in the French Market. "The lazy, unstudied attitude of these Red Roses,
these daughters of the forest, is not exactly in accordance with the poetic
idea one used to drink in." Choctaw women were described as "formless,"
with the covering over their heads having "no pretensions to fitting." The
guidebook authors also called them "professional 'deadheads'" because
they paid no rent for the space. "They lie on the stones at full length, or sit

on their feet, unheeding and unheeded by the crowd who are continually passing backward and forward."[7]

The ghostly image of American Indians retreating and receding from the foreground of life would persist in most references to Native people still seen in New Orleans toward the end of the nineteenth century. Mary Ashley Townsend, wife of a prominent New Orleans banker and merchant and one of the city's leading literary and philanthropic figures in the post–Civil War years, included this stanza in her 1882 poem "Down the Bayou":

> Now from some point of weedy shore
> An Indian woman darts before
> The light bow of our idle boat,
> In which, like figures in a dream,
> My Love, my Summer Love and I,
> Adown the sluggish bayou float;
> While she, in whose still face we see
> Traits of a chieftain ancestry,
> Paddles her pirogue down the stream
> Swiftly, and with the flexile grace
> Of some dusk Dian in the chase.[8]

It seems that extinction was the only way Indian people could truly satisfy the white observer's view of them. Adapting as resourcefully as possible in order to remain in their homeland, against endless odds, was far less acceptable. "It was," as C. Richard King has so aptly put it, "a paradoxical love of imagined Indians and a loathing of actual, embodied Indians that continues to this day." One of the most genocidal expressions of this paradox came from the pen of Frank Baum, best known as author of *The Wizard of Oz*, who only days before the Massacre at Wounded Knee in 1890 claimed in the *Aberdeen Pioneer* that "the proud spirit of the original owners of these vast prairies inherited through centuries of fierce and bloody wars for their possession, lingered last in the bosom of Sitting Bull." But now with the recent death of Sitting Bull at the hands of reservation police, "the nobility of the Redskin is extinguished, and what few are left are a pack of whining curs who lick the hand that smites them." "The Whites, by law of conquest, by justice of civilization," declared Baum, "are masters of the American continent," and "total annihilation of the few remaining Indians" now seemed necessary for their own good. "Their glory has fled, their spirit broken, their manhood effaced; better that they die than live the miserable wretches that they are," Baum concluded without regret.[9]

In *A History of Louisiana*, published in 1893 for use in schools, coauthors Grace King and John R. Ficklin offered a somewhat softer image of the vanishing Indian. "The Indians, from their manner of life and their traditions," they wrote, "were neither willing nor able to accept the laws of civilization. They possessed, however, many fine qualities, and the story of their gradual disappearance in Louisiana has a pathetic interest. The Indian women who to-day sell sassafras and herbs in the French market are descended from the once dreaded tribe of Choctaws; while those on the Teche, who make the wonderful baskets, are all that are left of the Attakapas." Seven years later Ficklin published "Indians of Louisiana" as a chapter in Henry Rightor's *Standard History of New Orleans, Louisiana*. Describing the Choctaws who peddled gumbo filé in New Orleans, the Tulane University professor of history emphasized how "they always sit in a group apart from the bustling Creoles and Americans around them, as if there were no amalgamation possible with this white race that for more than two hundred years has been forcing the red man to retire before the onward march of civilization." Ficklin declared that "the Indian is doubtless destined to gradual extinction," standing in Louisiana as "a shadowy figure from the past, and his gradual disappearance in pathetic isolation cannot but touch a sympathetic chord in the hearts of those who know his history."[10]

⋘

The World's Industrial and Cotton Centennial Exposition was a special occasion for including the Choctaw presence in publicity about New Orleans. "Of the many thousands of aborigines who once held, under the superior patent of Nature, the vast territory that composed old Louisiana," fairgoers read in the *Historical Sketch Book and Guide to New Orleans and Environs*, "the fifteen or twenty Choctaw women whom one sees at the French Market, sitting patiently, silent and motionless, waiting (with some contempt, if the truth were known) for the pale-face purchaser of their

pounded laurel and sassafras leaves, from which is derived that triumph
of Louisiana cookery, the *gombo filé;* their baskets, strongly woven from
the stalk and leaves of the latanier; their medicinal herbs—the drugs and
simples of natural man—are, with the males of their families, almost the
sole survivors of the race which inherited the land from their fathers. And
it seems strange that these representatives of the aborigines should belong
to that nation, the Choctaw, which was always hostile to the French." Although authors of this guidebook mistakenly summarized the Choctaws'
relationship with colonial Louisiana—except for a few years of civil war,
they had been its most important allies—they did faithfully report how
American Indians related to the Crescent City over the nineteenth century:

> Within a period as late as the memory of the old citizens of New
> Orleans, the remnant of the aboriginal population of Louisiana still fre-
> quented New Orleans in the wintertime in great numbers. They had been
> accustomed to gather in this city annually under the Spanish domination
> in order to receive a certain allowance of woolen goods, guns, powder
> and shot, vermillion, and other small presents, which were given them
> as evidence of friendship and goodwill. Each band had its village beyond
> the city limits, composed of huts covered with the skins of bears and of
> deer, or with the leaves of the latanier. During the daytime they spread
> about the city and among the neighboring plantations, and in the evening
> they returned, men, women, and children, to their camps. The women,
> then as now, brought their small wares to market; the men were hunters
> of deer, ducks, squirrels, and other game. In those days the men wore on
> their heads a sort of helmet furnished with large feathers, and they still
> retained enough of their old fashions to paint their faces, on a vermillion
> ground, with blue transverse and spiral lines which, united to their cos-
> tume, was in keeping with the Mardi-Gras season, the period in which
> they were found in greatest numbers in the city.[11]

Although readers of that guidebook were informed in passing that
"there are two or three very interesting Indian settlements in the neighborhood of New Orleans, one at Indian village near Bayou lacombe just
north of New Orleans, another at Bayou lacroix, and still another on the
Têche," local Native Americans were not a feature at the Crescent City's

world's fair.[12] Any Indian participation in the New Orleans world's fair was far below that in later international expositions like those in Chicago and St. Louis, with only a few Indian boarding-school students serving as assistants to exhibit organizers. The largest gathering of Indian people actually took place outside the fairgrounds, where Buffalo Bill Cody held Wild West shows that employed mostly Plains Indian performers. These performances of Indian battles and stagecoach attacks would of course reinforce popular perception of what authentic Indians were supposed to be like.[13]

Ethnological displays of Indian people and culture would become significant attractions at later international expositions in the United States. At the New Orleans fair, however, there was only one such exhibit. Alice Fletcher was a pioneer anthropologist who not only studied Indian societies but worked aggressively to implement the government's assimilation policy. For the World's Industrial and Centennial Cotton Exhibition, Fletcher was asked by the Office of Indian Affairs' education director to prepare an exhibit on "Indian Civilization." Because of budgetary constraints, "special agent" Fletcher decided to use photographs for an exhibit featuring the Omaha Indians. Along with sixteen large photos—showing Omaha people dressed in traditional clothing and performing customary activities—a map of their reservation and two drawings were placed in a balcony alcove of the federal government's fairground building. Fletcher went to this exhibit every day, explaining it to visitors and handing out pamphlets. She made sure also to praise the government's Indian boarding school in Carlisle, Pennsylvania, which had a nearby exhibit of its own. Julia Ward Howe, organizer of the Women's Exhibit, received the bulk of newspaper coverage devoted to women at the fair, but Alice Fletcher drew significant attention as well. She spoke to local church groups and larger audiences, like the International Educators Association, and gave an official "Noon Talk" at the Exposition. Fletcher's daily conversations with fairgoers and that talk, entitled "The Dark and Bright Side of Indian Social and Religious Life," undoubtedly contributed to a spread of interest in American Indians among New Orleans women.[14]

The only notable recognition of local Native American people at the World's Industrial and Cotton Centennial Exposition came in the form of their cultural objects. Basketry and other handiwork made by Choctaws and Chitimachas were prominently displayed in the Louisiana Exhibit. This collection of what the *New Orleans Times-Democrat* called "Indian curiosities" was loaned by one of that newspaper's own writers, Charles E. Whitney, "who has made a special study of the Indian tribes represented." Catering to fairgoers' desire for exotic and nostalgic things, a report on this display opened by surprising readers with "the fact that in a State so old and so thickly settled there should still exist tribes of Indians who retain their aboriginal habits and tribal relations." The persistence of these people was attributed "to the great forests and swamps in the State which could be inhabited by none save Indians, acclimated by centuries of residence therein." The news story also emphasized that the specimens of Indian handiwork on exhibit "were procured with infinite difficulty for one of their characteristics is an intense aversion to the whites," further remarking that "only by the most strenuous and diplomatic efforts" can a white man "gain an interview with an Indian." The irony here is that for Indigenous people like the Choctaws and Chitimachas of Louisiana, international expositions and other celebratory fairs were fast becoming an opportunity to advance new interest in marketable things like basketry, pottery, woodwork, textiles, and beadwork. A number of small Indian baskets, for example, were sent to St. Tammany Parish commissioner George W. Moorman by Louis Abadie of Covington "to be disposed of as souvenirs on Louisiana Day" at the New Orleans world's fair.[15]

<<<

When New Orleans writer John Dimitry was researching for the exposition guidebook, he relied heavily upon a Roman Catholic priest, Father Adrien Rouquette, for information about the Choctaws. Adrien Rouquette, like his brother Dominique Rouquette, had grown up along Bayou St. John and become a close friend of Choctaw Indians traveling back and forth between their north-shore communities and New Orleans markets. After becoming a priest in the Order of St. Dominic, Rouquette established several chapels among the St. Tammany Parish Choctaws and eventually devoted his life to this ministry across Lake Pontchartrain. He also wrote romantic poetry and prose heavily influenced by the work of François-René de Chateaubriand. During the US Civil War, jayhawkers and deserters destroyed Choctaw homes and fields along the headsprings

of Bayou Lacombe, scattering them into more dispersed groups and mak-
ing them dependent for a while on Father Rouquette's material assistance.
Whenever he was spending time back in New Orleans, between stays at
his mission home at Bayou Lacombe, Indians traveling to the city would
visit him in his small bedroom at the Archbishop's Palace near the French
Market. The priest became an advocate as well as a spiritual guide for the
Choctaws, providing information about them to such curious visitors as
Walt Whitman and nurturing interest in their crafts and customs. For the
Declaration of Independence Centennial Exposition in 1876, Rouquette
had sent a collection of garments, baskets, ceramics, and other objects for
the Smithsonian Institution's American Indian exhibit in Philadelphia.[16]

Father Adrien Rouquette's interviews and writings comprise the most
comprehensive documentation about Choctaws living near New Orleans.
In 1882 he counted eighty-six people in the Bayou Lacombe area who were
residing in "substantially built" log cabins and practicing Roman Catholicism to an increasing degree. The men worked for wages as woodchoppers
when not hunting, fishing, or farming. Seasonally, families would camp in
palmetto huts along the Bogue Chitto and Pearl Rivers to gather enough
sassafras for processing filé powder and enough river cane for weaving
baskets. Choctaws who traveled to the New Orleans French Market as
frequently as twice weekly enjoyed free passage across Lake Pontchartrain
and also paid no fare when taking the train into town from the landing
at Milneburg. For one ceremony held every year, Choctaws from other
communities—at Amite, Bayou Lacroix, Bay St. Louis, even as far away
as Biloxi—joined those at Bayou Lacombe to dance and dine in traditional clothing. Hereditary chiefs still governed the community. James
Mehataby was serving in that role in the mid-1880s. Identified by guides
and newspapers as *the* authority on local Indians, Rouquette became over-
whelmed by "many visits from travellers who come to New Orleans to
see the Exposition." Writing to John Dimitry from his room in the archbishop's residence on March 29, 1885, the priest lamented being "the Old
Sachem" tourists wanted to see in "the old building." "I wish I were in the
woods!" he moaned. "I long to be alone!"[17] When Rouquette passed away
at Hotel Dieu early in the morning of July 16, 1887, and his remains were
waked at St. Mary's Church later that day, there was too little time to inform Indians across the lake, so only those already present in the city were

able to attend the funeral. "These were a picturesque group of bare-footed Choctaw women," as the *Daily Picayune* reported, "one among them so old that she could barely walk. Her tribute was eloquent in its simplicity—a cross of the wild herbs of the forest, which she carried before her when she followed the hearse to the cemetery."[18]

In the years following Adrien Rouquette's death, the Choctaws at Bayou Lacombe and elsewhere in St. Tammany Parish continued to draw selective attention from people on both sides of Lake Pontchartrain. One Saturday in August 1895, for example, a large party of guests at Mandeville's Crescent Hotel and of residents along the beach took carriages and buggies "into the woods to witness the annual Indian war dance which occurs at the red man's settlement." By then most white onlookers conveniently assumed that any dance performed by American Indians was "a war dance." Two years later, the Florida Parishes Fair in Amite, Louisiana, engaged "a band of Indians" to "give war dances on the grounds." Other performers appearing at this fair included a tightwire and trapeze performer, a contortionist, and the "Punch and Judy" man.[19] Reporting in 1911 an excursion taken by some New Orleanians to unearth pottery and other artifacts near the site of Father Rouquette's main chapel, a *Times-Democrat* writer recalled how "some time back" motion picture representatives visited the area seeking to film Indian life. "Disappointed in not being able to find enough genuine Indians," as the reporter claimed, this film company did manage, though, to secure "an excellent reproduction of the famous mirror dance which played such a conspicuous part in the early Choctaw history."[20] Of course, there was plenty about St. Tammany Parish Indian life that went unnoticed or undervalued. Although mostly living apart from their non-Indian neighbors, Choctaw people did interact with other families. Jazz clarinetist George Lewis's father, Henry Louis Zeno, grew up around Mandeville as the son of a former slave and a Choctaw mother. George's own mother, Alice Williams, was a New Orleans housekeeper and laundress who had for a time worked for writer Grace King. Living with his mother after his parents separated, the young George Lewis spent summers across Lake Pontchartrain with his father, who worked at different times as a fisherman and trapper, a carpenter and handyman, and a cook on a lake steamer.[21]

American Indians who had come under Father Rouquette's ministry

around Bayou Lacombe were not the only Choctaws still living within a
day's journey from the Crescent City. The February 17, 1896, issue of the
Daily Picayune featured a lengthy article entitled "At the Markets You Saw
Indian Women and Asked Questions about their Lives and Stories," which
included some detailed information about other communities. Several
distinct groups of Native families lived between Slidell, Louisiana, and Bay
St. Louis, Mississippi, closely resembling in their livelihood and culture
the Choctaws around Bayou Lacombe. They were predominantly Roman
Catholic in faith, with most men working for lumber companies and some
women working inside white households for wages. Production of handcrafts, medicines, and seasonings persisted as an important source of income. An extended family at Indianville, six miles from Slidell, was headed
by Amelie, supposedly "the only one of her race" among Indians living
along the coast of Lake Pontchartrain and the Mississippi Sound who
"has not been christened and is not a professed Christian." A skilled basket weaver, this elderly woman now traveled to the New Orleans French
Market only about three times a year and always accompanied by grandchildren. Along with her baskets, Amelie sometimes sold game that two of
her grown grandsons hunted. One member of this community, Avery, was
"a paralytic who is an inmate of the charity hospital." A little farther east,
in the Pearl River estuary, was Bayou Lacroix, where "descendants of three
Choctaw families" lived. Rose, the youngest daughter of Auguste Makahal,
had died three years earlier at the age of thirty-five. Married in the Catholic
Church at Bay St. Louis to "a Mexican named Albane," Rose worked for
many years as housekeeper for a white family from New Orleans "whose
summer home was at the Bay." In a nearby community called "The Camp"
lived the "present head of the bayou Lacroix clan"—ninety-year-old Tekely
Yavi, who had nine married daughters, one son, and many grandchildren
and great-grandchildren. Closer to Bay St. Louis was the extended family
of seventy-five-year-old Marie Batiste, "the descendant of several generations of Indian doctors" and now "the only person living who knows the
names and medicinal virtues of all the plants, shrubs, grasses and trees
of the forests along the Mississippi sound." But as the reporter added,
Batiste's "unmarried granddaughter, who is about 15 years old, manifests
the traditional family interest in these secrets of nature, and probably will
learn from her grandmother the valuable hidden secrets which the latter

has steadfastly refused to divulge to the doctors." Women weavers at both this community and Bayou Lacroix did not travel to New Orleans, "but sell the baskets which they make for a livelihood to the Bay St. Louis store-keepers."[22]

⋘

The author of the above *Daily Picayune* article had "called upon a lady of this city who, by long knowledge of these people and by personal acquaintance with the best representatives of the race in Louisiana and Mississippi, was enabled to furnish much interesting and novel information concerning them." This lady is not identified, but by the end of the nineteenth century a number of upper- and middle-class women in New Orleans had mobilized and organized on behalf of American Indians, sharing with contemporary women in other American towns and cities an influential blend of philanthropic with aesthetic sentiments and literary with scientific pursuits. Better-known organizations in this period of New Orleans history include the Christian Woman's Exchange, the Quarante Club, the New Orleans chapter of the American Folklore Society, the Louisiana Historical Society, the Southern Art League, and the Newcomb Pottery Enterprise. But some of the women involved in these organizations also developed a special interest in American Indian issues, most notably Margaret Avery Johnston and Sarah Avery Leeds, their nieces Mary McIlhenny Bradford and Sara McIlhenny, Josephine (Mrs. E. John) Ellis, Eliza Nicholson, Martha Field, Ruth McEnery Stuart, Grace King, and Cora Bremer. Women in the Werlein, Richardson, Walmsley, and Dwyer families were also steady participants. Johnston and Leeds were early patrons of Chitimacha basket weavers as well as of Acadian textile weavers. In its downtown store near Lafayette Square, the Christian Woman's Exchange sold plenty of Choctaw and Chitimacha baskets. By catering to decorative tastes and social interests associated with the emerging Arts and Crafts movement, New Orleans ladies also helped Indian women in rural Louisiana earn much-needed income and attention.

As owner-editor of the New Orleans *Daily Picayune* and as a writer using the pen name of "Pearl Rivers," Eliza Nicholson—along with *Picayune* journalist Martha Field—robustly promoted a desire for local Indian basketry and regularly informed New Orleans readers about nearby Indian communities. Martha Field, whose pen name was Catherine Cole, was the daughter of a newspaperman who moved from Missouri to New Orleans in the 1860s. Pursuing her own career in journalism in California, she married a San Francisco stockbroker. Martha returned to New Orleans as a young widowed mother in the mid- to late 1870s and began writing full-time for the *Picayune* in 1881 as the first woman to hold a staff position at that paper. Her weekly column was called "Catherine Cole's Letter," and she also wrote an unsigned weekly column, "Women's World and Work," featuring news about women. In a "Catherine Cole's Letter" published on December 16, 1888, Field wrote a glimpse into how uptown New Orleans women at the time were beginning to venture more freely across town and thereby taking greater interest in the Vieux Carré. Two residents of the Garden District stayed for a week in "French Town," bringing easels, brushes, and pencils. Every morning, after a stop at "the Morning Star, the brightest, best and Frenchiest of all the bright and French coffee stalls in the French Market," these ladies would look over "the baskets, big and little, of the Choctaw women squatting on the stones in the market court" and then proceed to other Vieux Carré sights.[23]

Martha Field moved to the *Times-Democrat* in 1894, but illness caused her to seek water cures in Bavaria. She nevertheless continued to send travel pieces to this newspaper from Europe. At the age of forty-three she died from Parkinson's disease in a Chicago sanitarium. Before passing away in 1898, Field wrote a promotional pamphlet for the New Orleans Coffee Company, *The Story of the Old French Market, New Orleans*, in which she described Indian women regularly seen in the Crescent City in this way:

> At the end of the meat market a tiny flagged plaza spreads its twenty feet of width between the butcher stalls and the bazaar of the dry goods market.
>
> This little gray bit of foreground is one of the most picturesque places along the market side.
>
> It is here the Indian comes, that stolid, surly, usurped Queen of the St. Tammany Choctaws, accompanied by her women. And it is here they defer—but only for money's sake—to the appetites and esthetic tastes of the white woman and the white man, and sell them their garnerings of forest lore.

They sit on their fat haunches, their wiry black locks hanging over their flabby jowls. All about them are the wares they have for sale. Pounded leaves of sassafras and laurel, forming that dark green powder, "Gumbo File." Bricks of palmetto roots that the conservative minority of housewives still prefer for scrubbing brushes. Fragrant fagots of sassafras, so good for a tisane in springtime, with bunches of dried bay leaves for flavoring soups and sauces and so delicious to place among one's linen and let it grow lavender-sweet as the days go by.

Last and best of all, about them lie in green and bronze and amber piles, the sweet swamp canes and ribbon grasses woven into wonderful shapes and delicately dyed with the vegetable dyes, whose formula none but these Indians know.

These baskets are curious shapes. Here is one made in the sharp, three-cornered design, cut like a triangle. There is another like an elbow of a stovepipe; a third fashioned into a wall pocket for some lady's dressing case. Towering over all these are the huge Ali Baba baskets, square at the bottom, round at the top, and fitted with square covers that pull down like a Dutch smoker's cap. Each basket is amply large to hold a portly member of the Forty Thieves.

These Indians are staunch Catholics, made so by a good priest of blessed memory, one Pere Roquets, who died a while ago. To this day they hang his grave with bay leaves, wild lavender and sassafras.

They sit here stolid and dull, in true savage taciturnity, their babies on their breasts and backs, a queer row of amber idols interpreted into the heart of modern civilization.

When the market house bell rings at eleven-thirty to give notice that all must get ready for the closing, they rise, load up with their wares like typical beasts of burden, and—huge mountains of baskets, sacks of file, powdered sassafras leaves and bunches of bay—trudge off to their camp on the brown Tchefuncta river.[24]

Aesthetic interest in American Indian crafts, especially basketry, even drew some of these New Orleans women into a close involvement with local Indian communities' struggles for political recognition and cultural survival. They also facilitated ethnographic fieldwork and museum collection by anthropologists beginning to take an interest in Louisiana Indians.

Some joined like-minded women nationwide in a campaign for reform-
ing US Indian policy. In 1886 Josephine Ellis, wife of US congressman
Ezekiel John Ellis, brought New Orleans socialites together inside the
Christian Woman's Exchange to organize a New Orleans chapter of the
Women's National Indian Association (WNIA). This organization would
meet monthly, raising money and dry goods for select Indian reservations
and contributing their voices to the national movement to alter certain
aspects of federal Indian policy. For the Columbian Exposition of 1893,
members of the chapter initiated an effort to organize an exhibit in Chicago that would display Choctaws in their "peculiar industries" of basket
making and pounding gumbo filé. The actual presence of Louisiana Indian
women at the exposition never materialized, but Choctaw and Chitimacha basketry was displayed and sold at various places on the fairgrounds.
Inquiries related to baskets seen in Chicago also sparked some advocacy
for public education for Indian children in Louisiana and Mississippi.[25]
One of the New Orleans auxiliary's longest-lasting projects began in 1898,
when Ellis brought a Choctaw girl to the Poydras Female Orphan Asylum.
Ellis had just reorganized in Amite City, Louisiana, a WNIA branch whose
members were providing assistance and instruction to a nearby camp of
"destitute Choctaws." She then placed "the grandchild of a chief" under
the care of the New Orleans orphanage, later indicating that she had been
threatened with abuse from relatives. Ellis personally supported the education of this girl named Josephine Lilestan, "my Indian protégé" as she
called her, for eleven years. When Lilestan left the New Orleans orphanage in 1908, now eighteen years old, she began missionary work among
her people in Mississippi and would soon marry a Christian Choctaw.
Josephine Ellis served as southern vice president of the Women's National
Indian Association and regularly attended its annual meetings until her
death in 1912.[26]

Ellis was also an avid promoter of American Indian basketry, especially that woven by Choctaw women near her summer home over
Lake Pontchartrain in Amite. But Mary McIlhenny Bradford and Sara
McIlhenny, daughters of the Tabasco sauce founder, would play a truly
extraordinary role on behalf of the Chitimacha community at Charen-
ton, thirty miles from their home on Avery Island. Readers of the *Daily
Picayune* opened their Sunday morning newspaper on June 11, 1899, to

find a nearly half-page story entitled "The Chetimaches and Their Land Claims." The article was mostly an update about a case that lingered for years in the US Circuit Court in New Orleans. In 1897 the Chitimacha Indians in St. Mary Parish charged several of their neighbors along Bayou Teche with unlawful possession of lands. The defendants in *Chetimachas Indians v. Delhaye et al.* responded by stating that the Chitimachas had been citizens of Louisiana for many years and by further asserting that "there is not and never has been any nation known to and recognized by the United States as the Tchetimacha Indians with right to sue and plead as such in the courts of the United States." At first, judge Charles Parlange concurred with this opinion, but an amended plea was submitted in early 1898 with prominent New Orleans attorney Albert Voorhies serving as the Chitimachas' counsel.[27] While waiting for this trial to proceed, George Demarest of Franklin, Louisiana—self-appointed liaison between tribe and court—reported from New Orleans to John Paul, chief of the Chitimachas, that he had delivered "to our Friend" some baskets, made by the chief's daughter, and that "he was very much please with them."[28]

In a legal battle over land rights, the Chitimachas were putting to strategic use an aesthetic and ethnographic interest in their exquisite basketry, which influential white women had helped nurture since the New Orleans world's fair. "They hold that the sales were not valid," as readers learned in that Sunday morning article, "because no allotments were made, and, moreover, the lands in question belonged to the nation and not to individuals." John Paul was quoted saying, "we hold that the United States government should protect us in our grants. Our forefathers had no right to alienate the land. It is time that we should be permitted to enjoy the benefit of our inheritance." Prominently featured on the news page were sketches of tribal members, drawn from photographs sent by the Chitimacha chief: John Paul's daughter Pauline, his daughter-in-law Christine, Manuel Vulcin, and Clara Darden (figure 7). Darden was the oldest person in the community and its most skillful weaver of river-cane basketry; Christine and Pauline Paul were much younger, but were also talented basket makers. The *Daily Picayune* story ended by reporting that "baskets made by the Chetimaches are very pretty, ranging in size from large baskets for ordinary domestic use, to small fancy ones, to be used in the sewing-room, or to ornament the bric a brac table."[29] Eight months after the appearance of

Fig. 7. "Chetimaches and Their Land Claims," *New Orleans Daily Picayune,* June 11, 1899.

this article, Demarest wrote to Chief John Paul requesting that "the Girls" make more baskets, including one for the reporter "as he says he will write something good in the Paper for the Nation." Writing upside down on the top margin of this same letter, Demarest added, "John tell your Daughter to make me 2 Baskets and send them to me. I want to have them with me to show the court."[30]

By the beginning of the twentieth century, the Chitimacha Indians' possession of their remaining land had become extremely precarious. Lacking protection from the United States government, which was legally owed to them, the Chitimachas confronted a new surge of racial hostility as well as land grabbing from white neighbors. Under these circumstances, a relationship that Chitimacha women were forging at that moment with Mary Bradford and Sara McIlhenny would become crucial in this community's pursuit of federal recognition. Judge Parlange denied the Chitimachas' petition in April 1900, but the production and sale of exquisite baskets would give Chitimacha Indians special access to desperately needed political resources. Through a network of communication with distant dealers, collectors, anthropologists, and curators—facilitated by the McIlhenny sisters—the Chitimachas reached allies and officials in the nick of time and acquired federal recognition in 1916—two centuries after their ancestors had carried out the first calumet ceremony to be held in New Orleans.[31]

⋘

Meanwhile, African Americans in New Orleans were organizing what would become known as "Mardi Gras Indian tribes." Appropriating the popular image of dangerous yet free-spirited Plains Indian warriors as displayed in Wild West shows and other forms of entertainment, they seemed to be disguising their own defiance and prowess in Jim Crow New Orleans behind an acceptable mask of wild Indian behavior. As early as the 1880s the Creole Wild West Tribe began dressing in fancy Indian costumes every Mardi Gras. In contrast with Carnival's white merrymakers who donned "Indian" clothing and headdresses, however, these men were channeling African American song and dance into a new ceremonial pattern. A deep memory of fugitive slaves seeking freedom among Indian nations since colonial times, probably reinforced by more recent familiarity with the "Seminole Negro" experience, also influenced this association of Indianness with resistance. In her short story entitled "A Carnival Jangle," Alice Dunbar-Nelson depicted a Carnival gathering in Washington Square where blacks were performing "a perfect Indian dance." Spectators filled this square in Faubourg Marigny "to watch these mimic Redmen, they seemed so fierce and earnest."[32]

On Mardi Gras day in 1895, a group of black revelers, dressed as "a band of hostile Indians," made rounds in the neighborhood of Algiers and fell into a fight with "some white maskers." Eight African American men were arrested and held in jail overnight. "They feel very much aggrieved," according to the *Daily Picayune*, "and claim that they were out for fun, and that they have for the past four or five seasons made visits to Algiers and have always enjoyed themselves, and never before have been molested. They are all workingmen, and showed no signs of drunkenness when seen by a reporter. They with one accord say that they will shake the dust of Algiers from their feet when liberated, and that the denizens of this burg will be compelled to forego the pleasure of their visits in future Mardi Gras seasons." For arraignment the next day, these men received from some friends "their citizens' wearing apparel to enable them to appear in civilized costumes." In what was fast becoming a standard description of Mardi Gras Indians in city newspapers, the *Times-Democrat* reported in 1902 that bands of twenty to thirty men were "singing war songs and doing the war dance" and also noted how "the negroes are the only ones who came out as Indians, and they made good savages."[33]

Jelly Roll Morton told Alan Lomax about "the Indians, one of the biggest feats that happened in Mardi Gras." Whenever people heard the music produced by Mardi Gras Indian groups, they would even abandon "the parades with floats and costumes that cost millions" in order to see them perform. Wearing paint and blankets, these "Indians" danced and sang in an extraordinary manner, throwing their heads back and forth and bending their knees to refrains like "T'ouwais, bas q'ouwais, Ou tendais." During childhood Jelly Roll Morton "thought they really were Indians." As he explained it, "they wanted to act just like the old Indians did in years gone by and so they lived true to the traditions of the Indian style. They went armed with fictitious spears and tommyhawks and so forth and their main object was to make their enemy bow." Morton had once served as a tribe's "spy-boy," a member sent out to meet another tribe's "spy-boy" before the two groups would engage in a battle that sometimes resulted in injury or even death.[34] By the first decade of the twentieth century, as recorded by Marcus Bruce Christian, there were at least six "Negro Carnival clubs disporting themselves as Indian braves during Mardi Gras." Each associated with a particular New Orleans neighborhood. The "Yellow Pocahontas," for example, was based around the intersection of St. Bernard and North Claiborne Avenues. And Algiers was the home of "Eight Red Men."[35]

Mimicry of Indian people thought to be already gone, or on their way out, had no bounds in late nineteenth-century America, and the city of New Orleans was certainly no exception. At the very end of 1896, about a hundred white men gathered inside the Crescent Democratic Club to form a new organization. Regular Democrats, as they were called, wanted to revitalize their urban political machine and undercut serious reformist opposition from the Citizens' League of New Orleans. This assembly of mostly professional politicians and prominent businessmen decided to call their new group the "Choctaw Club," copying New York City's "Tammany Club" and Chicago's "Iroquois Club" as Indian-themed names for Democratic Party machines. Once the selection was made, as reported in city newspapers, stockbroker John Bach ran into the meeting hall wearing a feather duster in the back of his shirt and shouting an Indian war whoop.[36] During the formal start of the Choctaw Club four months later, Charles T. Madison, an attorney who had studied law at Tulane University, was making a strong appeal for Democratic Party unity across the state when he cited how the Choctaw Indians—"a true and steadfast set of men"—had always been loyal friends of the white man. Madison's historical overgeneralization aside, a major objective of this reorganized and reenergized urban machine was indeed to completely disfranchise African Americans throughout Louisiana. This and other pursuits guaranteed the Choctaw Club's control over New Orleans for the next half-century.[37]

Perhaps the most respectful form of homage paid to local Indian people, stickball or raquette games, which had long been popular occasions for cross-cultural interaction and competition in the city, continued to be played by black and white New Orleanians into the twentieth century. A brief revival was even occurring in time for Stewart Culin's visit in 1901. When Army of Northern Virginia veterans held a fundraising festival at the New Orleans Fair Grounds a few years before Culin came to town, one of the event's major attractions was a raquette contest between the La Villes and the Bayous. With thirty players on each team, the Bayous wore red caps and shirts and the La Villes blue caps and shirts. Only a couple of months later, a traveling troupe of Choctaws from Mississippi, called Chief Philup's Band, came to play a weekend of "Indian Ball" at New Orleans's Athletic Park. Ironically, while these Choctaw athletes appeared in the Crescent City to play the ball game, missionaries and officials in Mississippi were attempting to outlaw this traditional sport because it encouraged gambling and other social activities that defied assimilation. Anthropologists like Mark Harrington, at the same time, viewed the game as a vital cultural tradition (figures 8 and 9). Those two Choctaw

Fig. 8. "Agnes" Wallace, holding ball game sticks, photograph by Mark R. Harrington, 1908. National Museum of the American Indian, Smithsonian Institution (N02673).

teams in New Orleans, each with sixteen players, competed on the field for three consecutive afternoons and performed after every match a "War Dance," on an evening program of music that included the Chicago Marine Band—all for an admission price of two bits.[38] Excitement over this spectacle of Indian sport and dance, however, was quickly overshadowed by news that Chief Philup's Band was stranded in the city because their manager had been robbed of the Choctaws' train fare back to Meridian. After staying overnight in a jail, the athletes spent the next day across the street from city hall on Lafayette Square, where "they naturally attracted a large crowd" and waited for New Orleans citizens to donate sufficient funds for their return home. Within an hour, according to the *Daily Picayune,* a sufficient sum was collected.[39] Although a far cry from that Chitimacha peace ceremony back in 1718, this sequence of events dramatically showed that American Indians would not stop improvising their presence in New Orleans—a city famous for cultural improvisation. Nationwide, the early twentieth century was a time when urban residents were being treated to stories about, and even visits by, a rising number of celebrated

Fig. 9. Will E. Morris with drum for ball game dance, photograph by Mark R. Harrington, 1908. National Museum of the American Indian, Smithsonian Institution (No2678).

Indian athletes. Jim Thorpe (Sac and Fox), of course, is best known today, but also competing at football and baseball contests and at track-and-field events in major cities were such stars as Thomas Longboat (Onondaga), Lewis Tewanima (Hopi), Frank Mount Pleasant (Tuscarora), John Meyers (Cahuilla), Frank Pierce (Seneca), and Bill Davis (Mohawk). On a gridiron in New Orleans, Louisiana State University's football team faced an all-Indian team from the Haskell Indian School (Lawrence, Kansas) in 1908 and again in 1914. The Tigers defeated the Haskell Indians in the first game, 32–0, but lost to them the next time, 31–0.[40]

By the time of the Crescent City's bicentennial, baseball and football would completely replace the ancient Indian sport of raquette on its urban landscape. And as popular attention turned more and more toward college and professional sports, the dynamic role that stickball had played in the city's public life over a long span of time quickly faded from New Orleanians' memory and history.[41] More generally, white Americans were gravitating to popular spectacles that represented American Indians in only stereotypical ways. The Louisiana State Fair in 1899 even included on its schedule demonstrations of an "Indian Attack on Settlers" and a "Burning of Cabins and Capture of Indians." Shows like Buffalo Bill Cody's Wild West and Joseph Miller's 101 Ranch Wild West continued to tour through New Orleans into the 1910s. American Indians in those shows, mostly from Northern Plains reservations, were performing as Indians, for needed income, in a way that audiences expected—donning war bonnets and paint, whooping on horseback, and attacking stagecoaches.[42] Sometimes Native performers would end up staying in a city through which the Wild West toured. White Eagle, a Crow Indian working for the 101 Ranch Wild West and "regarded as the best rider of the outfit," fell ill in New Orleans. A former student at the Carlisle Indian School in Pennsylvania, White Eagle converted to the Presbyterian faith during his prolonged hospitalization in the Crescent City. "On account of his patient suffering and gentle demeanor," the *Times Picayune* reported, "he won for himself many friends in New Orleans." In 1916, sadly, White Eagle passed away in the tuberculosis building at Charity Hospital and received funeral service at the Esplanade Presbyterian Church.[43]

Earlier in the same year of White Eagle's death, the New Orleans department store Maison Blanche held for two weeks on its third floor "The Wonderful Hiawatha Indian Village." Customers were invited to see, for free, "a complete picture of real Indian life" in "a beautiful woodland setting." Ten "real Ojibways" performed war dances every half hour and during the intervals demonstrated leatherwork, basketry, and other crafts. Also a graduate of Carlisle Indian School, "Princess Neawanna" gave talks about Indian life to the shoppers. Indian arts and crafts were, of course, available for purchase at low prices. Ironically, Native American performers who played "Indian" in accordance with white assumptions about premodern Indianness were pursuing one of the limited avenues available to them in the early twentieth century for actually doing modern things—like traveling from city to city or selling products to urban consumers—and also for exhibiting pride in their Indian identity.[44]

Watching real American Indian people play "Indian" was never enough for white urban Americans, who were themselves also playing "Indian" for entertainment and recreation during these early years of the twentieth century. The New Orleans City Park, for example, celebrated its seasonal opening in 1913 with a festival that featured an "Indian water carnival." In what organizers considered "an almost exact reproduction of the annual games of the Indians," about fifty young men and women formed two teams with the names of "Choctaws" and "Sioux." "The legend of the carnival," as reported in the *Times-Democrat*, "is to the effect that after many years of war, the two tribes have smoked the pipe of peace, and instead of a war of extermination, will hold a grand water carnival." For the city park festival, "the 'Braves' and their 'Squaws' will emerge from their picturesque wigwams, on the north shore of Lake Grandjean," assuming such names as "Rainbow," "Laughing Water," "Minnehaha," and "Pocahontas." Then they would "enter their canoes and proceed to the western end of Bayou Delgado, where the proper program will begin."[45]

❦

While US citizens found amusement in watching, even playing, stereotypical Indians in American cities like New Orleans, their government still pursued policies threatening Indian societies with destruction. For the New Orleans area, this resulted in a precipitous decline in the number of American Indians whose presence in the city had endured for so long against so many odds. Committed to terminating the Choctaw Nation's government in what would soon become the state of Oklahoma—where Indian people had once been promised sovereignty and territory in perpetuity—the Office of Indian Affairs insisted upon allotting their land in Indian Territory to tribal members once and for all. In order to qualify for allotment before the government closed the tribal roll, Choctaws remaining in the Southeast were being pressured to relocate. Over several months in 1902 and 1903, nearly three hundred Choctaws departed from their homes in Louisiana and Mississippi. Cora Bremer, a New Orleans artist with a family home in Florenville who like other Crescent City women held a keen interest in Louisiana Indian basketry, reported to Mary McIlhenny Bradford that "sixty-five of my Choctaw left here for Indian Territory last week." With "only a very few" remaining behind, Bremer wrote, "I am disappointed." Altogether nearly fifteen hundred Choctaws left Mississippi and Louisiana by the time the tribal roll closed in 1907. About a thousand remained in Mississippi and way below a hundred in Louisiana.[46]

Just when the federal government was evacuating Lake Pontchartrain's north shore of most of its Choctaw people, anthropologists—somewhat ironically—began to appear on the scene. Small communities of American Indians scattered across their eastern homelands had largely gone unnoticed by ethnologists, especially those engaging in ethnographic fieldwork. Larger populations located on western reservations drew most of the anthropologists' attention. But during the first decade of the twentieth century, a few anthropologists began taking interest in communities like those in Louisiana. Wanting to capture whatever remained of traditional culture before it vanished, John Swanton, M. Raymond Harrington, and David Bushnell traveled among Choctaws, Houmas, Chitimachas, Tunicas, Biloxis, and Coushattas in Louisiana—"hunting for Indians" as Christine Paul put it when reporting Swanton's arrival in her Chitimacha community to Mary Bradford.[47] Working for the Smithsonian Institution, Swanton visited Louisiana on two separate trips in 1907–1908 and three years later published *Indian Tribes of the Lower Mississippi Valley and Adjacent Coast of the Gulf of Mexico*, a thick book based mostly on ambitious and comprehensive reading of published and unpublished documents. This and several subsequent bulletins written by Swanton for the Bureau of American Ethnology would heavily influence southeastern Indian studies for years to come. Harrington spent several weeks among Louisiana Indians in 1908, employed by George Heye to acquire objects for his growing collection in New York City. Reflecting their profession's preoccupation with gathering information about what they considered authentic customs and beliefs, anthropologists at that time showed relatively little interest in what Native people were actually experiencing during their fieldwork.

Nevertheless, like some of the New Orleans women who actually assisted them in their museum and fieldwork, anthropologists visiting the area would help communities there to gain much needed attention from the federal government.[48]

During the winter of 1908–1909, working for the Smithsonian's Bureau of American Ethnology, David Bushnell carried out fieldwork among the small group of Choctaws still living at Bayou Lacombe. Like Stewart Culin, whose visit to Mandeville preceded his by several years, this St. Louis–born anthropologist was quite experienced at aggressively acquiring Native American things. At Bayou Lacombe Bushnell excavated a mound near Chinchuba Creek, gathering mostly pieces of pottery and bones of deer, rabbit, and alligator. Although wishing for more information about foods and medicines used by precontact Choctaws, he did observe that "many of the primitive beliefs and customs of the people" have persisted, "notwithstanding the fact that the Choctaw have been in close contact with Europeans for about two centuries, and under the direct influence of Christian missionaries for several generations." In a short Bureau of American Ethnology bulletin, Bushnell described games, dances, and ceremonies, recorded myths and legends, and included photographs of community members and their handcrafts (figures 10–13). Although ethnographers emphasized collective aspects of information provided by their informants, at the expense of their own personhood, Bushnell's close-up photographs of named Choctaw persons in the Bayou Lacombe community offer a rare sense of their individuality and identity. And a dozen or so stories were told to him by those same individuals: Pisatuntema (Emma), Ahojeobe (Emil John), and Heleema (Louisa). According to an article that Bushnell published in the *American Anthropologist,* fifty-year-old Pisatuntema, oldest member of the community, was "recognized as a chief" ever since her father's death some years earlier. Writing that "the Choctaw are excellent basket makers, although their work at the present time is greatly inferior to that of a generation ago," Bushnell did notice that Bayou Lacombe weavers brought "large numbers of small baskets provided with handles" to the stores of nearby towns in exchange for merchandise.[49] He brought back to the Smithsonian a sizable array of material objects and photographs from Louisiana, and several years later he sold to the American Museum of Natural History in New York City, for five hundred dol-

Fig. 13. Choctaw boy in pack
basket, photo by Bushnell.
National Anthropological
Archives, Smithsonian Institution,
BAE GN 01102b16b.

lars, a large personal collection of American Indian objects that included
more than fifty Choctaw, Chitimacha, and Atakapa baskets. Asserting
the particular value of the Louisiana basketry, Bushnell reported to Clark
Wissler that "it would be impossible to duplicate some of the specimens,
especially the old Attacapa, the majority of which were made before 1850.
I learned the age of these from the old lady from whom I obtained them,
not an Indian, but a member of one of the old families of New Orleans."[50]

Because of the removal of Choctaws from the region only a few years
before his visit, David Bushnell found only two settlements in St. Tammany Parish, the one he visited at Bayou Lacombe and the other at Pearl
River about twelve miles from its mouth. He also seemed unaware of
the fact that some of his hosts at Bayou Lacombe wanted to leave for
the Choctaw Nation, hoping to improve their condition, but had failed
to meet the government's deadline. Illness had prevented Pisatuntema
(Emma) from traveling to Indian Territory. Five years after Bushnell's visit,
Ahojeobe (Emil John) would join two Mississippi Choctaws on a special
mission to Washington DC—even meeting President Woodrow Wilson
in a diplomatic appeal for the government's attention to Choctaws left
behind and denied their rights.[51] With the sudden reduction of nearby
Choctaws, the Chitimacha Tribe of Louisiana would become the Indian

nation closest to New Orleans to eventually receive recognition from the federal government. The greater distance from their reservation along Bayou Teche, however, did not permit an ongoing or regular presence by Chitimacha people in the city. When Bushnell presented an update of his work on the St. Tammany Parish Choctaws to the Louisiana Historical Society, the anthropologist hoped that "others may become interested in preserving notes on the Indians scattered throughout Louisiana." Referring to "small groups and individuals" one might meet in widely scattered locations, he figured they "may represent the last of a little-known tribe, and may possess knowledge of inestimable value to the historian and ethnologist at the present time." Bushnell concluded by urging his readers to gather and preserve such information because "little will remain" in "another generation." Thankfully, the anthropologist was wrong in making this prediction about the future of American Indians in Louisiana. On a Sunday in 1917, nearly one year following publication of Bushnell's Louisiana Historical Society paper, "the Indian basketmakers of Lacombe" were acknowledged in a local newspaper for selling their baskets to benefit the Red Cross. Choctaws in St. Tammany Parish were obviously still participating in some of the area's public events.[52] Through their own persistent struggles for survival and self-determination, and with support from allies near and far, Native communities across the state would actually begin to recover and grow soon after David Bushnell delivered his somber forecast. After all, the first two centuries of their relationship with New Orleans had already demonstrated noteworthy resilience and perseverance.[53]

EPILOGUE

A t the dawn of the twentieth century, New Orleans druggist and painter Alphonse J. Gamotis produced a painting entitled *Indian Village on the Shores of Lake Pontchartrain*. Near the mouth of a bayou, the artist placed a few human figures in front of a palmetto-covered cabin. A large pack-basket rests in front of a standing woman (plate 8). Although several known landscape paintings, like this one in the personal collection of Roger H. Ogden, include glimpses of American Indian camps or families on the outskirts of the Crescent City, historians and art historians have tended to ignore or downplay the presence of American Indians in such images. About Gamotis's painting, for example, Randolph Delehanty wrote, "By 1900 there were few Native Americans left in the New Orleans area, and this scene may be wholly imagined."[1] Hopefully my readers now realize that the scene painted by Gamotis, a member of the Artists' Association of New Orleans, more likely depicts an actual rather than an imaginary camp. Like many observers of American Indians in towns and cities over the nineteenth century, this painter can be held partly responsible for the common impression that Indigenous people disappeared a long time ago. The very descriptions and pictures comprising the present-day historian's archive tended to blend them ghostlike into a natural landscape and to render them into fading remnants of a once nobler people. But the problem is largely our unwillingness or inability to see through this imperialist gaze and find the real people who persisted in being American Indians in and around New Orleans. Having demonstrated in this book the dynamic continuity of their presence across the city's first two centuries, I hope it provides some groundwork for greater attention to the ensuing years.

The history of American Indians in cities like New Orleans is very much a case of people hiding in plain sight. No matter how much resourceful adaptation and determined survival they put into their presence, others kept insisting that they were nothing but remnants of people on their way out. And even as more and more American Indians became permanent residents of the Greater New Orleans area over the twentieth century, too many people still held tightly to that myth. Insistence upon Indian people looking and behaving in ways narrowly defined by others continued to impose challenges and obstacles, most particularly in the pursuit of federal recognition.

The third century of American Indians in the Crescent City would be shaped by a confluence of new circumstances, most notably persistence and growth among Houma Indians in parishes adjacent to Orleans Parish. Metropolitan sprawl and Houma movement into the city began to raise the number of American Indians residing in the Greater New Orleans area by World War II. Decennial censuses throughout the nineteenth and early twentieth centuries counted few American Indians as residents of New Orleans. In 1870 fewer than sixteen were enumerated, in 1900 only two, and in 1920 about ten. Inconsistency in how census takers identified someone's race was a perennial problem, but not until 1930—when twenty-nine American Indians were enumerated for Orleans Parish—do we begin to see slow but steady growth in Native American residency.[2] The thousand or so American Indians residing in New Orleans today include members of Louisiana tribes as well as migrants from more distant Native American nations. And they come from all walks of life, working in industry, education, business, law, medicine, and other occupations in and around the city. In 1980 the total population of people identified as American Indian alone (not in combination with another identity) across the state of Louisiana was nearly thirteen thousand. Three decades later, it exceeded thirty thousand. Both Baton Rouge and New Orleans have an Indian residential population of a thousand or more. More than half of all American Indians in Louisiana live within a few hours of the Crescent City.[3]

Like many groups of Native Americans scattered across the Southeast, American Indians in Louisiana entered the twentieth century lacking formal recognition from the federal government. Having signed no treaties with the United States, they suffered from the Bureau of Indian Affairs' refusal to even consider protecting their land rights—even when those rights were sometimes recognized by federal courts.[4] This situation put American Indians in and around New Orleans at the mercy of state and local governments whenever their interests, and sometimes even their lives, fell into danger, but it never terminated their efforts to pursue justice and autonomy. As the largest group living nearest the Crescent City, the Houma people's endless struggles against local discrimination and federal neglect are most relevant. Throughout much of the twentieth century, Houmas living along the bayous and in the marsh country south and southwest of New Orleans engaged in trapping, fishing, shrimping, oystering, and oil-industry work. But no matter how resourceful and adaptable they proved to be, encroachment by powerful economic interests combined with environmental destruction have threatened Houma communities with dispossession.[5]

During the second decade of the twentieth century, Houma families began appealing for admission to public schools in their part of the Jim Crow South. Denied access to white-only schools and refusing enrollment in poorly funded schools for black students, they eventually persuaded Terrebonne Parish to open schools for Indian children by 1939. These public educational facilities, however, were inadequately supported and were staffed with mostly unqualified teachers. By then several other Houma schools were being operated by Baptists, Methodists, and Catholics. Desegregation of public education in the parish, though, resulted only from *Naquin v. Terrebonne School Board*, a lawsuit brought to federal court in 1961 on behalf of fifty-six Houma students and a case that actually contributed to success of African Americans in finally gaining open access to the parish's public schools. New Orleans civil rights attorney John Nelson prepared the case and represented the Houmas in court. Along the way, anthropologists from various research institutions as well as special agents from the federal government had been affirming in reports and letters that the Houmas are American Indian people who deserved access to educational and other support from the US government.[6]

Federal recognition of Louisiana Indians, however, did not easily follow. Going into the 1970s, the only federally recognized group in the state was the Chitimacha Tribe in St. Mary Parish, thanks to congressional action that began in 1916. The only additional group to gain recognition by Congress was the Coushatta Tribe of Louisiana in Allen Parish, and that did not occur until 1971.[7] In 1978 the Bureau of Indian Affairs opened its Branch of Acknowledgment Research, establishing rigid and lengthy guidelines for a growing number of groups around the country seeking recognition. With these rules and requirements in place, the Department of the Interior assumed nearly exclusive authority over the process. Two Louisiana groups acquired recognition this way, the Tunica-Biloxi Tribe in Avoyelles Parish in 1981 and the Jena Band of Choctaws in LaSalle Parish in 1995. The Louisiana government was meanwhile identifying these and other Native peoples as state-recognized tribes. Additional groups receiving state recognition are the Clifton Choctaw Tribe in Rapides Parish, the Louisiana Tribe of Choctaw in West Baton Rouge Parish, the Choctaw-Apache Community in Sabine Parish, and the United Houma Nation, along with a few other communities along the Gulf Coast: the Pointe-au-Chien Tribe, the Isle de Jean Charles Indian Band of Biloxi-Chitimacha, and the Grand Caillou/Dulac Band. In 1972 Louisiana opened an Office of Indian Affairs to represent state-recognized tribes, and in 1974 the groups established the Inter-Tribal Council of Louisiana to enhance alliance among themselves.[8]

During the 1970s Houma people formed the Houma Tribe, Inc. and the Houma Alliance, merging these two organizations into the United Houma Nation by 1979. The United Houma Nation then invited Mennonite researchers to compile materials required by the Bureau of Indian Affairs and submitted their petition in 1985. After nearly a decade of waiting, the Houmas were told that they failed the preliminary stage of their request. They appealed that denial in 1996 and are still waiting for a decision. With its future still uncertain, the Houma case is nationally important because it has exposed serious flaws and biases written into the federal government's acknowledgment process. For such a large population living in dispersed communities from St. Bernard Parish to St. Mary Parish, the Branch of Acknowledgment Research makes an exacting demand for records only erratically generated by real-life circumstances of migration and adaptation. While the Houmas awaited a decision, Louisiana's delegation to the US Senate and House of Representatives did initiate congressional action during the late 1980s that might have resulted in federal recognition. But opposition from oil companies fearful of potential land claims as well as from the Bureau of Indian Affairs killed the effort.

The Houmas' ongoing relationship with New Orleans throughout the twentieth century served many needs and interests, as families moved toward and into the urban center for work without abandoning ties to their bayou and coastal communities. The Branch of Acknowledgment Research, however, even turned this dynamic Houma presence in the Crescent City against the tribe's petition. Urbanization naturally facilitated Houma people's nationwide outreach to other Indian tribes and to pan-tribal organizations. Helen Gindret was born in Golden Meadow, Louisiana, and moved to New Orleans at the age of ten, growing up in a family network linking small communities with the city. In 1961 Gindret attended the American Indian Chicago Conference in Chicago and returned to south Louisiana energetically committed to helping organize a tribal government. She became the United Houma Nation's first vice chairperson in 1979 and held the executive directorship of the Louisiana Office of Indian Affairs from 1980 to 1983. Another American Indian who grew up in New Orleans, Diana Williamson of the Chitimacha nation, became executive director of the Louisiana Office of Indian Affairs in 1986. In response to such effective intercommunity networking, the Bureau of Indian Affairs actually used residency of Houma people in New Orleans as one of its excuses for denying them federal recognition. Branch of Acknowledgment Research officials grossly exaggerated both the percentage of Houmas living in the city and the city's distance from rural Houma communities. And, not surprisingly, they failed to notice the city's intricate and age-old relationship with wetlands communities.[9]

Louisiana Indians also advanced self-representation of their history, culture, and status in ways that included New Orleans. The New Orleans Jazz and Heritage Festival, held annually in the city, became an important venue for vendors and performers from local Indian nations. At the Native American Village on the festival grounds, basketry and other crafts are sold. In 1982 the United Houma Nation worked with various Crescent City agencies to hold the Tricentennial Indian Festival in City Park Stadium, marking the anniversary of La Salle's journey down the Mississippi. The very next year, the New Orleans French Market Board sought assistance from the Louisiana Office of Indian Affairs to involve American Indians in celebrating the two-hundred-year anniversary of the market's official beginning. Their contributions to the market's history were again recognized in 1987, when members of the Coushatta, Chitimacha, Choctaw, Tunica-Biloxi, and Houma communities sold crafts and demonstrated cooking at the French Market as part of the city's bicentennial celebration of the US Constitution. Over these same years, the National Park Service included participation by the region's Native peoples in developing its Jean Lafitte National Historical Park at New Orleans and several other sites across south Louisiana. Within their own communities, Louisiana Indians have been pursuing a range of cultural projects that include creation of tribal museums and historical centers, and retention and recovery of languages.[10]

Along with the damaging effects of delayed recognition by the federal government, the Houmas and other Native people in south Louisiana are confronting rapid deterioration of their coastal environment. Consequently, in 2005, Hurricanes Katrina and Rita added environmental injustice to political neglect on the list of New Orleans–area issues that face many Indigenous and non-Indigenous peoples around the world.[11] Those two storms alone, as T. Mayheart Dardar of the United Houma Nation has written, "were the culmination of centuries of abuse and neglect. Two hundred years of non-recognition by the United States had left the tribe in its scattered settlements at the edges of the Gulf of Mexico." And although "for many years the Houma prospered as the land sustained us" even without federal support, "the avarice of empire eventually made its way into our isolated bayou homeland." As described by Dardar with generations of his family's own experience behind him, "the dawn of the twentieth century brought the land speculators, oil companies, and politicians, and the process of taking and exploiting Houma land began. Levee systems were built, bayous were blocked, and canals were dug into the marshlands and swamps to allow access to the oil industry." The impact was slowly felt by the still resilient Houma people, but with coastal erosion accelerating from climate change and with US Army Corps of Engineers projects doing more harm than good, destruction and displacement of communities are the more likely consequence of hurricanes.[12]

As we now head into New Orleans's fourth century, the unfolding story of American Indians in and around the city continues to reveal plenty about important themes in global as well as national history. With that Chitimacha calumet ceremony in 1718, Lower Mississippi Valley Indians began decades-long alliance and commerce with the French Atlantic world. Toward the end of the eighteenth century, they negotiated skillfully with shifting and competing colonial governments in and around New Orleans. While quite suddenly losing land and leverage after the Louisiana Purchase, the region's Native inhabitants innovatively transformed the Crescent City from a stage for political engagement into a marketplace for cultural expression as well as for economic exchange. As prisoners of war in exile from their homelands, Creek and Seminole people endured a painful passage through the Crescent City that drew a vexing mix of public attention but nevertheless demonstrated remarkable resilience and determination. After the American Civil War, American Indians from scattered communities across south Louisiana forged valuable public and personal relations with New Orleans residents that could possibly assist them in ongoing struggles over sovereignty and territory. And now, through campaigns for federal recognition and environmental protection, they are challenging powerful authorities and interests to take action that can save cultures and ecologies essential for all of us.

NOTES

PREFACE

1. *The WPA Guide to New Orleans: The Federal Writers' Project Guide to 1930s New Orleans* (Boston: Houghton Mifflin, 1938), 41, 403, 405, 407.

2. For a comprehensive study of American Indian experiences in cities since World War II, based on written sources and oral history, see Donald L. Fixico, *The Urban Indian Experience in America* (Albuquerque: University of New Mexico Press, 2000).

3. Timothy R. Pauketat, *Ancient America's Great City on the Mississippi* (New York: Viking, 2009); Stephen H. Lekson, *A History of the Ancient Southwest* (Santa Fe, NM: School for Advance Studies Press, 2009). The relationship between American Indians and colonial towns is examined variously in Colin Calloway, ed., *After King Philip's War: Presence and Persistence in Indian New England* (Hanover, NH: University Press of New England, 1997); Jean M. O'Brien, *Dispossession by Degrees: Indian Land and Identity in Natick, Massachusetts, 1650–1790* (New York: Cambridge University Press, 1997); Steven C. Hahn, *The Life and Times of Mary Musgrove* (Gainesville: University Press of Florida, 2012); Dawn G. Marsh, *A Lenape among the Quakers: The Life of Hannah Freeman* (Lincoln: University of Nebraska Press, 2014); Lucy Eldersveld Murphy, *Great Lakes Creoles: A French-Indian Community on the Northern Borderlands, Prairie du Chien, 1750–1860* (New York: Cambridge University Press, 2014).

4. For a sample of work about the Atlantic crossings to European cities, see Bunny McBride, *Molly Spotted Elk: A Penobscot in Paris* (Norman: University of Oklahoma Press, 1995); Alden T. Vaughan, *Transatlantic Encounters: American Indians in Britain, 1500–1776* (New York: Cambridge University Press, 2006); Jace Weaver, *The Red Atlantic: American Indigenes and the Making of the Modern World, 1000–1927* (Chapel Hill: University of North Carolina Press, 2014); and Coll Thrush, *Indigenous London: Native Travelers at the Heart of Empire* (New Haven, CT: Yale University Press, 2016). Tracing movement by American Indian sailors and whalemen brings even wider oceanic crossings into view. See Nancy Shoemaker, *Native Whalemen and the World: Indigenous Encounters and the Contingency of Race* (Chapel Hill: University of North Carolina Press, 2016).

5. Edmund J. Danziger Jr., *Survival and Regeneration: Detroit's American Indian Community* (Detroit: Wayne State University Press, 1991); Joan Weibel-Orlando, *Indian Country, LA: Maintaining Ethnic Community in Complex Society* (Urbana: University of Illinois Press, 1991); James B. LaGrand, *Indian Metropolis: Native Americans in Chicago, 1945–75* (Urbana: University of Illinois Press, 2005); Karl A. Hoerig, *Under the Palace Portal: Native American Artists in Santa Fe* (Albuquerque: University of New Mexico Press, 2003); Coll Thrush, *Native Seattle: Histories from the Crossing-Over Place* (Seattle: University of Washington Press, 2007); Renya K. Ramirez, *Native Hubs: Culture, Community, and Belonging in Silicon Valley and Beyond* (Durham, NC: Duke University Press, 2007); Richard L. Carrico, *Strangers in a Stolen Land: Indians of San Diego County from Prehistory to the New Deal* (San Diego: Sunbelt Publications, 2008); Penelope Edmonds, *Urbanizing Frontiers: Indigenous Peoples and Settlers in 19th-Century Pacific Rim Cities* (Seattle: University of Washington Press, 2010); Myla Vicenti Carpio and P. Jane Hafen, *Indigenous Albuquerque* (Lubbock: Texas Tech University Press, 2011); Nicolas G. Rosenthal, *Reimagining Indian Country: Native American Migration and Identity in Twentieth-Century Los Angeles* (Chapel Hill: University of North Carolina Press, 2012); Julie L. Davis, *Survival Schools: The American Indian Movement and Community Education in the Twin Cities* (Minneapolis: University of Minnesota Press, 2013); Rosalyn R. Lapier and David R. M. Beck, *City Indian: Native American Activism in Chicago, 1893–1934* (Lincoln: University of Nebraska Press, 2015); John Mack Faragher, *Eternity Street: Violence and Justice in Frontier Los Angeles* (New York: W. W. Norton, 2016).

6. Robert W. Rydell, *All the World's a Fair: Visions of Empire at American International Expositions, 1876–1916* (Chicago: University of Chicago Press, 1987); L. G. Moses, *Wild West Shows and the Images of American Indians, 1883–1933* (Albuquerque: University of New Mexico Press, 1996); Paige Raibmon, "Theatres of Contact: The Kwakwaka'wakw Meet Colonialism in British Columbia and at the Chicago World's Fair," *Canadian Historical Review* 81 (June 2000): 157–90; Joy S. Kasson, *Buffalo Bill's Wild West: Celebrity, Memory, and Popular History* (New York: Hill and Wang, 2000); Louis S. Warren, *Buffalo Bill's America: William Cody and the Wild West Show* (New York: Alfred A. Knopf, 2005); Nancy J. Parezo and Don D. Fowler, *Anthropology Goes to the Fair: The 1904 Louisiana Purchase Exposition* (Lincoln: University of Nebraska Press, 2007); Theda Perdue, *Race and the Atlanta Cotton States Exposition of 1895* (Athens: University of Georgia Press, 2010).

7. Peter Nabokov, *How the World Moves: The Odyssey of an American Indian Family* (New York: Viking, 2015), 290.

8. Robert Berkofer Jr., *The White Man's Indian: Images of the American Indian from Columbus to the Present* (New York: Alfred A. Knopf, 1978).

9. Recent coverage of the first two centuries of New Orleans history can be sampled in Richard Campanella, *Bienville's Dilemma: A Historical Geography of New Orleans* (Lafayette: University of Louisiana at Lafayette Press, 2008); Emily Clark, *The Strange History of the American Quadroon: Free Women of Color in the Revolutionary Atlantic World* (Chapel Hill: University of North Carolina Press, 2013); Shannon Lee Dawdy, *Building the Devil's Empire: French Colonial New Orleans* (Chicago: University of Chicago Press, 2008); Nathalie Des-

sens, *Creole City: A Chronicle of Early American New Orleans* (Gainesville: University Press of Florida, 2015); Freddi Williams Evans, *Congo Square: African Roots in New Orleans* (Lafayette: University of Louisiana at Lafayette Press, 2011); Eberhard L. Faber, *Building the Land of Dreams: New Orleans and the Transformation of Early America* (Princeton, NJ: Princeton University Press, 2015); x; Dianne Guenin-Lelle, *The Story of French New Orleans: History of a Creole City* (Jackson: University Press of Mississippi, 2016); Rashauna Johnson, *Slavery's Metropolis: Unfree Labor in New Orleans during the Age of Revolutions* (New York: Cambridge University Press, 2016); Ari Kelman, *A River and Its City: The Nature of Landscape in New Orleans* (Berkeley: University of California Press, 2003); Alecia P. Long, *The Great Southern Babylon: Sex, Race, and Respectability in New Orleans, 1865–1920* (Baton Rouge: Louisiana State University Press, 2004); Carolyn Morrow Long, *Madame Lalaurie, Mistress of the Haunted House* (Gainesville: University Press of Florida, 2012); Scott P. Marler, *The Merchants' Capital: New Orleans and the Political Economy of the Nineteenth-Century South* (New York: Cambridge University Press, 2013); Justin Nystrom, *New Orleans after the Civil War: Race, Politics, and a New Birth of Freedom* (Baltimore: Johns Hopkins University Press, 2010); Lawrence N. Powell, *The Accidental City: Improvising New Orleans* (Cambridge, MA: Harvard University Press, 2012); Adam Rothman, *Beyond Freedom's Reach: A Kidnapping in the Twilight of Slavery* (Cambridge, MA: Harvard University Press, 2015); Judith Kelleher Schafer, *Brothels, Depravity, and Abandoned Women: Illegal Sex in Antebellum New Orleans* (Baton Rouge: Louisiana State University Press, 2009); Jennifer M. Spear, *Race, Sex, and Social Order in Early New Orleans* (Baltimore: Johns Hopkins University Press, 2009); Shirley Elizabeth Thompson, *Exiles at Home: The Struggle to Become American in Creole New Orleans* (Cambridge, MA: Harvard University Press, 2009); Sophie White, *Wild Frenchmen and Frenchified Indians: Material Culture and Race in Colonial Louisiana* (Philadelphia: University of Pennsylvania Press, 2012); Urmi Engineer Willoughby, *Yellow Fever, Race, and Ecology in Nineteenth-Century New Orleans* (Baton Rouge: Louisiana State University Press, 2017).

10. Daniel H. Usner, "Romance and Reality: American Indians in 19th-Century New Orleans," *The Historic New Orleans Collection Quarterly* 17 (Summer 1999): 2–4; Usner, "Glimpses of an Overshadowed People: American Indians in 19th-Century Louisiana," *Louisiana Cultural Vistas* 10 (Summer 1999): 34–35; Siona LaFrance, "'Romance and Reality': Images of Louisiana Indians take center stage at Historic New Orleans Collection," *New Orleans Times-Picayune,* July 17, 1999.

11. C. Richard King, *Colonial Discourses, Collective Memories, and the Exhibition of Native American Cultures and Histories in the Contemporary United States* (New York: Garland Publishing, 1998); Amy Lonetree, *Decolonizing Museums: Representing Native America in National and Tribal Museums* (Chapel Hill: University of North Carolina Press, 2012); Raney Bench, *Interpreting Native American History and Culture at Museums and Historic Sites* (Lanham, MD: Rowman and Littlefield, 2014); and Scott Manning Stevens, "Collectors and Museums: From Cabinets of Curiosities to Indigenous Cultural Centers," *The Oxford Handbook of American Indian History,* ed. Frederick E. Hoxie (New York: Oxford University Press, 2016), 475–97.

1. PLACE OF FOREIGN LANGUAGES

1. Richebourg Gaillard McWilliams, trans. and ed., *Iberville's Gulf Journals* (Tuscaloosa: University of Alabama Press, 1981), 57.

2. Marco J. Giardino, "Documentary Evidence for the Location of Historic Indian Villages in the Mississippi Delta," in *Perspectives on Gulf Coast Prehistory,* ed. Dave D. Davis (Gainesville: University Press of Florida, 1984), 232–57; Tristram R. Kidder, "Making the City Inevitable: Native Americans and the Geography of New Orleans," in *Transforming New Orleans and Its Environs: Centuries of Change,* ed. Craig E. Colten (Pittsburgh: University of Pittsburgh Press, 2000), 9–21.

3. Richard J. Shenkel, *Oak Island Archaeology: Prehistoric Estuarine Adaptations in the Mississippi River Delta* (New Orleans: Jean Lafitte National Historical Park, 1980); Daniel H. Usner, "A Cycle of Lowland Forest Efficiency: The Late Archaic-Woodland Economy of the Lower Mississippi Valley," *Journal of Anthropological Research* 39 (Winter 1983): 433–44; "FEMA Archeologists Find American Indian Pottery, Other Items by Bayou St. John," *New Orleans Times-Picayune,* February 20, 2013; "FEMA Archaeologists Discover Native Artifacts in New Orleans," *Indian Country Today,* February 21, 2013.

4. Mary Christine Morkovsky and Patricia Galloway, eds., *La Salle, the Mississippi, and the Gulf: Three Primary Documents,* trans. Ann Linda Bell and Robert S. Weddle (College Station: Texas A&M University Press, 1987), 53–54, 57. For the widespread effects of slave-raiding for trade with British Carolina, see Christina Snyder, *Slavery in Indian Country: The Changing Face of Captivity in Early America* (Cambridge, MA: Harvard University Press, 2010), 46–79.

5. Jean Baptiste Bernard de La Harpe, "Historical Journal of the Establishment of the French in Louisiana," trans. from the French, presented to the American Philosophical Society by William Darby, in *Historical Collections of Louisiana,* ed. B. F. French (New York: Appleton, 1851), 5:35–36; Bienville to Pontchartrain, February 20, 1707, Bienville to Cadillac, June 23, 1716, *Mississippi Provincial Archives: French Dominion,* ed. Dunbar Rowland, Godfrey Sanders, and Patricia K. Galloway (5 vols.), vols. 1–3, Jackson: Mississippi Department of Archives and History, 1929–32, vols. 4–5, Baton Rouge: Louisiana State University Press, 1984, 3:38, 214; André Pénicaut, *Fleur de Lys and Calumet: Being the Pénicaut Narrative of French Adventure in Louisiana,* trans. and ed. Richebourg Gaillard McWilliams (Tuscaloosa: University of Alabama Press, 1953), 70–72, 101–2, 216–20.

6. Antoine Le Page du Pratz, *Histoire de la Louisiane,* 3 vols. (Paris: Du Bure, Delaguette, Lambert, 1758), 1:106–14; *Pénicaut Narrative,* 218–19.

7. For a more general and detailed description of the ceremony from a colonial observer, see Jean-François-Benjamin Dumont de Montigny, *The Memoire of Lieutenant Dumont, 1715–1747: A Sojourner in the French Atlantic,* trans. and ed. Gordon M. Sayre, ed. Carla Zecher (Chapel Hill: University of North Carolina Press, 2012), 341–44. A calumet ceremony performed by Quapaw Indians for René Robert Cavelier de La Salle on his journey down the Mississippi in 1682 is vividly reported in *La Salle, the Mississippi, and the Gulf: Three Primary Documents,* 46–47. Also see McWilliams, *Iberville's Gulf Journals,* 58–59, 66–69, for

description of Bayogoula and Houma versions. The spread of the ritual among Indian nations is discussed in Ian W. Brown, "The Calumet Ceremony in the Southeast as Observed Archaeologically," in *Powhatan's Mantle: Indians in the Colonial Southeast*, ed. Gregory S. Waselkov, Peter H. Wood and Tom Hatley, rev. and expanded ed. (Lincoln: University of Nebraska Press, 2006), 371–419.

8. François Gerard Jollain, "Le Commerce que les Indiens du Mexique font avec les François au Port de Missisipi," hand-colored engraving, ca. 1719–20, The Historic New Orleans Collection, New Orleans; May Rush Gwinn Waggoner, ed., *Le Plus Beau Païs du Monde: Completing the Picture of Proprietary Louisiana, 1699–1722* (Lafayette: Center for Louisiana Studies, 2005), 49. For the use of propaganda by John Law's company encouraging colonization and exaggerating the promise of Louisiana, see Dianne Guenin-Lelle, *The Story of French New Orleans: History of a Creole City* (Jackson: University Press of Mississippi, 2016), 21–22.

9. Stephen Greenblatt, *Marvelous Possessions: The Wonder of the New World* (Chicago: University of Chicago Press, 1991), 71; Patricia Seed, *Ceremonies of Possession in Europe's Conquest of the New World, 1492–1640* (Cambridge: Cambridge University Press, 1995), 60–61.

10. D. Anthony Tyeeme Clark and Malea Powell, "'Resisting Exile in the Land of the Free': Indigenous Groundwork at Colonial Intersections," *American Indian Quarterly* 32 (Winter 2008): 1–15. There is a long and deep scholarship on how performance of Indianness by non-Indians shaped the evolution of American identity and culture, from theatrical stages and middle-class men's clubs to sports mascots and motion pictures. Performance of Indianness by American Indians in Europe has also received plenty of attention lately. When it comes to the study of Indians performing Indianness on this side of the Atlantic, however, far less has been written, with the exception of work on Wild West shows and world's fairs.

11. Corin C. O. Pursell, "Colored Monuments and Sensory Theater among the Mississippians," in *Making Senses of the Past: Toward a Sensory Archaeology*, ed. Jo Day (Carbondale: Southern Illinois University Press, 2013), 69–89; LeAnne Howe, "Embodied Tribalography—First Installment," in *Choctalking on Other Realities* (San Francisco: Aunt Lute Books, 2013), 173–95; LeAnne Howe, "The Story of Movement: Natives and Performance Culture," in *The Oxford Handbook of Indigenous American Literature*, ed. James H. Cox and Daniel Heath Justice (New York: Oxford University Press, 2014), 250–65.

12. Erin M. Greenwald, ed., *A Company Man: The Remarkable French-Atlantic Voyage of Marc Antoine Caillot* (New Orleans: The Historic New Orleans Collection, 2013), 112–13.

13. "Journal of d'Artaguiette," in *Travels in the American Colonies*, ed. Newton D. Mereness (New York: Macmillan, 1916), 29–39; James F. Barnett Jr., *The Natchez Indians: A History to 1735* (Jackson: University Press of Mississippi, 2007), 88–89; and George Edward Milne, *Natchez Country: Indians, Colonists, and the Landscapes of Race in French Louisiana* (Athens: University of Georgia Press, 2015), 104–5. For an outstanding analysis of how these early performances of Indian diplomacy shaped public life and culture in New Orleans during and after the colonial period, see Shane Lief, "Singing, Shaking, and Parading at the Birth of New Orleans," *Jazz Archivist* 28 (2015): 15–25.

14. Frank Norall, *Bourgmont, Explorer of the Missouri, 1698–1723* (Lincoln: University of Nebraska Press, 1988); Cuthbert Morton Girdlestone, *Jean-Philippe Rameau, His Life*

and Work (London: Cassell, 1957), 8–9, 320–49, quote from 344–46; Michael V. Pisani, *Imagining Native America in Music* (New Haven, CT: Yale University Press, 2005), 37–43.

15. "Journal of d'Artaguiette," 41–45.

16. Bienville, Memoire on Louisiana [1726], *Mississippi Provincial Archives: French Dominion*, 3:526–39; Marcel Giraud, *A History of French Louisiana. Volume Five: The Company of the Indies, 1723–1731,* trans. Brian Pearce (Baton Rouge: Louisiana State University Press, 1987), 316, 333; Greenwald, *A Company Man*, 83–84; Shannon Lee Dawdy, *Patina: A Profane Archaeology* (Chicago: University of Chicago Press, 2016), 89, 117–19.

17. David I. Bushnell Jr., "Drawings by A. DeBatz in Louisiana, 1732–1735," *Smithsonian Miscellaneous Collections* 80, no. 5 (Washington, DC: Smithsonian Institution, 1927): 1–15.

18. Charles R. Maduell Jr., comp. and ed., *The Census Tables for the French Colony of Louisiana from 1699 through 1732* (Baltimore: Genealogical Publishing, 1972), 88, 92–93; *Memoire of Lieutenant Dumont*, 208.

19. Among recent advances in early American history, the study of American Indian slavery has been significant. See, for some of the leading works, Alan Gallay, *The Indian Slave Trade: The Rise of the English Empire in the American South, 1670–1717* (New Haven: Yale University Press, 2002); Robbie Ethridge and Sheri M. Shuck-Hall, eds., *Mapping the Mississippian Shatter Zone: The Colonial Indian Slave Trade and Regional Instability in the American South* (Lincoln: University of Nebraska Press, 2009); Christina Snyder, *Slavery in Indian Country: The Changing Face of Captivity in Early America* (Cambridge, MA: Harvard University Press, 2010); Brett Rushforth, *Bonds of Alliance: Indigenous and Atlantic Slaveries in New France* (Chapel Hill: University of North Carolina Press, 2012); Margaret Ellen Newell, *Brethren by Nature: New England Indians, Colonists, and the Origins of American Slavery* (Ithaca, NY: Cornell University Press, 2015); and Andrés Reséndez, *The Other Slavery: The Uncovered Story of Indian Enslavement in America* (Boston: Houghton Mifflin Harcourt, 2016).

20. Maduell, *Census Tables*, 16–27, 50–76.

21. For the dispersal of Chitimacha slaves among colonial inhabitants, see Gregory A. Waselkov and Bonnie L. Gums, eds., *Plantation Archaeology at Rivière aux Chiens, ca. 1725–1848* (Mobile: University of South Alabama Center for Archaeological Studies, 2000), 35; James F. Barnett Jr., *The Natchez Indians: A History to 1735* (Jackson: University Press of Mississippi, 2007), 77; H. Sophie Burton and F. Todd Smith, *Colonial Natchitoches: A Creole Community on the Louisiana-Texas Frontier* (College Station: Texas A&M University Press, 2008), 30, 39–41, 55; Dayna Bowker Lee, "From Captives to Kin: Indian Slavery and Changing Social Identities on the Louisiana Colonial Frontier," in *Native American Adoption, Captivity, and Slavery in Changing Contexts*, ed. Max Carocci and Stephanie Pratt (New York: Palgrave, 2012), 79–96. For Indian contributions to the knowledge, circulation, and collection of plants, see Lake Douglas, *Public Spaces, Private Gardens: A History of Designed Landscapes in New Orleans* (Baton Rouge: Louisiana State University Press, 2011), 135–47; and Mary Louise Christovich and Roulhac Bunkley Toledano, *Garden Legacy* (New Orleans: The Historic New Orleans Collection, 2016), 50–53, 61–67.

22. Surgeon's Report, August 10 and 12, 1724, Slave Suit, August 14, 1724, "Records of the Superior Council," *Louisiana Historical Quarterly* 1 (January 1918): 242–43.

23. Jennifer M. Spear, *Race, Sex, and Social Order in Early New Orleans* (Baltimore: Johns Hopkins University Press, 2009), 40, 241n116.

24. The Crown vs. Jeanne Marie Negress, June 21, 1749, Superior Council Records, Louisiana Historical Center, Louisiana State Museum, New Orleans; Sale of a savagess of the Panis nation, July 27, 1743, "Records of the Superior Council," *Louisiana Historical Quarterly* 11 (October 1928): 644; Sale of a savagess to the Ursuline nuns, February 27, 1744, "Records of the Superior Council," *Louisiana Historical Quarterly* 12 (October 1929): 667; Auction sale of a savage woman, August 17, 1746, "Records of the Superior Council," *Louisiana Historical Quarterly* 14 (July 1931): 458. For information about d'Orgon's military career, see *Mississippi Provincial Archives: French Dominion,* 4:181.

25. Cattle plunder reported, May 24, 1723, "Records of the Superior Council," *Louisiana Historical Quarterly* 1 (January 1917): 109; Criminal procedure against Sansoucy, March 31, 1727, Motion to try runaway Indians, April 9, 1727, "Records of the Superior Council," *Louisiana Historical Quarterly* 3 (July 1920): 443–44.

26. "Report on Louisiana," n.d. [ca. 1750], Louisiana Miscellany Collection, Library of Congress, Manuscripts, f. 1493, quoted in Samuel Wilson, *The Vieux Carré, New Orleans: Its Plan, Its Growth, Its Architecture* (New Orleans: Marcou O'Leary and Associates, 1968), 37. For coverage of similar interaction in other colonial towns, see Billy G. Smith, *The "Lower Sort": Philadelphia's Laboring People, 1750–1800* (Ithaca, NY: Cornell University Press, 1990), 21–26; Joyce D. Goodfriend, *Before the Melting Pot: Society and Culture in Colonial New York City, 1664–1730* (Princeton, NJ: Princeton University Press, 1992), 114–15, 121, 126–27; Clare A. Lyons, *Sex among the Rabble: An Intimate History of Gender and Power in the Age of Revolution, Philadelphia, 1730–1830* (Chapel Hill: University of North Carolina Press, 2006), 193–95; Margaret Ellen Newell, *Brethren by Nature: New England Indians, Colonists, and the Origins of American Slavery* (Ithaca, NY: Cornell University Press, 2015), 60–130.

27. Daniel H. Usner, "Indian-Black Relations in Colonial and Antebellum Louisiana," in *Slave Cultures and the Cultures of Slavery,* ed. Stephan Palmié (Knoxville: University of Tennessee Press, 1995), 145–61.

28. Attorney General on desertions, August 17, 1726, "Records of the Superior Council," *Louisiana Historical Quarterly* 3 (July 1920): 414; Criminal Trial of Guillory, Bontemps, and Jean Baptiste, June 4–14, 1728, "Records of the Superior Council," *Louisiana Historical Quarterly* 4 (October 1921): 489; Shannon Lee Dawdy, *Building the Devil's Empire: French Colonial New Orleans* (Chicago: University of Chicago Press, 2008), 189–94. Dawdy suggests, in a footnote, that Bontemps was hanged and that Guillory was flogged or beaten in prison. The fate of the third captured runaway is not known.

29. Petition to Recover a Runaway Slave, November 13, 1730, Superior Council Records.

30. M. R. Ailenroc, *The White Castle of Louisiana* (Louisville, KY: John P. Morton & Co., 1903), 37–50, quotes from 42–43, 48. The author of this reminiscence was Cornelia Randolph Murrell (1851–1931), daughter of John Hampden Randolph. According to her account, Juda was not found at the camp but was eventually captured. He joined the Union army as soon as it occupied the area.

31. *Memoire of Lieutenant Dumont,* 232–33, 238–39, 250.

32. Ory to Perier, November 1, 1730, *MPAFD*, 4:46–47; Daniel H. Usner, *Indians, Settlers, and Slaves in a Frontier Exchange Economy: The Lower Mississippi Valley before 1783* (Chapel Hill: University of North Carolina Press, 1992), 18–20, 65, 72–74, 77–79.

33. Father [Mathurin] le Petit, Missionary to Father d'Avaugour, Procurator of the Missions in North America, at New Orleans, July 12, 1730, *Jesuit Relations and Allied Documents: Travels and Explorations of the Jesuit Missionaries in New France, 1610–1791*, ed. Reuben Gold Thwaites, 68:201–3 (Cleveland: Barrows Brothers Co., 1900); Robert Michael Morrissey, *Empire by Collaboration: Indians, Colonists, and Governments in Colonial Illinois Country* (Philadelphia: University of Pennsylvania Press, 2015), 110–38.

34. *Jesuit Relations*, 68:209–11. For an outstanding study of Roman Catholicism as practiced by American Indians in French North America, see Tracy Neal Leavelle, *The Catholic Calumet: Colonial Conversions in French and Indian North America* (Philadelphia: University of Pennsylvania Press, 2012).

35. Diron d'Artaguette to Maurepas, June 24, 1731, Jadart de Beauchamp to Maurepas, November 5, 1731, *Mississippi Provincial Archives: French Dominion*, 4:77, 79; Greenwald, *A Company Man*, 146–48, and plate 6. For a detailed and deep analysis of this episode, see Sophie White, "Massacre, Mardi Gras, and Torture in Early New Orleans," *William and Mary Quarterly* 3d ser., 70 (July 1013): 497–538, esp. 518–34. Also see Milne, *Natchez Country*, 198–99.

36. Bienville to Maurepas, January 28, 1733, *Mississippi Provincial Archives: French Dominion*, 3:581. The exportation of enslaved Natchez people and traces of their survival are closely examined in Edward Noel Smyth, "The Natchez Diaspora: A History of Indigenous Displacement and Survival in the Atlantic World" (PhD diss., University of California, Santa Cruz, 2016), 54–80. For coverage of the enslavement of American Indians in upper Louisiana, see Carl J. Ekberg, *Stealing Indian Women: Native Slavery in the Illinois Country* (Urbana: University of Illinois Press, 2007); Rushforth, *Bonds of Alliance*; and Morrissey, *Empire by Collaboration*.

37. King Louis XV to Bienville, February 2, 1732, Beauchamp to Maurepas, November 5, 1731, *Mississippi Provincial Archives: French Dominion*, 3:556, 4:81–82.

38. *Memoire of Lieutenant Dumont*, 232–33, 238–39, 250; Philibert Ory to Périer, ca. November 1, 1730, Jadart de Beauchamp to Maurepas, November 5, 1731, Vaudreuil to Rouillé, June 24, 1750, *Mississippi Provincial Archives: French Dominion*, 4:46–47, 81–82, 5:49; Interrogation of François and Joseph, May 18–26, 1748, "Records of the Superior Council," *Louisiana Historical Quarterly* 19 (July 1936): 769–71.

39. Shannon Lee Dawdy and Christopher N. Matthews, "Colonial and Early Antebellum New Orleans," in *Archaeology of Louisiana*, ed. Mark A. Rees (Baton Rouge: Louisiana State University Press, 2010), 273–305; Investigation of a theft committed at Sr. Delaunay's, "Records of the Superior Council," *Louisiana Historical Quarterly* 12 (October 1929): 651–52.

40. Cyrus Byington, *A Dictionary of the Choctaw Language*, ed. John R. Swanton and Henry S. Halbert (Washington, DC: US Government Printing Office, 1915), 87, 506; James H. Howard and Victoria Lindsay Levine, *Choctaw Music and Dance* (Norman: University of Oklahoma Press, 1990), 24–27; Kenneth Blanchard, *The Mississippi Choctaws at Play: The Serious Side of Leisure* (Urbana: University of Illinois Press, 1981), 35–36.

41. Usner, *Indians, Settlers, and Slaves in a Frontier Exchange Economy*, 244–75; Alexandre Dubé, "Tisser les liens de l'alliance: réseaux commerciaux et étatiques franco-amérindiens en Louisiane," in *Interculturalité: La Louisiane au Carrefour des Cultures*, ed. Nathalie Dessens and Jean-Pierre Le Glaunec (Québec, Canada: Presses de l'Université Laval, 2016), 65–92; Dubé, "The Seller King: Revisiting Control and Authority in French Louisiana," in *European Empires in the American South: Colonial and Environmental Encounters*, ed. Joseph P. Ward (Jackson: University Press of Mississippi, 2017), 87–121.

42. AC, C13A, 25:226, 35:39–52; AC, C13A, 35:322, translated and published in Charles Gayarré, *History of Louisiana*, 3d ed., 4 vols. (New Orleans: A. Hawkins, 1885), 2:361–63.

43. Memoir on Indians by Kerlérec, December 12, 1758, *Mississippi Provincial Archives: French Dominion*, 5:212–13.

44. R. E. Chandler, "Life in New Orleans in 1798," *Revue de Louisiane/Louisiana Review* 6 (Winter 1977): 183–84; François-Xavier Martin, *A General Digest of the Acts of the Legislatures of the Late Territory of Orleans and of the State of Louisiana, and the Ordinances of the Governor under the Territorial Government*, 3 vols. (New Orleans: Peter K. Wagner 1816), 2:438. See Peter C. Mancall, *Deadly Medicine: Indians and Alcohol in Early America* (Ithaca, NY: Cornell University Press, 1995), for a careful study of alcohol's impact on Indigenous societies during the colonial period.

2. BORDERLAND

1. *A Comparative View of French Louisiana, 1699 and 1762: The Journals of Pierre Le Moyne d'Iberville and Jean-Jacques-Blaise d'Abbadie*, trans. and ed. Carl A. Brasseaux (Lafayette: University of Southwestern Louisiana Press, 1979), 122–24. This Tunica delegation departed New Orleans only three days short of witnessing a very different public spectacle—the gruesome execution of a slave named César in the city's public square. For running away from a Chapitoulas plantation owned by Joseph Zerangue and firing upon militiamen in pursuit of him, César "was condemned by decree of the Council to make honorable amends before the church door, to have his hand amputated, and then to be broken on the wheel; his corpse was to be exhibited on the highway along the bayou." For understanding the full context of Tunica diplomacy, see Elizabeth Ellis, "Petite Nation with Powerful Networks: The Tunicas in the Eighteenth Century," *Louisiana History* 58 (Spring 2017): 133–78.

2. Kerlérec to Rouillé, March 8, 1753, Kerlérec to Peirèiine de Moras, May 13, 1757, *MPAFD*, 5:122, 183.

3. *The Adams-Jefferson Letters: The Complete Correspondence Between Thomas Jefferson and Abigail and John Adams*, ed. Lester J. Cappon, 2 vols. (Chapel Hill: University of North Carolina Press, 1959), 2:307–8; John Galt, *The Life, Studies and Works of Benjamin West, Esq., President of the Royal Academy* (London: T. Cadell and W. Davies, 1820), 18.

4. *Comparative View*, 96, 100–2, 111, 114.

5. *Comparative View*, 113–14; Robin F. A. Fabel, *Colonial Challenges: Britons, Native Americans, and Caribs, 1759–1775* (Gainesville: University Press of Florida, 2000), 95–96.

6. *Comparative View*, 116, 118–19.

7. *Comparative View*, 121–22.

8. *Comparative View*, 127, 135–37. For comprehensive information about d'Abbadie's life and career, including evidence of his knowing about his government's cession of Louisiana to Spain before he left France, see Donald E. Pusch, "Jean-Jacques-Blaise d'Abbadie, Director General of Louisiana, 1763–1765," *Louisiana History* 58 (Summer 2017): 263–99.

9. *Comparative View*, 137–38.

10. Journal of the Commons House, Mon., March 19, 1770, *The Minutes, Journals, and Acts of the General Assembly of British West Florida*, comp. Robert R. Rea with Milo B. Howard Jr. (University: University of Alabama Press, 1979), 230.

11. Pierre Juzan to Gálvez, July 11, 1780, *Spain in the Mississippi Valley, 1765–1794*, trans. and ed. Lawrence Kinnaird, 3 vols. (Washington, DC: US Government Printing Office, 1946–1949), 2:382–83.

12. Alejandro O'Reilly to Arriaga, October 17, 1769, *Spain in the Mississippi Valley*, 1:101–2, 154–55.

13. Bernardo de Gálvez to José de Gálvez, October 16, 1779, Confidential Despatches of Don Bernardo de Gálvez, Fourth Spanish Governor of Louisiana, Sent to his Uncle Don José de Gálvez, Secretary of State and Ranking Official of the Council of the Indies [from National Archives of Cuba], Translated from Spanish transcriptions in Tulane University's Howard Memorial Library by Adolph Baum, Survey of Federal Archives in Louisiana, Louisiana and Lower Mississippi Valley Collections, Hill Memorial Library, Louisiana State University, Baton Rouge; Kathleen DuVal, *Independence Lost: Lives on the Edge of the American Revolution* (New York: Random House, 2015), 161–64; Frances Bailey Kolb, "Contesting Borderlands: Policy and Practice in Spanish Louisiana, 1765–1803" (PhD diss., Vanderbilt University, 2014), 207–10, 240–42.

14. Memorandum of merchandise, which is needed at the warehouses of New Orleans, to entertain the friendship of the Indians and furnish the traders, who are sent to trade with them. New Orleans, October 16th, 1779, Confidential Despatches.

15. W. Adolphe Roberts, *Lake Pontchartrain* (Indianapolis: Bobbs-Merrill, 1946), 98; John Caughey, *Bernardo de Gálvez in Louisiana, 1776–1783* (Berkeley: University of California Press, 1934), 160.

16. Gálvez to Gálvez, New Orleans, June 5, 1780, Confidential Despatches of Don Bernardo de Gálvez. Also see DuVal, *Independence Lost*, 161–64.

17. Agreement made for the purchase of three hundred eighty thousand pesos of merchandise for gifts and commerce with the Indians. March 18th, 1782, Despatches of Don Bernardo de Gálvez; Joseph de Gálvez to Bernardo de Gálvez, San Lorenzo, October 30, 1782, Confidential Despatches of Don Bernardo de Gálvez. For more detailed information about Maxent's military service and business career, see James J. Coleman Jr., *Gilbert Antoine de St. Maxent: The Spanish-Frenchman of New Orleans* (Gretna, LA: Pelican Publishing House, 1968); John G. Clark, *New Orleans, 1718–1812: An Economic History* (Baton Rouge: Louisiana State University Press, 1970), 173–74, 183, 196–97, 225; Thomas D. Watson, "A Scheme Gone Awry: Bernardo de Gálvez, Antonio de Maxent, and the Southern Indian Trade," *Louisiana History* 17 (Winter 1976): 5–17; and Pusch, "Jean-Jacques-Blaise d'Abbadie," 294–95.

18. Antonio Maxent to Francisco Bouligny, September 24, 1782, *Spain in the Mississippi Valley*, 2:59.

19. Antonio Maxent to Esteban Miró, December 5, 1782, *Spain in the Mississippi Valley*, 2:67–68.

20. Marios de Villiers to Esteban Miró, August 30, 1787, *Spain in the Mississippi Valley*, 2:233–34.

21. Inhabitants of Pascagoula to Carondelet, June 15, 1792, *Spain in the Mississippi Valley*, 3:53–54.

22. Frederick S. Ellis, *St. Tammany Parish: L'Autre Côte du Lac* (Gretna, LA: Pelican Publishing, 1981), 58–60.

23. William Panton to Carondelet, Pensacola, April 16, 1792, *Georgia Historical Quarterly* 22 (December 1938): 393; John Forbes to Carondelet, Mobile, October 31, 1792, *East Tennessee Historical Society Papers* 28 (1956): 131. For information about Turnbull, see John Caughey, *McGillivray of the Creeks* (Norman: University of Oklahoma Press, 1938), 85–86; and Christopher Morris, *Becoming Southern: The Evolution of a Way of Life, Warren County and Vicksburg, Mississippi, 1770–1860* (New York: Oxford University Press, 1995), 14–15.

24. Carondelet to the Conde de Maranda, New Orleans, October 1, 1792, *East Tennessee Historical Society Papers* 28 (1956): 130; Panton to Carondelet, Pensacola, November 6, 1792, *East Tennessee Historical Society Papers* 28 (1956): 132–33; Carondelet to Panton, New Orleans, November 21, 1792, Panton, Leslie & Co. Papers, University Archives and West Florida History Center, University of West Florida, Pensacola; Panton to Carondelet, Pensacola, January 1, 1793, *Georgia Historical Quarterly* 23 (June 1939): 198–99; Villebeuvre to Carondelet, Boukfouca, February 7, 1793, *East Tennessee Historical Society Papers* 29 (1957): 152.

25. Henry P. Dart, "A Savage Law of the French Regime in Louisiana," *Louisiana Historical Quarterly* 15 (July 1932): 482–85. Two decades after the death of his Indian slave Jean Baptiste, Robert Antoine Robin de Lorgny, one of the region's wealthiest indigo planters, would contract with a free man of color named Charles Pacquet to build upriver from New Orleans a new plantation house. This became the Destrehan Plantation, one of the oldest and most visited plantation houses in Louisiana. When Robin de Lorgny died in 1792, he owned about sixty slaves at Destrehan.

26. Proclamation by O'Reilly, December 7, 1769, *Spain in the Mississippi Valley*, 1:125–26; Stephen Webre, "The Problem of Indian Slavery in Spanish Louisiana, 1769–1803," *Louisiana History* 25 (Spring 1984): 117–35. Also see Dayna Bowker Lee, "Indian Slavery in Lower Louisiana during the Colonial Period, 1699–1803," MA thesis, Northwestern State University, 1989.

27. *Ulzere et al. v. Poeyfarre* (Eastern District, May Term, 1820), Louisiana Supreme Court Records, UNO; François-Xavier Martin, *Louisiana Term Reports or Cases Argued and Determined in the Supreme Court of the State of Louisiana* (New-Orleans: Roche Brothers, 1820; Annotated Edition, St. Paul: West Publishing Co., 1913), 6:156–60; Webre, "Problem of Indian Slavery in Spanish Louisiana," 130–31.

28. Daniel H. Usner, *Indians, Settlers, and Slaves in a Frontier Exchange Economy: The Lower Mississippi Valley before 1783* (Chapel Hill: University of North Carolina Press, 192), 105–44.

29. Charles Stuart, List of the Several Tribes of Indians inhabiting the banks of the Mississippi, Between New Orleans and Red River, with their number of gun men & places of residence, January 1, 1773, Haldimand Papers, British Museum; Thomas Hutchins, *An Historical Narrative and Topographical Description of Louisiana and West Florida*, facsimile reproduction of the 1784 edition (Gainesville: University Press of Florida, 1968), 39–45.

30. Sargent to Pickering, March 1, 1800, *The Mississippi Territorial Archives, 1798–1803: Executive Journals of Governor Winthrop Sargent and Governor William Charles Cole Claiborne*, ed. Dunbar Rowland (Nashville, 1905), 210–12; Pierre Clément de Laussat, *Memoirs of My Life to My Son During the Years 1803 and After . . .*, trans. Sr. Agnes-Josephine Pastwa and ed. Robert D. Bush (Baton Rouge: Louisiana State University Press, 1978), 39.

3. BACK-OF-TOWN ACTION

1. Mathé Allain, ed., *The Festival of the Young Corn; or, The Heroism of Poucha-Houmma by LeBlanc de Villeneuvfre* (Lafayette: Center for Louisiana Studies, 1964), i–vii.

2. *Festival of the Young Corn*, vii–xix.

3. *Festival of the Young Corn*, 2–4, 7.

4. Dunbar Rowland, ed., *Official Letter Books of W. C. C. Claiborne, 1801–1816*, 6 vols. (Jackson, MS: State Department of Archives and History, 1917), 4:356; *Festival of the Young Corn*, xviii–xx.

5. *Official Letter Books of W. C. C. Claiborne*, 3:347, 4:223–24.

6. Corinne L. Saucier, *The History of Avoyelles Parish, Louisiana* (New Orleans: Pelican Publishing, 1943), 522; Mattie Austin Hatcher, "The Louisiana Background of the Colonization of Texas, 1763–1803," *Southwestern Historical Quarterly* 24 (January 1921): 187; Grant Foreman, *Indians and Pioneers: The Story of the American Southwest before 1830* (New Haven, CT: Yale University Press, 1930), 30; *American State Papers: Public Lands* (Washington: Duff Green, 1834), 3:232.

7. David Andrew Nichols, *Engines of Diplomacy: Indian Trading Factories and the Negotiation of American Empire* (Chapel Hill: University of North Carolina Press, 2016), 50, 65, 76, 79, 87, 97, 134.

8. Arsène LaCarrière Latour, *Historical Memoir of the War in West Florida and Louisiana in 1814–15*, ed. Gene A. Smith (New Orleans and Gainesville: The Historic New Orleans Collection and University Press of Florida, 1999), Appendix No. 18–1: Copies of letters from the secretary of war to general Jackson, 209–10.

9. Jane Lucas de Grummond, *The Baratarians and the Battle of New Orleans* (Baton Rouge: Louisiana State University Press, 1961), 55, 84–89, 106–13; Greg O'Brien, "Choctaw recruits fight with the U.S. Army," National Park Service Jean Lafitte National Historical Park and Preserve, accessed June 19, 2017, https://www.nps.gov/articles/choctaw-indians-and-the-battle-of-new-orleans.htm.

10. *A Comparative View of French Louisiana, 1699 and 1762: The Journals of Pierre Le Moyne d'Iberville and Jean-Jacques-Blaise d'Abbadie*, trans. and ed. Carl A. Brasseaux (Lafayette: University of Southwestern Louisiana Press, 1979), 116; Guy Soniat du Fossat, *Synopsis of*

the *History of Louisiana, From the Founding of the Colony to the End of the Year 1791*, trans. Charles T. Soniat (New Orleans: Louisiana Historical Society, 1903), 35; Pierre Clément de Laussat, *Memoirs of My Life to My Son During the Years 1803 and After . . .,* trans. Sr. Agnes-Josephine Pastwa and ed. Robert D. Bush (Baton Rouge: Louisiana State University Press, 1978), 53–54.

11. For descriptions of Choctaw stickball in colonial accounts, see "Relation de la Louisiane, c. 1755," an anonymous manuscript in the Newberry Library's Ayer Collection and partly translated in John R. Swanton, *Source Material for the Social and Ceremonial Life of the Choctaw Indians, Smithsonian Institution Bureau of American Ethnology Bulletin* 43 (Washington, DC: US Government Printing Office, 1911): 140; Jean Bernard Bossu, *Nouveaux Voyages aux Indes occidentales*, 2 vols. (Paris: Chez Le Jay, 1768), 2:100–3; and Bernard Romans, *A Concise Natural History of East and West Florida* (New York: R. Aitken, 1776), 79.

12. Swanton, *Source Material for the Social and Ceremonial Life of the Choctaw Indians,* 152–55.

13. Donna L. Akers, *Culture and Customs of the Choctaw Indians* (Santa Barbara, CA: Greenwood, 2013), 133–40, uses *ishtaboli* as the Choctaw word for the stickball game and explains it as "Little Brother of War"—played to settle conflict and avoid war. Marcia Haag and Henry Willis, *Choctaw Language and Culture: Chahta Anumpa* (Norman: University of Oklahoma Press, 2001), 338, 368, uses *kapucha* for the game and *ishtaboli* for the playing field. Anthony Michael Krus, "Bridging History and Prehistory: The Possible Antiquity of a Native American Ballgame," *Native South* 4 (2011): 136–45, traces this game to the Mississippian period through historical records dating to the 1560s. For insight into the record of stickball among Mississippi Choctaws from colonial times to the present, see James F. Barnett Jr., "Ferocity and Finesse: American Indian Sports in Mississippi," *Southern Quarterly* 51 (Summer 2014): 9–19; Tammy Greer and Harold Comby, "Photo Essay: Stickball Fever," *Southern Quarterly* 51 (Summer 2014): 21–27. Charles Lesueur was a French naturalist and artist who traveled down the Mississippi River to New Orleans several times during the 1820s and 1830s. Among his rough sketches of American Indians capturing features of their itinerant presence in and around Mississippi River towns, his *Jeu de Peaume indian à la Nelle Orleans* depicts a stickball game being played at New Orleans. See Daniel H. Usner, *American Indians in the Lower Mississippi Valley: Social and Economic Histories* (Lincoln: University of Nebraska Press, 1998), p. 28 and plate 4.

14. "Report on Louisiana," n.d. [ca. 1750], Louisiana Miscellany Collection, Library of Congress, Manuscripts, f. 1493, quoted in Samuel Wilson, *The Vieux Carré, New Orleans: Its Plan, Its Growth, Its Architecture* (New Orleans: Marcou O'Leary and Associates, 1968), 37.

15. "The Choctaws of Louisiana: Father Rouquette and His Wards in St. Tammany," *New Orleans Daily Picayune*, September 22, 1882, series 2, box 2, Adrien Emmanuel Rouquette Papers, 1842–1942, Louisiana Research Collection, Howard-Tilton Memorial Library, Tulane University, New Orleans.

16. Fortescue Cuming, *Sketches of a Tour through the Western Country, through the States of Ohio and Kentucky: A Voyage down the Ohio and Mississippi Rivers, and a Trip through the Mississippi, and Part of Western Florida* (originally published Pittsburgh: Cramer, Spear &

Eichbaum, 1810); *Early Western Travels, 1748–1846,* ed. Reuben Gold Thwaites, Volume 4: *Cuming's Tour to the Western Country (1807–1809)* (Cleveland: Arthur H. Clark Co., 1904), 365–66; Berquin-Duvallon, *Travels in Louisiana and the Floridas in the Year, 1802, Giving a Correct Picture of those Countries,* trans. John Davis (New York: J. Riley & Co., 1806), 96–99; Paul Alliot, "Historical and Political Reflections on Louisiana, July 1, 1803–April 13, 1804," *Louisiana Under the Rule of Spain, France, and the United States, 1785–1807: Social, Economic, and Political Conditions of the Territory Represented in the Louisiana Purchase,* ed. James Alexander Robertson, 2 vols. (Cleveland: Arthur Clark, 1911), 1:81–83; Christian Schultz Jr., *Travels on an Inland Voyage through the States of New York, Pennsylvania, Virginia, Ohio, Kentucky and Tennessee, and through the Territories of Indiana, Louisiana, Mississippi and New-Orleans; Performed in the Years 1807 and 1808; Including a Tour of Nearly Six Thousand Miles,* 2 vols. (New York: Isaac Riley, 1810), 2:198.

17. Mather's report to the City Council, dated June 3, 1807, was quoted in Isadore Dyer's "Endemic Leprosy in Louisiana," originally published in the *Philadelphia Medical Journal* 2:12 (May 26, 1898) and reprinted in the *New Orleans Daily Picayune,* September 29, 1898, in an article entitled "A Leprosy Study for Louisiana." Dyer was a professor of skin disease in New Orleans and president of the state's leper board. His paper included information about the leper hospital that had been established in 1785 on Metairie Ridge in the rear of New Orleans and occupied until 1807. Additional information from Clare D'Artois Leeper, *Louisiana Place Names: Popular, Unusual, and Forgotten Stories of Towns, Cities, Plantations, Bayous, and Even Some Cemeteries* (Baton Rouge: Louisiana State University Press, 2012), 148.

18. *New Orleans Times,* June 6, 1867; Henry Castellanos, *New Orleans as It Was: Episodes of Louisiana Life,* Facsimile of 1895 Edition with an Introduction by Judith Kelleher Schafer (Baton Rouge: Louisiana State University Press, 2006), 339.

19. John Adams Paxton, *New Orleans Directory and Register: Containing the Names, Professions, & Residences, of all the Heads of Families, and Persons in Business, of the City and Suburbs; Notes on New-Orleans; with Other Useful Information* (New Orleans: Benjamin Levy & Co., 1822), 37. For more about the significance of the Carondelet Canal and Basin for back-of-town interaction, see Daniel H. Usner, "Colonial Projects and Frontier Practices: The First Century of New Orleans History," in *Frontier Cities: Encounters at the Crossroads of Empire,* ed. Jay Gitlin, Barbara Berglund, and Adam Arenson (Philadelphia: University of Pennsylvania Press, 2013), 27–45. The African influence on and African American presence at these social gatherings are more closely explored in Freddi Williams Evans, *Congo Square: African Roots in New Orleans* (Lafayette: University of Louisiana at Lafayette Press, 2011).

20. David C. Hunt and Marsha V. Gallagher, eds., *Karl Bodmer's America* (Lincoln: University of Nebraska Press, 1984), 109, 111–12, 119–20.

21. Georges J. Joyaux, ed., "Forest's *Voyage aux Etats-Unis de l'Amérique en 1831,*" *Louisiana Historical Quarterly* 39 (October 1956): 468–69.

22. *New Orleans Daily Picayune,* December 4, 10, 12, 17, 18, 24, 26, 27, 30, 1850.

23. Friedrich Wilhelm von Wrede, *Sketches of Life in the United States of North America and Texas,* trans. and ed. Chester W. Geue (Waco, TX: Texian Press, 1970), 59.

24. "The Choctaws of Louisiana."

25. *Official Letter Books of W. C. C. Claiborne*, 3: 50–51, 4:145–46; Proceedings of Council Meetings, vol. 2, no. 1, p. 263.

26. Castellanos, *New Orleans as It Was*, 221, 222.

27. Edouard de Montulé, *Travels in America, 1816–1817*, trans. Edward D. Seeber (Bloomington: Indiana University Press, 1950), 84–85; Louis Moreau-Lislet, comp., *A General Digest of the Acts of the Legislature of Louisiana: Passed from the Year 1804, to 1827, Inclusive, and In Force at This Last Period, with An Appendix and General Index*, 2 vols. (New Orleans: B. Levy, 1828), 1:128–29.

28. Benjamin Henry Boneval Latrobe, *Impressions Respecting New Orleans: Diary and Sketches 1818–1820*, ed. Samuel Wilson Jr. (New York: Columbia University Press, 1951), 75–76. Captain Walsh was probably Antonio Patrick Walsh, a native of Dublin, Ireland, who served in the Spanish military and Louisiana colonial militia, became a shipping merchant, and owned a cotton plantation in West Feliciana Parish. See Walsh (Antonio Patrick) Papers (Mss. 887, 1208), Louisiana and Lower Mississippi Valley Collections, Hill Memorial Library, Louisiana State University, Baton Rouge.

29. Gordon M. Sayre, *The Indian Chief as Tragic Hero: Native Resistance and the Literatures of America, From Moctezuma to Tecumseh* (Chapel Hill: University of North Carolina Press, 2005); Daniel H. Usner, *Indian Work: Language and Livelihood in Native American History* (Cambridge, MA: Harvard University Press, 2009), 59–67; Jean M. O'Brien, *Firsting and Lasting: Writing Indians Out of Existence in New England* (Minneapolis: University of Minnesota Press, 2010); Miles A. Powell, *Vanishing America: Species Extinction, Racial Peril, and the Origins of Conservation* (Cambridge, MA: Harvard University Press, 2016), 119–24. For a sample of "last Indian" stories contemporaneous with Choctaw execution narratives in and around New Orleans, see A. M., "The Last of the Lenni Lenape," *New-Yorker*, June 10, 1837; Poems: Anonymous, "Pe-Wa-Tem: Or the Last Chief Huron," *New-Yorker* 7, no. 2 (1839), 17; S. Compton Smith, "The Last of his Tribe," *The Rural Repository Devoted to Polite Literature*, October 12, 1839; "The Last of the Mohegans Gone," *Niles' National Register*, December 31, 1842; Mary Hartman, "The Last of His Tribe," *Monthly Literary Miscellany*, October 1852; "The Last of the Pequods," *Scribner's Monthly*, October 1871.

30. Castellanos, *New Orleans as It Was*, 222–24.

31. *New Orleans Picayune*, Thursday, April 6, 1837.

32. John C. Calhoun to James Monroe, January 24, 1825, *American State Papers. Documents, Legislative and Executive, of the Congress of the United States: Indian Affairs* (Washington, DC: Gales and Seaton, 1834), 2:542. Herring is quoted in Wilcomb Washburn, ed., *The American Indian and the United States: A Documentary History*, 4 vols. (New York: Random House, 1973), 1:18.

33. William Rounseville Alger, *Life of Edwin Forrest, the American Tragedian*, 2 vols. (1877; repr., New York: Benjamin Blom, 1972), 1:113–39, 237–49, quotes from 126, 128, 138; Jill Lepore, *The Name of War: King Philip's War and the Origins of American Identity* (New York: Alfred A. Knopf, 1998), 201–15; Matthew Rebhorn, "Edwin Forrest's Redding Up: Elocution, Theater, and the Performance of the Frontier," *Comparative Drama* 40 (Winter 2006–2007): 455–81.

34. Louis Moreau Gottschalk, *Notes of a Pianist*, ed. Jeanne Behrend (New York: Alfred A. Knopf, 1964), 291–92.

35. This strategy of forging personal relationships with local non-Indians through seasonal exchange and work is closely studied in Erik M. Redix, *The Murder of Joe White: Ojibwe Leadership and Colonialism in Wisconsin* (East Lansing: Michigan State University Press, 2014), 65–99. Also see William J. Bauer Jr., *We Were All Like Migrant Workers Here: Work, Community, and Memory on California's Round Valley Reservation, 1850–1941* (Chapel Hill: University of North Carolina Press, 2009); and Dawn G. Marsh, *A Lenape among the Quakers: The Life of Hannah Freeman* (Lincoln: University of Nebraska Press, 2014).

36. Laussat, *Memoirs of My Life*, 68, 124; Claiborne to Judge Cantrelle, June 14, 1811, *Official Letter Books*, 5:275; Claiborne to William Eustis, N.O., 3 August 1811, *Official Letter Books*, 5:322–23.

37. Howard Corning, ed., *Journal of John James Audubon Made During His Trip to New Orleans in 1820–1821* (Boston: The Club of Odd Volumes, 1929), 170.

38. Deiler, *Settlement of German Coast*, 62; Meloncy C. Soniat, "The Tchoupitoulas Plantation," *Louisiana Historical Quarterly* 7 (April 1924): 309–10.

39. James Morris Morgan, *Recollections of a Rebel Reefer* (Boston and New York: Houghton Mifflin, 1917), 3.

40. Berquin-Duvallon, *Travels in Louisiana and the Floridas in the Year, 1802*, 103. For insightful discussion of representations of American Indian women, see Rayna Green, "The Pocahontas Perplex: The Image of Indian Women in American Culture," *Massachusetts Review* 16 (Autumn 1975): 698–714.

41. Daniel H. Usner, "Frontier Exchange and Cotton Production: The Slave Economy in Mississippi, 1798–1836," in *From Slavery to Emancipation in the Atlantic World*, ed. Sylvia R. Frey and Betty Wood (London: Frank Cass, 1999), 24–37; Usner, "'The Facility Offered by the Country': The Creolization of Agriculture in the Lower Mississippi Valley," *Creolization in the Americas*, ed. David Buisseret and Steven G. Rehnhardt (College Station: Texas A&M University Press, 2000), 35–62.

42. John Francis McDermott, ed., *Tixier's Travels on the Osage Prairies*, trans. Albert J. Salvan (Norman: University of Oklahoma Press, 1940), 55–59, 69, 81–83. After spending summer months in the lower Missouri Valley, Victor Tixier (1815–1885) returned to France toward the end of 1840. Four years later he published *Voyage aux Prairies Osages, Louisiane et Missouri, 1839–40*, best known for its details about Osage life and culture. Tixier resumed his medical studies and practiced medicine in the village of Saint Pont. He also pursued and published research in philology and archaeology.

43. François Dominique Rouquette, "The Choctaws," translation by Olivia Blanchard from original transcript, 11–12, 50, François Dominique Rouquette Papers, Louisiana Research Collection, Howard-Tilton Memorial Library, Tulane University, New Orleans.

44. Lady Emmeline Stuart-Wortley, *Travels in the United States, Etc. During 1849 and 1850* (New York: Harper & Brothers, 1851), 130–31; Victoria Welby-Gregory, *A Young Traveller's Journal of a Tour in North and South America During the Year 1850* (London: T. Bosworth, 1852), 133–34.

45. For analysis of comparable performance antics among another Indian group, see Thomas Vennum, "The Ojibwe Begging Dance," in *Music and Context: Essays for John M. Ward*, ed. Anne Dhu Shapiro (Cambridge, MA: Harvard University Department of Music, 1985), 54–78.

46. *New Orleans Daily Picayune*, December 16, 1837, April 2, 1839.

47. *New Orleans Daily Picayune*, May 17, 1839.

48. *New Orleans Daily Picayune* April 3, 1844, January 26, 1845.

49. Castellanos, *New Orleans as It Was*, 328–29.

50. *New Orleans Daily Picayune*, January 3, August 11, 1839.

51. *New Orleans Daily Picayune*, August 29, 1838.

52. *New Orleans Daily Picayune*, April 9, 1842.

53. Jean Boze (1753–1839) to Jean-François Henri de Sainte-Gême, New Orleans, May 1830, quoted in Nathalie Dessens, *Creole City: A Chronicle of Early American New Orleans* (Gainesville: University Press of Florida, 2015), 166–67; Samuel Wilson, ed., *Southern Travels: Journal of John H. B. Latrobe, 1834* (New Orleans: Historic New Orleans Collection, 1986), 41.

54. George Washington Cable, "The Dance in Place Congo," *The Century Magazine* 31 (February 1886), 518–19; Rouquette, "The Choctaws," 53–54. For analysis of what this game meant to both black players and white spectators, see Rashauna Johnson, *Slavery's Metropolis: Unfree Labor in New Orleans during the Age of Revolutions* (New York: Cambridge University Press, 2016), 112–17.

55. "Rare Sport at the Union Race Course," *New Orleans Times-Democrat*, April 25, 1853.

56. "Raquette," *New-Orleans Commercial Bulletin*, April 13, 1868.

57. Rouquette, "The Choctaws," 51–53. Dale A. Somers, in *The Rise of Sports in New Orleans, 1850–1900* (Baton Rouge: Louisiana State University Press, 1972), was the first professional historian to explore the importance of American Indian stickball in the city's history. Historians of Indian lacrosse, however, have ignored the sport's long-lasting presence in New Orleans. See, for example, Thomas Vennum Jr., *American Indian Lacrosse: Little Brother of War* (Washington, DC: Smithsonian Institution Press, 1994).

58. "Indian Ball Play," *New Orleans Bee*, July 1, 1848 (from the *Alexandria Republican*); Walter Prichard, ed., "A Tourist's Description of Louisiana in 1860," *Louisiana Historical Quarterly* 21 (October 1938): 1150–51. Matches between Biloxis and Choctaws were still being played at the end of the nineteenth century. For a detailed description, see "Louisiana, Alexandria," *New Orleans Daily Picayune*, February 18, 1894.

4. PAINFUL PASSAGE

1. *Proceedings of the Physico-Medical Society of New-Orleans, in Relation to the Trial and Expulsion of Charles A. Luzenberg* (New Orleans: Physico-Medical Society of New-Orleans, 1838), quotes from 5, 6, 17–18, 30; John Duffy, ed., *The Rudolph Matas History of Medicine in Louisiana*, 2 vols. (Baton Rouge: Louisiana State University Press, 1962), 2:82–92. In April 2000 a rare ceremonial event took place at Jackson Barracks in New Orleans. Delegations of

seventy-five men, women, and children from the Seminole Tribe of Florida and thirty-one from the Seminole Nation of Oklahoma visited the site to memorialize the imprisonment of their ancestors. A monument was dedicated and gifts were exchanged in remembrance of the forced relocation of three thousand Seminole people from Florida to Oklahoma. Major General Bennett C. Landreneau of the Louisiana National Guard hosted the Seminole visitors, including Seminole Tribe of Florida president Mitchel Cypress and Chief Jerry Haney of the Seminole Nation of Oklahoma. See Steve Cannizaro, "Seminoles Honored by National Guard," *New Orleans Times-Picayune,* April 7, 2000.

2. Herman J. Viola, *Diplomats in Buckskins: A History of Indian Delegations in Washington City* (Norman: University of Oklahoma Press, 1995); Suzan Shown Harjo, ed., *Nation to Nation: Treaties Between the United States and American Indian Nations* (Washington, DC: Smithsonian Institution, 2014); Michael V. Pisani, *Imagining Native America in Music* (New Haven, CT: Yale University Press, 2005), 79–125.

3. Carolyn Thomas Foreman, *Indians Abroad, 1493–1938* (Norman: University of Oklahoma Press, 1943), 132–33, 145; John Joseph Mathews, *The Osages: Children of the Middle Waters* (Norman: University of Oklahoma Press, 1961), 539–47; Tracy N. Leavelle, "The Osage in Europe: Romanticism, the Vanishing Indian, and French Civilization during the Restoration," in *National Stereotypes in Perspective: Americans in France, Frenchmen in America,* ed. William L. Chew III (Amsterdam: Rodopi, 2001), 89–112; Michael V. Pisani, *Imagining Native America in Music* (New Haven, CT: Yale University Press, 2005), 117–19.

4. *New Orleans Daily Picayune,* January 19, 1860.

5. Edwin McReynolds, *The Seminoles* (Norman: University of Oklahoma Press, 1957), 210.

6. William Duval to Elbert Herring, January 20, 1834, *American State Papers: Military Affairs* (Washington: Gales & Seaton, 1861), 6:458.

7. *Negroes, &c., Captured from Indian in Florida, &c.,* 25th Congress, 3d Session, 1838, House Document No. 225 (Washington, 1839), 52; Kevin Mulroy, *The Seminole Freedmen: A History* (Norman: University of Oklahoma Press, 2007), 44–50. For an exceptionally insightful look into the complexity of Seminole-Black relations in Florida, see Christina Snyder, *Slavery in Indian Country: The Changing Face of Captivity in Early America* (Cambridge, MA: Harvard University Press, 2010), 213–43. Various dimensions of Seminole conflict with the United States are innovatively explored in William S. Belko, ed., *America's Hundred Years' War: U.S. Expansion to the Gulf Coast and the Fate of the Seminole, 1763–1858* (Gainesville: University Press of Florida, 2011).

8. Christopher D. Haveman, "Final Resistance: Creek Removal from the Alabama Homeland," *Alabama Heritage* 89 (Summer 2008): 9–19. For a comprehensive investigation of this war's causes and consequences, see John T. Ellison, *The Second Creek War: Interethnic Conflict and Collusion on a Collapsing Frontier* (Lincoln: University of Nebraska Press, 2010).

9. Audubon to the John Bachman Family, Mobile, Alabama, February 24, 1837, in Richard Rhodes, ed., *The Audubon Reader* (New York: Alfred A. Knopf, 2006), 504–5.

10. Christopher D. Haveman, *Rivers of Sand: Creek Indian Emigration, Relocation, and Ethnic Cleansing in the American South* (Lincoln: University of Nebraska Press, 2016), 207–8, 234–41, 250–60.

11. *New Orleans Daily Picayune,* October 17, 18, 25, 1837.

12. *New Orleans Daily Picayune,* November 3, 1837; *New Orleans True American,* November 7, 1837; Haveman, *Rivers of Sand,* 258–60; Cecil Meares, "When the Steamboat *Monmouth* Sank in the Mississippi, Creek Indian Passengers Paid the Price," *Wild West* 11 (October 1998): 10–12.

13. Angie Debo, *The Road to Disappearance* (Norman: University of Oklahoma Press, 1941), 105–6. Joy Harjo's poem "New Orleans" also represents Creek memory of this and other tragic episodes of removal. *Words in the Blood: Contemporary Indian Writers of North and South America,* ed. Jamake Highwater (New York: Plume, 1984), 212.

14. *New Orleans Daily Picayune,* March 18, 21, 1838; Coll Thrush, *Indigenous London: Native Travelers at the Heart of Empire* (New Haven, CT: Yale University Press, 2016), 80.

15. Dan L. Thrapp, *Encyclopedia of Frontier Biography in Three Volumes* (Lincoln: University of Nebraska Press, 1988), 3:754. Representatives of the Seminole Nation of Oklahoma visited Fort Pike on June 14, 2009, and placed a plaque there to honor Chief Jumper. The plaque reads: "It is with honor and gratitude the Seminole Nation returns to this historic site to pay tribute to a great warrior who served his family, relatives and fellow Seminoles in a time of great upheaval as a resistance leader in the war against Indian Removal. Seminole War Chief Jumper epitomizes the Spirit of the Seminole and the undying will to serve his country and his people. The Seminole Nation honors all of its men and women who died at Fort Pike and Jackson Barracks while in route to Indian Country as prisoners of war. The Seminole Nation honors all of our ancestors whose will and determination was to be free. The Seminole Nation Honor Color Guard recognizes and honors this Freedom Spirit in its service to the Defense of the United States of America and thanks the Louisiana Office of State Parks and Louisiana National guard for its participation in the military ceremonies conducted in honor of Chief Jumper." Unfortunately, Fort Pike was closed to the public in 2015 because of budget cuts and layoffs by Louisiana's state legislature. When Fort Pike was evacuated by Confederate troops during the Civil War, it became the site for training former slaves who volunteered to fight for the Union army. Many of those African American soldiers bravely participated in the forty-eight-day Battle of Port Hudson, the longest siege in American history and the engagement that completed recapture of all of the Mississippi River for the United States. *New Orleans Advocate,* February 3, 2015. To view photos of Fort Pike, a state historic site currently closed to the public, visit http://www.drbronsontours.com/bronsonseminolefortpike.html; and https://www.crt.state.la.us/louisiana-state-parks/historic-sites/fort-pike-state-historic-site/index.

16. *New Orleans Daily Picayune,* May 15, 1838. For an insightful look at the Seminole presence in New Orleans during these years, particularly in regard to its significant impression upon the city's African American population, see Jerry Brock, "Chula Bungo! The Seminoles in New Orleans," *The Jazz Archivist* 29 (2016), 50–64.

17. Mrs. [Matilda Charlotte] Houstoun, *Texas and the Gulf of Mexico; or Yachting in the New World,* 2 vols. (London: John Murray, 1844), 2:24–35.

18. Thomas Lorraine McKenney and James Hall, *History of the Indian Tribes of North America* (Philadelphia: D. Rice and J. G. Clark, 1842–1844), 2:71–74, plate opposite p. 95.

19. My narrative of this dispute is based primarily on *Negroes, &c., Captured from Indian in Florida, &c.*, 25th Congress, 3d Session, 1838, House Document No. 225; and *The Congressional Globe: Containing the Debates, Proceedings, and Laws, of the First Session of the Thirty-Second Congress* (City of Washington: John G. Rives, 1852), vol. 24, part 1, 611–16, 791–800. For other scholars' coverage, see McReynolds, *Seminoles*, 182–89, 210–13; and Ellison, *Second Creek War*, 319–29, 388–95. Important insight into the life of Abraham can be found in Jane G. Landers, *Atlantic Creoles in the Age of Revolutions* (Cambridge, MA: Harvard University Press, 2010), 175–203.

20. *New Orleans Courier*, April 2, 1835. For data on the commerce of buffalo robes through New Orleans and the impact of the 1837 smallpox epidemic, see Andrew C. Isenberg, *The Destruction of the Bison* (New York: Cambridge University Press, 2000), 105, 114–19.

21. Charles Lyell, *A Second Visit to the United States of North America*, 2 vols. (New York: Harper & Sons, 1849), 2:91–92; New Orleans *Daily Picayune*, February 22, 1885; "The Carnival Was Its Merry Self," New Orleans *Daily Picayune*, Wednesday, February 15, 1899.

22. Houstoun, *Texas and the Gulf of Mexico*, 2:23–24; Walt Whitman, "New Orleans in 1848," *Prose Works 1892*, ed. Floyd Stovall, 2 vols. (New York: New York University Press, 1964), 2:606. This was Whitman's response to a request in 1887 to write some remembrance of several months in New Orleans, when he worked for *The Crescent*. It was published in the *New Orleans Daily Picayune* on January 25, 1887.

23. George Combe, *Notes on the United States of America, During a Phrenological Visit in 1838-9–40*, 2 vols. (Edinburgh: Maclachlan, Stewart, & Co., 1841), 1:98.

24. Samuel George Morton, *Crania Americana; or, a Comparative View of the Skulls of Various Aboriginal Nations of North and South America* (Philadelphia: J. Dobson, 1839), 160, 162–64, 170. For official notice from the Department of Interior to the Chitimacha Tribe of Louisiana regarding human remains left in the University of Pennsylvania Museum of Archaeology and Anthropology from Morton's collection, see *Federal Register*, 76:93 (May 13, 2011), 28072–73. When Osceola died of what was likely malaria as a prisoner of war at Fort Moultrie, South Carolina, army surgeon Frederick Weedon cut off his head and embalmed it before closing the coffin. Weedon displayed Osceola's head like a trophy in his St. Augustine drugstore window. In 1843 Weedon's son-in-law Dr. Daniel Whitehurst sent it to his former professor of medicine at New York University, Dr. Valentine Mott. This phrenologist's collection of human skulls was destroyed when the Medical College in New York City caught fire. Patricia R. Wickman, *Osceola's Legacy* (Tuscaloosa: University of Alabama Press, 1991), 144–53.

25. Josiah C. Nott and George R. Glidden, *Types of Mankind: or, Ethnological Researches, Based Upon the Ancient Monuments, Paintings, Sculptures, and Crania of Races, and Upon their Natural, Geographical, Philological, and Biblical History* (Philadelphia: Lippincott, Grambo & Co., 1854), 441–44; Reginald Horsman, *Josiah Nott of Mobile: Southerner, Physician, and Racial Theorist* (Baton Rouge: Louisiana State University Press, 1987), 58, 177, 207. For information about the Choctaw community around Mobile at this time, see Jacqueline Anderson Matte, *They Say the Wind is Red: The Alabama Choctaws—Lost in Their Own Land* (Montgomery, AL: New South Books, 2002), 32–68.

26. John Forbes to the Marquis de Casa Irujo, April 28, 1804, Panton, Leslie and Company Collection, 1739–1847, University of West Florida University Archives and West Florida History Center, Pensacola.

27. Dayna Bowker Lee, *Choctaw Communities along the Gulf Coast: Louisiana, Mississippi, and Alabama*, Final Report Prepared for the National Park Service and the Federal Emergency Management Agency, September 2009, Contract Number P5038090018, pp. 20–21.

28. Katherine M. B. Osburn, *Choctaw Resurgence in Mississippi: Race, Class, and Nation Building in the Jim Crow South* (Lincoln: University of Nebraska Press, 2014), is a thorough and insightful study of the Mississippi Choctaws' ordeals and struggles after removal. For an equally valuable work on the Jena Choctaws in Louisiana, see Brian R. Klopotek, *Recognition Odysseys: Indigeneity, Race, and Federal Tribal Recognition Policy in Three Louisiana Indian Communities* (Durham, NC: Duke University Press, 2011).

29. McReynolds, *Seminoles*, 220, 233, 266–67, 287; Jane F. Lancaster, *Removal Aftershock: The Seminoles' Struggle to Survive in the West, 1836–1866* (Knoxville: University of Tennessee Press, 1994), 76–77, 123–24.

30. Paige Raibmon, *Authentic Indians: Episodes of Encounter from the Late-Nineteenth-Century Northwest Coast* (Durham, NC: Duke University Press, 2005), 116. Also see Daniel H. Usner, *Indian Work: Language and Livelihood in Native American History* (Cambridge, MA: Harvard University Press, 2009).

5. ACROSS THE LAKE

1. Stewart Culin, Report of Archaeological and Ethnological Collecting Trips in 1901, Culin Archival Collection, Department of Ethnology, Brooklyn Museum of Art, Brooklyn, NY.

2. For information about this painting, see Theodore E. Stebbins Jr. and Melissa Renn, *American Paintings, Watercolors, and Pastels by Artists Born Before 1826* (rev. ed., Cambridge, MA: Harvard Arts Museums, 2014), 90–91.

3. "Up the Mississippi," *Emerson's Magazine and Putnam's Monthly* 5 (October 1857), 438, illustration of Indians in N.O. market by Richardson Cox on p. 441; A. R. W., "Pictures of the South. The French Market, New Orleans," *Harper's Weekly* 10 (August 18, 1866), 526, illustration on p. 517; Giulio Adamoli, Letters From America: 1867. 3. From *Nuova Antologia*, February 1 (Literary and Political Semi-Monthly), *The Living Age*, Eighth Series, vol. 313, no. 4056 (April 1, 1922), 36.

4. Léon H. Grandjean, *Crayon Reproductions of Fremaux's New Orleans Characters* (1876), n.p.: text accompanying sketch "Choctaw Indian Squaws" by engineer Léon J. Frémaux; "Two baskets woven of colored split cane made by Indians and sold in market place at New Orleans," Accession No. 269, Museum Archives, Gantz Family Collections Center, Field Museum of Natural History, Chicago.

5. *Martin Behrman of New Orleans*, ed. Kemp, 1–2. Also see James S. Zacherie, *New Orleans Guide and Exposition Hand Book* (New Orleans: New Orleans News Co., 1885), 212; and David I. Bushnell Jr., *The Choctaw of Bayou Lacomb, St. Tammany Parish, Louisiana* (Washington, DC: Government Printing Office, 1909), 8.

6. Alfred R. Waud, "Sunday in New Orleans—The French Market," *Harper's Weekly,* August 18, 1866, p. 517; Frank Hamilton Taylor, *Records of the Southern Excursion of the American Society of Civil Engineers, 1877* (Philadelphia: Merrihew, 1877), 17; Nancy L. Gustke, *The Special Artist in American Culture: A Biography of Frank Hamilton Taylor (1846–1927)* (New York: Peter Lang, 1995), 49–51. Hamilton's original drawing and the Wilson and Hammersmith photographs are held in the Historic New Orleans Collection, New Orleans. At the opening reception for an exhibit that I guest-curated at the Historic New Orleans Collection two decades ago, Thomas Colvin of Mandeville, Louisiana, recognized the anonymous Choctaw woman in Hammersmith's photograph as Sally Lewis, mother of the woman who had taught him basket-making skills. For information about Colvin and his basketry, see Janice Dee Gilbert, "Tom Colvin, Mandeville," in *People of the Florida Parishes: Their Arts, Crafts, and Traditions, Folklife in Louisiana: Louisiana's Living Traditions,* accessed August 25, 2017, http://www.louisianafolklife.org/LT/Virtual_Books/Fla_ Parishes/book_florida_people.html; Thomas A. Colvin, "Cane and Palmetto Basketry of the Choctaw of St. Tammany Parish," in *The Work of Tribal Hands: Southeastern Indian Split Cane Basketry,* ed. Dayna Bowker Lee and H. F. Gregory (Natchitoches, LA: Northwestern State University Press, 2006), 73–94.

7. Stewart Stehlin, *Sketches of Urban and Cultural Life in North America: Friedrich Ratzel* (New Brunswick, NJ: Rutgers University Press, 1988), 210; Frederic Trautmann, "New Orleans, the Mississippi, and the Delta Through a German's Eyes: The Travels of Emil Deckert, 1885–1886" [Notes and Documents], *Louisiana History* 25 (Winter 1984): 86, 87; Lafcadio Hearn to H. E. Krehbiel, New Orleans, 1877, *The Life and Letters of Lafcadio Hearn,* ed. Elizabeth Bisland, 2 vols. (Boston: Houghton, Mifflin, 1906), 1:168–69; *Historical Sketch Book and Guide to New Orleans and Environs,* Edited and Compiled by Several Leading Writers of the New Orleans Press (New York: Will H. Coleman, 1885), 258, 263.

8. Mary Ashley Townsend, *Down the Bayou and Other Poems* (Boston: James R. Osgood and Co., 1882), 14.

9. C. Richard King, *Redskins: Insult and Brand* (Lincoln: University of Nebraska Press, 2016), 4, 18–19.

10. Grace King and John R. Ficklen, *A History of Louisiana* (New York and New Orleans: University Publishing Co., 1893), 164–65; Ficklin, "The Indians of Louisiana," in *Standard History of New Orleans, Louisiana,* ed. Henry Rightor (Chicago: Lewis Publishing, 1900), 56–57.

11. *Historical Sketch Book and Guide to New Orleans and Environs* (1885), 169–70.

12. *Historical Sketch Book and Guide to New Orleans and Environs* (1885), 169–70.

13. Richard Henry Pratt to Spencer F. Baird, Carlisle Indian Industrial School, October 7, 1884, A. J. Standing, Asst. Supt., Carlisle, to G. Brown Goode, August 4, 1884, Folder 15, Box 19, Series 6, World's Industrial and Cotton Centennial Exposition, Record Unit 70 (Exposition Records of the Smithsonian Institution and the United States National Museum, 1867–1940), Smithsonian Institution Archives, Washington, DC; William E. Deahl Jr., "Buffalo Bill's Wild West Show in New Orleans," *Louisiana History* 16 (Summer 1975): 289–98.

14. *New Orleans Daily Picayune,* January 29, February 1, February 15, March 4, 1885; Herbert S. Fairall, *The World's Industrial and Cotton Centennial Exposition, New Orleans, 1884–1885* (Iowa City, IA: Republican Publishing Co., 1885), 412. For more information about Fletcher, see Joan Mark, *A Stranger in Her Native Land: Alice Fletcher and the American Indians* (Lincoln: University of Nebraska Press, 1988).

15. Hon. C. J. Barrow, US Commissioner for Louisiana, March 15, 1885, list of articles on exhibition in the Agricultural Division, New Orleans–World's Industrial and Cotton Centennial Exposition, Department of Louisiana, Report to Gov. S. D. McEnery, February 23, 1885, pp. 21–23; "World's Industrial and Cotton Centennial Exposition," *New Orleans Times-Democrat,* April 6, 1885; *St. Tammany Farmer* (Covington, LA), April 25, 1885.

16. Adrien Rouquette to John Dimitry, December 1, 1884, folder 6, box 1, Adrien Emmanuel Rouquette Papers, 1842–1942, Louisiana Research Collection, Howard-Tilton Memorial Library, Tulane University, New Orleans; Letter written by Pierre Alphonse Chocarne (born in Dijon, 1826) describing his visit to Father Rouquette's Choctaw mission at Bayou Lacomb in May 1867, from Susan Blanchard Elder, *Life of the Abbe Adrien Rouquette,* 142–45; "In Search of a Word—A Visit to Pere Rouquette. _____ Whitman," *New Orleans Bulletin,* August 6, 1875, folder 3, box 1, Adrien Emmanuel Rouquette Papers; Blaise C. D'Antoni, "Chahta-Ima and St. Tammany's Choctaws," St. Tammany Historical Society, Inc., Mandeville, LA, 1986, series 2, box 1, Adrien Emmanuel Rouquette Papers; Label Collection, Folder 9, Box 39, Series 10, World's Columbian Exposition, Record Unit 70 (Exposition Records of the Smithsonian Institution and the United States National Museum, 1867–1940), Smithsonian Institution Archives, Washington, DC; "The Choctaws of Louisiana: Father Rouquette and His Wards in St. Tammany," *New Orleans Daily Picayune,* September 22, 1882, series 2, box 2, Adrien Emmanuel Rouquette Papers; "Catherine Cole's Letter," *New Orleans Daily Picayune,* Sunday, March 1, 1883.

17. "Choctaws in Louisiana—A Talk with Father Rouquette about His Favorite Charge," *New Orleans Daily Picayune,* August 4, 1882; Rouquette to John Dimitry, March 29, 1885, folder 6, box 1, Adrien Emmanuel Rouquette Papers; "At the Markets You Saw Indian Women and Asked Questions about their Lives and Stories," *New Orleans Daily Picayune,* February 17, 1896.

18. "Father Rouquette: The Burial of the Poet Priest," *New Orleans Daily Picayune,* July 17, 1887; John Dimitry, "Chahta-Ima, Father Adrien Rouquette," *Harper's Weekly* 31, no. 1597 (July 30, 1887), 537–38. A couple of valuable book-length biographies of Rouquette were written over the early twentieth century, but I have found a few more recent explorations into his life to be particularly useful: Blaise C. D'antoni, *Chahta-Ima and St. Tammany's Choctaws* (Mandeville, LA: St. Tammany Historical Society, 1986); Dominic Braud, "Père Rouquette, Missionnaire Extraordinaire: Father Adrien Rouquette's Mission to the Choctaw," in *Cross, Corzier and Crucible: A Volume Celebrating the Bicentennial of a Catholic Diocese in Louisiana,* ed. Glenn R. Conrad (Lafayette: The Archdiocese of New Orleans in cooperation with the Center for Louisiana Studies, 1993), 314–27; Rien Fertel, "Catholic Priest and Poet Adrien Rouquette Bridges the Atlantic Ocean," in *Imagining the Creole City: The*

Rise of Literary Culture in Nineteenth-Century New Orleans (Baton Rouge: Louisiana State University Press, 2014), 31–48.

19. "Personal and General Notes," *New Orleans Daily Picayune,* August 18, 1895; "Florida Parishes Fair," *New Orleans Daily Picayune,* November 29, 1897. Before a meeting of the Louisiana Historical Society in 1941, André Lafargue would share his boyhood memory of watching, from concealed branches of a tree with two friends, what he thought had been the last Indian gathering at Bayou Bonfouca. André Lafargue, "Louisiana Linguistic and Folklore Backgrounds," *Louisiana Historical Quarterly* 24 (July 1941): 749–50.

20. "Many Persons Visit Mission," *New Orleans Times-Democrat,* April 24, 1911.

21. Tom Bethell, *George Lewis: A Jazzman from New Orleans* (Berkeley: University of California Press, 1977), 14–17, 46–47.

22. "At the Markets You Saw Indian Women and Asked Questions about their Lives and Stories," *New Orleans Daily Picayune,* February 17, 1896. For comprehensive information about these and other Choctaw communities along the Gulf Coast and Lake Pontchartrain, see Dayna Bowker Lee, *Choctaw Communities along the Gulf Coast: Louisiana, Mississippi, and Alabama,* Final Report Prepared for the National Park Service and the Federal Emergency Management Agency, September 2009, Contract Number P5038090018. A concise overview can be found in H. F. "Pete" Gregory, "Indians and Folklife in the Florida Parishes of Louisiana," Louisiana's Living Traditions, accessed July 9, 2017, http://www.louisiana-folklife.org/LT/Virtual_Books/Fla_Parishes/book_florida_country.html.

23. "Catherine Cole's Letter," *New Orleans Daily Picayune,* December 16, 1888, printed in Martha R. Field, *Louisiana Voyages: The Travel Writings of Catherine Cole,* ed. Joan B. McLaughlin and Jack McLaughlin (Jackson: University Press of Mississippi, 2006), 192–93.

24. Catherine Cole [pseudonym of Martha R. S. Field, 1855–1898], *The Story of the Old French Market, New Orleans* (New Orleans: Compliments of the New Orleans Coffee Company, ca. 1916), not paginated. In a letter written by Field's son, Frederick Field, to Mrs. O'Keefe, dated 1934, he said: "The little book was written by my mother—probably fifty years ago—yet it seemed as fresh—as charming and as modern as if it were yesterday. It was written as an advertisement—but the coffee company is gone—and the little book has some added value as being out of print—and rare. Remembering our talk of old New Orleans at the tea party, I thought you might care to read 'The Story of French Market.' With very best wishes for the Christmas season." Historic New Orleans Collection.

25. *New Orleans Daily Picayune,* February 17, 1893, October 2, 1898; *New Orleans Times-Democrat,* May 12, 1893. An article appearing in the January 15, 1893, issue of the *Chicago Daily Tribune,* entitled "Last of Their Race, Remnant of the Mighty Choctaw Tribe Near New Orleans," described both Choctaw and Chitimacha communities in Louisiana and offered especially high praise for Chitimacha basketry.

26. "News and Notes," *Indian's Friend* 10 (July 1898), 4–5; "Women Defenders of Indian Rights," *New Orleans Daily Picayune,* April 13, 1899; *Annual Report of the National Indian Association, December, 1908* (Philadelphia: National Indian Association, n.d.), 19. For enlightening exploration into particular dimensions of WNIA membership in the South, see

Rose Stremlau, "WNIA Chapters in the South," *The Women's National Indian Association: A History,* ed. Valerie Sherer Mathes (Albuquerque: University of New Mexico Press, 2015), 173–91.

27. *New Orleans Daily Picayune,* December 10, 1896, January 3, 1897, March 21, 1897, January 8, 1898, March 9, 1898.

28. George Demarest to Chief John Paul, December 4, 1898, Chitimacha Papers, McIlhenny Company and Avery Island, Inc., Archives, Avery Island, Louisiana.

29. "Chetimaches and Their Land Claims," *New Orleans Daily Picayune,* June 11, 1899.

30. George A. Demarest to Chief John Paul, December 4, 1898, February 11, 1900, Chitimacha Papers.

31. Daniel H. Usner, *Weaving Alliances with Other Women: Chitimacha Indian Work in the New South* (Athens: University of Georgia Press, 2015).

32. Alice Ruth Moore, "A Carnival Jangle," in *Violets and Other Tales* (Boston: Monthly Review, 1895), 80–81.

33. "Maskers Visit Algiers and a Free Fight Lands Them in Jail," *New Orleans Daily Picayune,* February 27, 1895; *New Orleans Times-Democrat,* February 12, 1902.

34. Alan Lomax, *Mister Jelly Roll: The Fortunes of Jelly Roll Morton, New Orleans Creole and "Inventor of Jazz"* (Berkeley: University of California Press, 1950), 14–15, 280.

35. Marcus Bruce Christian Manuscript for a Black History of Louisiana, Chapter 42, pp. 5–6, Typescript in Marcus Bruce Christian Collection, Archives and Manuscripts Department, Earl K. Long Library, University of New Orleans. For insightful treatments of the origins of Mardi Gras Indians, see Samuel Kinser, *Carnival, American Style: Mardi Gras at New Orleans and Mobile* (Chicago: University of Chicago Press, 1990), 151–94; Reid Mitchell, *All on a Mardi Gras Day: Episodes in the History of New Orleans Carnival* (Cambridge, MA: Harvard University Press, 1995), 113–30; Joseph Roach, *Cities of the Dead: Circum-Atlantic Performance* (New York: Columbia University Press, 1996), 192–211; and Richard Brent Turner, *Jazz Religion, the Second Line, and Black New Orleans* (Bloomington: Indiana University Press, 2009), 39–68.

36. *New Orleans Times-Democrat,* December 30, 1896; *New Orleans Daily Picayune,* December 30, 1896, January 2, 1897.

37. *New Orleans Daily Picayune,* May 2, 1897; *New Orleans Times-Democrat,* May 2, 1897; Edward F. Haas, *Political Leadership in a Southern City: New Orleans in the Progressive Era, 1896–1902* (Ruston, LA: McGinty Publications, 1988), 22–23, 28, 37, 93–94.

38. Advertisement, *New Orleans Daily Picayune,* August 27, 1897; "Amusements," *New Orleans Daily Picayune,* August 28, 1897.

39. "Virginia Veterans," *New Orleans Daily Picayune,* July 12, 1897; "Hungry Choctaws. The Indian Ball Players Suffer by Their Manager's Loss," *New Orleans Daily Picayune,* Wed., September 1, 1897; "Indians in a Hole," *New Orleans Daily Picayune,* September 2, 1897.

40. *New Orleans Times-Democrat,* February 8, 1914; Scott Rabalais, *The Fighting Tigers, 1993–2008: Into a New Century of LSU Football* (Baton Rouge: Louisiana State University Press, 2008), 201–5.

41. Laurence M. Hauptman, "Tom Longboat: Onondaga Champion Marathon Runner," *American Indian* 17 (Summer 2016), 36–38. Demonstrating the amnesia over stickball's long-lasting presence in New Orleans, reports about the current spread of lacrosse to New Orleans schools and clubs fail to mention the city's past record. See Sarah Carr, "Lacrosse Catches on in N.O. Charter Schools," *New Orleans Times-Picayune*, April 14, 2009; and Melanie Warner Spencer, "Take Me Out to the Lacrosse Game: A New Generation Is Having Kicks with Sticks," *New Orleans Magazine* (June 2014).

42. *New Orleans Daily Picayune*, May 25, 1899, October 29, 1900; *New Orleans Times-Democrat*, November 14, 1908, October 19, 22, 1910. See Linda Scarangella McNenly, *Native Performers in Wild West Shows: From Buffalo Bill to Euro Disney* (Norman: University of Oklahoma Press, 2012), for an informative study of why and how American Indians participated in Wild West shows and other performances of Indianness. Various dimensions are also keenly analyzed in Clyde Ellis, "Five Dollars a Week to Be 'Regular Indians': Shows, Exhibitions, and the Economics of Indian Dance, 1880–1930," in *Native Pathways: American Indian Culture and Economic Development in the Twentieth Century*, ed. Brian Hosmer and Colleen O'Neill (Boulder: University Press of Colorado, 2014), 184–208.

43. "White Eagle, Dies, in Christian Faith. Educated Indian Expired in Tuberculosis Building of Charity Hospital," *New Orleans Times-Picayune*, August 9, 1916.

44. *New Orleans Times-Picayune*, January 16, 1916. For a keen analysis of Indian women performing Indianness during this period, see Ruth B. Phillips, "Performing the Native Woman: Primitivism and Mimicry in Early Twentieth-Century Visual Culture," *Antimodernism and Artistic Experience: Policing the Boundaries of Modernity*, ed. Lynda Jessup (Toronto: University of Toronto Press, 2001), 26–49. While urban stages for Indian performance represented a rising nostalgic romance among white Americans, helping justify conquest and dispossession of Indian nations, they also channeled an influence by Indian people upon scripts and songs being produced and performed by non-Indians. Composers like Antonín Dvořák, Edward MacDowell, and Charles Cadman included elements of "Indianism" in pieces meant to capture a uniquely American music. Also by the close of the nineteenth century, this "contact zone" included folklorists and anthropologists seeking to salvage what they considered the last remnants of Indian culture. Transcribing and recording Indian songs and photographing Indian dances became a vital part of ethnographic fieldwork, and performance of Native dance even reached the film industry's earliest work. At Thomas Edison's studio in West Orange, New Jersey, a "Sioux Buffalo Dance" and a "Sioux Ghost Dance" were captured on silent film in September 1894. The dancers were performers in Buffalo Bill's Wild West, showing in Brooklyn's Ambrose Park at the time. We need to learn more about the motives behind Indian participation in these performances as well as the effects that resulted from it. See Michael V. Pisani, *Imagining Native America in Music* (New Haven, CT: Yale University Press, 2005), 182–239; and Kathleen M. German, "American Indians in Silent Film, 1894–1929," in *American Indians and Popular Culture, vol. 1: Media, Sports, and Politics*, ed. Elizabeth DeLaney Hoffman (Santa Barbara, CA: Praeger, 2012), 17–32.

45. *New Orleans Times-Democrat,* May 11, 1913. For insight into white Americans pretending to be American Indians across the centuries, see Philip J. Deloria, *Playing Indian* (New Haven, CT: Yale University Press, 1998).

46. Cora Bremer to Mary Bradford, December 1, 1902, Mary Bradford Papers, McIlhenny Company and Avery Island, Inc., Archives, Avery Island, Louisiana. For more information about this Choctaw removal, see John H. Peterson Jr., "Louisiana Choctaw Life at the End of the Nineteenth Century," in *Four Centuries of Southern Indians,* ed. Charles H. Hudson (Athens: University of Georgia Press, 1975), 101–12; Charles Roberts, "The Second Choctaw Removal, 1903," in *After Removal: The Choctaws in Mississippi,* ed. Samuel J. Wells and Roseanna Tubby (Jackson: University Press of Mississippi, 1986), 94–111; Katherine M. B. Osburn, *Choctaw Resurgence in Mississippi: Race, Class, and Nation Building in the Jim Crow South* (Lincoln: University of Nebraska Press, 2014), 36–56; Mikaëla M. Adams, *Who Belongs? Race, Resources, and Tribal Citizenship in the Native South* (New York: Oxford University Press, 2016), 96–131.

47. Christine Paul to Mary Bradford, May 2, 1907, Mary Bradford Papers.

48. John R. Swanton, *Indian Tribes of the Lower Mississippi Valley and Adjacent Coast of the Gulf of Mexico* (Washington, DC: Smithsonian Institution, 1911); M. Raymond Harrington, "Among Louisiana Indians," *Southern Workman* 37 (December 1908): 656–61; Usner, *Weaving Alliances with Other Women,* 19–20, 24–25, 42–47.

49. David I. Bushnell Jr., *The Choctaw of Bayou Lacomb, St. Tammany Parish, Louisiana,* Bureau of American Ethnology Bulletin 48 (Washington, DC: Smithsonian Institution, 1909), quotes from 8, 13, 15–16; Bushnell, "Myths of the Louisiana Choctaw," *American Anthropologist* 12 (October–December 1910), 526–35, quote from 526.

50. David Bushnell to Clark Wissler, January 17, 1916, Wissler to Bushnell, February 11, 1916, Receipt to David Bushnell for $500, February 15, 1917, Accession Number 1917–10, Division of Anthropological Archives, American Museum of Natural History, New York; "Museum Notes," *American Museum Journal* 17 (March 1917): 215.

51. Adams, *Who Belongs?,* 115–16, 120–22.

52. David I. Bushnell Jr., "The Choctaw of St. Tammany Parish," *Louisiana Historical Quarterly* 1 (January 1917): 11–20, quote from 19–20; *St. Tammany Farmer,* November 3, 1917.

53. Since the landmark publication of Fred B. Kniffen, Hiram F. Gregory, and George A. Stokes, *The Historic Indian Tribes of Louisiana: From 1542 to the Present* (Baton Rouge: Louisiana State University Press, 1987), a steady stream of scholarship has been devoted to American Indians in the region over the twentieth century. See, for a sample, Bruce Duthu, "The Houma Indians of Louisiana: The Intersection of Law and History in the Federal Acknowledgement Process," *Louisiana History* 38 (Fall 1997): 409–36; Brian R. Klopotek, *Recognition Odysseys: Indigeneity, Race, and Federal Tribal Recognition Policy in Three Louisiana Indian Communities* (Durham, NC: Duke University Press, 2011); Roger Emile Stouff, *Native Waters* (rev. ed., Shadowfire Books, 2012); Jay Precht, "Coushatta Basketry and Identity Politics: The Role of Pine-Needle Baskets in the Federal Recognition of the Coushatta Tribe of Louisiana," *Ethnohistory* 62 (January 2015): 145–67.

EPILOGUE

1. Randolph Delehanty, *Art in the American South: Works from the Ogden Collection* (Baton Rouge: Louisiana State University Press, 1996), 133.

2. Dayna Bowker Lee, *Choctaw Communities along the Gulf Coast: Louisiana, Mississippi, and Alabama,* Final Report Prepared for the National Park Service and the Federal Emergency Management Agency, September 2009, Contract Number P5038090018, pp. 89–91.

3. For an informative and convenient overview of all Native groups in the state, see Dayna Bowker Lee, "Louisiana Indians in the 21st Century," *Folklife in Louisiana: Louisiana's Living Traditions,* accessed October 17, 2017, http://www.louisianafolklife.org/LT/Articles_Essays/nativeams.html.

4. For a close-up look at what this meant for one Louisiana Indian nation, see Daniel H. Usner, "Weaving Material Objects and Political Alliances: The Chitimacha Indian Pursuit of Federal Recognition," *Native American and Indigenous Studies* 1 (Spring 2014): 25–48; Daniel Usner, "'They Don't Like Indian Around Here': Chitimacha Struggles and Strategies for Survival in the Jim Crow South," *Native South* 9 (2016): 89–124.

5. Bruce Duthu and Hilde Ojibway, "Future Light or Feu Follet? Louisiana Indians and Federal Recognition," *Southern Exposure* 13 (November/December 1985): 24–32; Bruce Duthu, "The Houma Indians of Louisiana: The Intersection of Law and History in the Federal Acknowledgement Process," *Louisiana History* 38 (Fall 1997): 409–36; J. Daniel D'Oney, "The Houma Nation: A Historiographical Overview," *Louisiana History* 47 (Winter 2006): 63–90.

6. Kimberly Krupa, "'So-Called Indians': Stand Up and Fight: How a Jim Crow Suit Thrust a Louisiana School System into the Civil Rights Movement," *Louisiana History* 51 (Spring 2010): 171–94.

7. Fred B. Kniffen, Hiram F. Gregory, and George A. Stokes, *The Historic Indian Tribes of Louisiana: From 1542 to the Present* (Baton Rouge: Louisiana State University Press, 1987), 299–314; Frye Gaillard, *As Long as the Waters Flow: Native Americans in the South and East* (Winston-Salem, NC: John F. Blair, 1998), 167–83.

8. Hiram F. Gregory, "The Louisiana Tribes: Entering Hard Times," *Indians of the Southeastern United States in the Late 20th Century,* ed. J. Anthony Paredes (Tuscaloosa: University of Alabama Press, 1992), 162–82; Denise E. Bates, *The Other Movement: Indian Rights and Civil Rights in the Deep South* (Tuscaloosa: University of Alabama Press, 2012), 11–22. Information about Louisiana groups can also be found in these articles appearing in the *Handbook of North American Indians: Volume 14 Southeast,* ed. Rayond D. Fogelson (Washington, DC: Smithsonian Institution, 2004); Jeffrey P. Brain, George Roth, and William J. de Reuse, "Tunica, Biloxi, and Ofo," 586–97; Jack Campisi, "Houma," 632–41; Brightman, "Chitimacha," 642–52; Gregory, "Survival and Maintenance Among Louisiana Tribes," 653–58.

9. Mark Edwin Miller, *Forgotten Tribes: Unrecognized Indians and the Federal Acknowledgment Process* (Lincoln: University of Nebraska Press, 2004), 156–208; Bates, *The Other Movement,* 63–64, 70–98, 201.

10. "Indian Craft Display Sunday," *New Orleans Times-Picayune*, September 18, 1987; Bates, *The Other Movement*, 150–71. For glimpses into language projects, see Daniel W. Hieber, "Reborn on the Bayou: A Lost Language of Louisiana. How Software and Schools are Reviving Chitimacha," *Houston Chronicle*, July 28, 2015; Mark Guarino, "Young Members of Louisiana's Houma Nation Try to Reclaim Tribe's Lost Language," *Washington Post*, January 3, 2015.

11. Andrew Jolivette, "Indigenous Locations Post-Katrina: Beyond Invisibility and Disaster," special issue of *American Indian Culture and Research Journal* 32 (no. 2, 2008): 1–108. The Isle de Jean Charles community has become the United States' first beneficiary of a federally funded program to relocate communities fleeing climate change. Faimon A. Roberts III, "State Chooses Site Near Thibodaux for Isle de Jean Charles Residents," *New Orleans Advocate*, December 22, 2017.

12. T. Mayheart Dardar, "Tales of Wind and Water: Houma Indians and Hurricanes," *American Indian Culture and Research Journal* 32, no. 2 (2008): 27–34, quote from 32–33.

INDEX

Note: Page numbers in *italics* refer to illustrations; those followed by "n" indicate endnotes.